ANANSE

THE WEB OF LIFE IN AFRICA

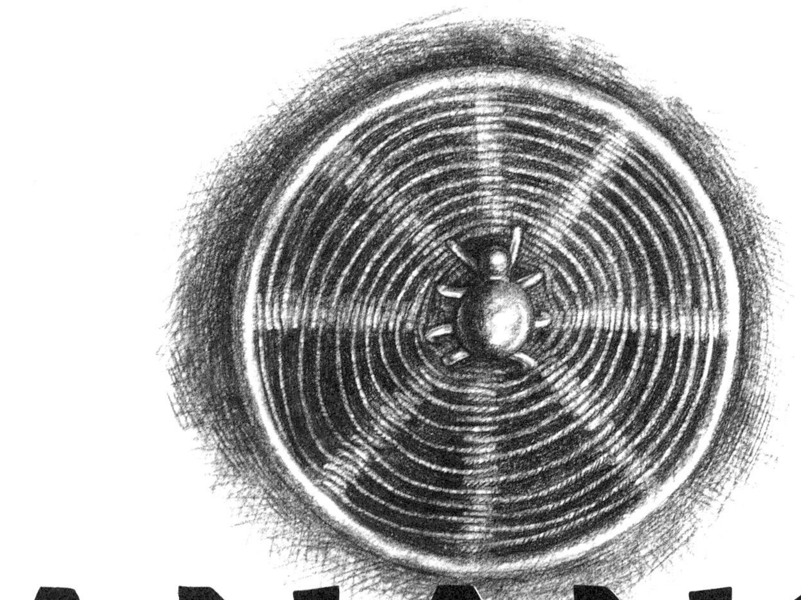

ANANSE

THE WEB OF LIFE IN AFRICA

Ananse is the spider, a heroic character in African folklore. Like Br'er Fox, he outwits all the other creatures of the forest. He depicts every kind of hero. There is an Ananse story for every situation in life. God gave Ananse the meaning of order. He taught him architecture, the structure of dwellings, and the structure of life and society. This is symbolized by his web, which stands also for the sun and its rays, and the sun personifies God.

DRAWINGS AND TEXT BY JOHN BIGGERS

UNIVERSITY OF TEXAS PRESS • AUSTIN

Requests for permission to reproduce material from this work should be sent to Permissions, University of Texas Press, P.O. Box 7819, Austin, TX 78713-7819.

∞ The paper used in this publication meets the minimum requirements of American National Standard for Information Sciences—Permanence of Paper for Printed Library Materials, ANSI Z39.48-1984.

International Standard Book Number 0-292-70345-7
Library of Congress Catalog Card Number 78-68777
Copyright © 1962, 1979 by John Biggers

All rights reserved

Printed in the United States of America

Second Paperback Printing, 1996

CONTENTS

FOREWORD

AS A WRITER AND ARTIST, John Biggers conveys graphically, sensitively, and efficiently the West Africa of his 1957 visit. His poetic depiction enables the reader to visit a place and people under the tutelage of a gentle guide of talent and acute perception.

John Biggers introduced himself to me through his art—my initial memory of Texas Southern University is the muraled hallway for which he was responsible. Because of this man and his enthusiasm, "culturally deprived" youth became artistically privileged. *Ananse* serves to lessen the cultural deprivation of a wider audience.

Barbara Jordan
Lyndon B. Johnson Public Service Professor
Lyndon B. Johnson School of Public Affairs
University of Texas at Austin

INTRODUCTION

THE TITLE OF THIS BOOK is the African word for spider, hence the subtitle, "The Web of Life in Africa." The spider is an excellent symbol of African life, for this core of African folklore that Ananse represents has spread throughout the Black Diaspora to every corner of our modern world. My father as a child heard spider stories in his native Jamaica and in turn he told them to his children in our native Southland here in these United States.

This folk philosophy of Black people as represented by the spider is expressed with great sensitivity and sensibility by a splendid artist, John Biggers. The unity of all life and all knowledge; the search for truth, freedom, peace, and human dignity; the concepts of time, of God, and of man, and all the spiritual values attenuating therefrom, are portrayed here in the actual life of Black West Africa. They are perceived and portrayed both in the text and in the descriptive drawings. The work appears in pencil, charcoal, and crayon.

This is a new edition of the book first published in 1962 and based on Dr. Biggers' African journeys in Ghana, Nigeria, and other parts of West Africa during the late 1950s. A new generation awaits this important work. Those who first read it can understand a growing demand for its reappearance.

Dr. Biggers has written and drawn this life with realistic and faithful delineations. Not only has he observed it with the uncanny accuracy of the artist's pen and brush, but he has also lovingly dipped his pencil into a welter of familiar Black life and given us a book of great magnitude, one of immeasurable power and sheer beauty.

John Biggers has the imaginative scope of the muralist—big and panoramic, yet painstaking in minute detail. The life of people far away becomes as immediate as one's neighbor next door. You see the farmer with his produce, the fisherman with his nets, and the women over their pots, with their distinctive native dress and their variety of hair styles and head coverings: corn rows, braids, plaits, and geylas. All Black people recognize a mutual kinship in these Black faces. The heritage of a great Black culture inspires us with its eternal strength, its durability, its fresh and versatile creativity, and its powerful humanity—all communicated in these timeless vignettes. Dr. Biggers' comprehensive knowledge of anatomy makes his pen appear sure and skillful, and there is a definite polarity of cultural expressions showing the relationship of Black America to Black Africa.

This book should be widely distributed and better known in both literary and artistic circles, but most of all it should be known to the general public. All will appreciate it. Emotions and intellect will immediately fuse to an aesthetic reaction, and what better test of great art can there be than that?

Margaret Walker Alexander
Professor of English
Director of the Institute for the Study of History, Life, and Culture of Black People
Jackson State University
Jackson, Mississippi

TO THOSE WHO SEEK DIGNITY
AND FREEDOM FOR ALL MEN

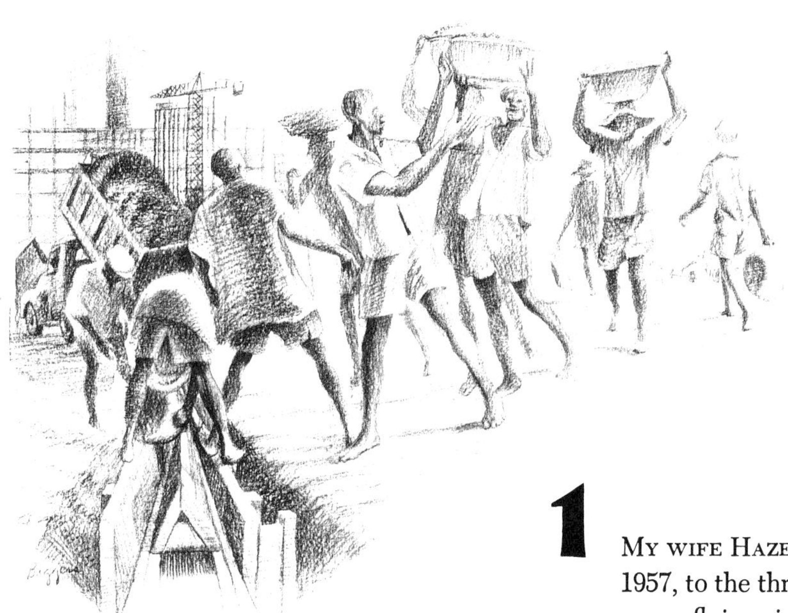

1

My wife Hazel and I awoke at daybreak on July 3, 1957, to the throb of the great four-engine plane. We were flying into a sapphire-blue virgin morning somewhere over West Africa. Our destination was Accra, the capital of Ghana.

Soon after we awoke the sun burst over the eastern horizon. Elusive arrows of orange bounced off the ceiling and reflected a warm red glow on rumpled, sleeping passengers. I sat up to get a better view of the countryside.

Far below, a bluish vapor crawled among the black-greens of the earth, filling us with restless anticipation of what bright daylight would reveal there. Even as we watched, the sun slowly climbed higher, pushing the darkness westward. We saw below us now a velvet green carpet of vegetation occasionally broken by patches and threads of iron red that we knew were clearings and connecting roads. The great silver plane thundered on in a southeasterly direction, and I slumped back meditatively.

As an American Negro, my lifelong desire had been to bridge the gap between African and American culture. When I was an art student at Hampton Institute in Virginia during the early forties our art master, Viktor Lowenfeld, taught us something about the noble meaning of African sculpture. But African art—in fact, African culture generally—remained devoid of significance in our lives. I felt cut off from my heritage, which I suspected was estimable and something to be embraced, not an ignobility to be scorned. I believed that many of my American brothers, in their flight from the stereotyped concepts of our race, had also flown from their real selves and had created a grotesque, unattainable image based on Caucasian attributes, a development that must surely prove a hindrance in the struggle to achieve dignity and self-respect in contemporary society.

Sorrowfully I recalled the dismissal from an American Negro college of a classmate of mine—a sensitive Negro girl with excellent intellectual and creative abilities—because she refused to take the kinks out of her hair with grease and pressing irons. And I remembered the self-conscious questions asked me and my students by other members of our race: "But why do you paint Negroes?" Our answers—"Whom should we portray? Whom do we know best? Are we not Negroes?"—failed to satisfy them.

My musing was interrupted by a change in the tempo of the engines. Again I sat up for a better view and observed Accra Bay, its shore lined with palm trees that waved their green crowns leisurely back and forth against a background of glaring white sand. Scattered for miles beyond, over the vastness of the Gulf of Guinea, were tiny fishing boats, salmon-pink dots on a blue-green sea.

The boats were so distant that they might have been in another world, and I was glad that the plane was losing altitude for the landing. I wanted to observe those boats more carefully, to know the fishermen intimately. One reason was that I was traveling on a UNESCO fellowship to do an artist's study of West African life. Another reason was that I wanted to embrace Africa. I was searching for roots.

The passengers began to stir and shift in their seats. Other faces besides Hazel's and mine pressed hard against windows to observe the spectacle. Gleaming white buildings near the edge of the ocean shot into view. And there were red-tiled roofs, green lawns, and asphalt streets, all in a checkerboard pattern. We stared at downtown Accra below us and saw, to our surprise, that it looked like an American city.

The plane dipped its left wing slowly and circled downward. Then it settled into a gentle glide. With a soft thump it met a concrete runway and taxied to the Accra terminal. At 7:00 A.M. we disembarked in Africa.

The morning air was a cool seventy degrees. We saw small groups of Africans, Europeans, and Americans waiting calmly at the gates as we entered customs. The officials—courteous, efficient, and patient—were dressed in crisp blue uniforms, and we noticed that they were all Africans. To see these black men attending to their duties with poise and obvious pride was inspiring to us.

At the terminal we were met by Mr. Edward Read, a UNESCO representative who directed the Ghana Vernacular Literature Bureau. He was smartly dressed for the tropical climate in freshly laundered white clothes—a short-sleeved shirt with an open collar, walking shorts, socks, and sandals. The spotless white attire accentuated the deep tan of his skin and the gold tinge of his blond hair, which had begun to gray around the temples.

Mr. Read helped us load our luggage into the trunk of his English-made automobile; then Hazel slipped into the rear seat, and I climbed into the front seat beside our host. We drove along an asphalt highway toward Accra, six miles from the airport. Trucks, buses, cars, and bicycles jammed the road, and along the shoulders of the highway flowed a stream of humanity—Africans carrying tremendous loads on erect heads and shoulders. Women, men, and children were on the move, down the highway to Accra. They moved with purpose and determination, with energetic, rhythmical steps. They held their bodies as straight as poles, their necks and heads erect; and they swung their arms freely—a movement that helped to propel themselves and their burdens forever forward. Mr. Read, perceiving our wonder, remarked that we would soon become accustomed to the African personality and to the atmosphere.

Entering the Accra suburbs, we passed two-story brick residences set behind wide green lawns. Mr. Read told us that these estates once housed British colonials, but that since independence, Africans—or anybody else who had the money—could live in them. We also passed many one- and two-story modern apartments being constructed of reinforced concrete; in Accra, as in all Ghana, there was a housing shortage.

The highway became more congested, and at the intersections the multitude swarmed in every direction. Policemen, smartly dressed in dark blue uniforms, white helmets, and elbow-length gloves, directed traffic. We met a platoon of khaki-attired soldiers marching in bold military rhythm. Next came a group of boisterous, barefooted teen-age boys riding by on spirited white and brown ponies; the people hesitated, then let the ponies have plenty of room. Ed Read told us that these were racing ponies, that horse racing was a popular sport in Ghana.

Along the road old men and women set up market on tables and boxes, selling raw products, manufactured articles, and cooked food. Many of the men wore short togas with walking shorts. Some were dressed in brilliantly striped togas that flowed to the ankles, and still others wore garments made of expensive *kente* cloth stitched with silk and gold threads. Many people, however, wore cheap imported cloth draped across bare shoulders. The clothing blended into a magnificent bunting-like display that flapped and waved in the morning air.

We saw no idle people; along the streets and sidewalks an atmosphere of purposefulness prevailed. Destiny was being met head on.

Farther on we witnessed a beehive of building activity. A new order of architecture was being raised in steel, concrete, stone, and glass. The unfinished structures foretold new office buildings, industries, library and school buildings, hospitals, hotels, and residences. A new way of life was supplanting another which was centuries old.

On Ring Road we turned right and drove a mile farther to the hotel. Along the road, repair gangs toiled, working picks and shovels in cadence. Another group of about twenty workers cleared brush along the embankment, swinging machetes to the rhythm of an instrument resembling a *maracá,* which was being shaken at a quick tempo by the foreman. It all reminded us of work gangs we used to see in North Carolina when we were children; they toiled to rhythm too. But here there were also bulldozers rumbling around, pushing tons of earth before them.

We pulled off the road onto a driveway that made a half-circle and stopped in front of the hotel, a two-story building of white stucco. Two boys dressed in white jackets and trousers opened the car doors and took our bags. We climbed several wide cement steps to a porch, then entered the lobby. Behind the desk stood a handsome, polite girl who looked to be in her early twenties. Her brightly colored dress was laundered and stiffly starched; her black skin reflected a clean, soft, silvery glow. Her hair was tightly braided in narrow rows, a hair style that we had known in North Carolina—"corn rows."

The girl's dark eyes measured us curiously but amiably. She asked if we were American Negroes, and if we had come to live in Ghana. I answered that we were American Negroes, but that we had come for only a few months—to learn something about her country. She wished us a pleasant visit.

Then Ed Read left us in the care of the desk clerk and the house boys. We went to our room eagerly; we wanted to unpack and to shower, then to have breakfast.

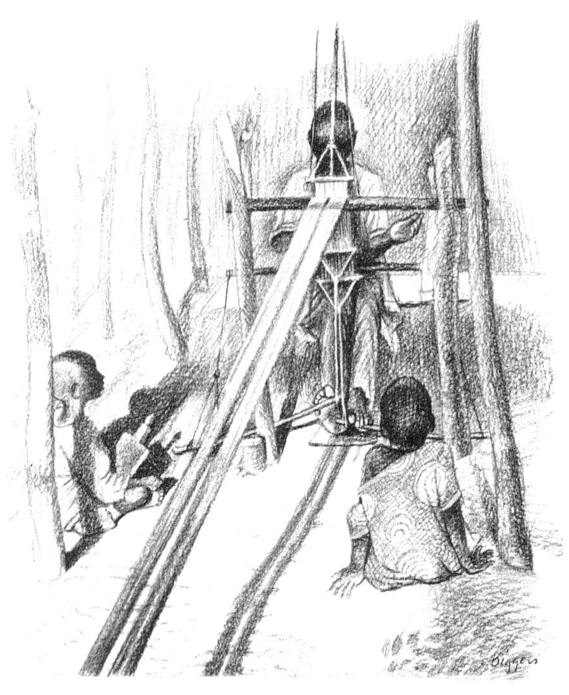

2

My immediate desire was to see as much of the country as possible, to acquire a broad vision. I had already read enough about the geography and history of Ghana to have an idea of what to expect:

Ghana is located in West Africa, facing the Gulf of Guinea to the south. Its coast line, stretching for some four hundred miles over low sandy beaches and bold rocky headlands, is characterized by a flat belt called the Accra plains, but this quickly gives way to mountainous country which covers most of central Ghana and reaches an altitude of more than two thousand feet. Farther on, in the Northern Territories, the mountains level off into rolling hills and vast plains. The total area of Ghana is about ninety-two thousand square miles, the population five million.

Inhabitants of the coastal plains and the foothills are the Fanti, Ga, and Ewe tribes. Ashanti inhabit the central forest region, Brong and other tribes (mostly of Moslem faith) the more sparsely settled Northern Territories.

Most of these people were for five centuries victims of the European lust for gold—gold in one form or another. In the fifteenth century the presence of the precious metal itself lured Portuguese ships to the coast of "Guinea," as it was then called. In the sixteenth century there arose a demand for slaves for shipment to the recently conquered West Indies, and for the next three hundred years all the leading European nations conducted a lively business selling human beings taken from this area. In the twentieth century another commodity supplanted gold and slaves; as a British Colony (the Gold Coast) the country became the world's leading producer of cocoa. But in 1957, a few months before our visit, the Gold Coast was given independence, and it was renamed "Ghana."

Now, having read about Ghana, I wanted to see it; so various officials arranged for Hazel and me an itinerary and a crowded schedule of activities that would exhibit the country geographically and culturally. Our first trip, however, was to take us into French Togo and Dahomey as well as through southeastern Ghana, because we had been advised to visit sections of French West Africa to gain a broader view of the region.

Permanent quarters were assigned us at the College of Technology in Kumasi, Ghana, about 180 miles northwest of Accra and thus more centrally located. Kumasi was the old capital of the Ashanti nation and afforded us an intimate contact with one of the more permanent and vigorous cultures of West Africa.

We made the first trip to Kumasi on July 7, our first Sunday in Ghana. Aidoo, a professional chauffeur, raced the little European sedan along a good asphalt highway that curved and climbed constantly. Occasionally the highway cut through a village; porches and steps extended almost to the shoulder. Along the way we passed people dressed for church —in robes, suits, dresses. But other people worked. A few market stalls were open, although business was generally slow. Railroad workers laid track, and road gangs put down new pavement and cut away brush from the shoulders. Farmers harvested fresh corn, cassava, pineapple, groundnuts, and oranges.

We climbed higher into a dense mountain forest that was cool and damp. Overhead, thick clouds piled up, shutting out much of what little sunlight had filtered through to us. A mist began falling, then a hard shower. Aidoo slowed his speed until the rain ceased.

Still we climbed. The trees grew taller, the foliage thicker. Soon we could not see beyond the shoulders; we were speeding through a tunnel with green walls. Not even the sky was visible for long periods. We became subdued by nature's architecture, and it was a relief to arrive at the village of Kibi. There Aidoo left the highway momentarily and drove through the village streets. We saw a well-ordered town with new, freshly painted mud and cement houses, green lawns, and towering palms that lined the roads. Crowning a nearby hill was the two-story, colonial-style palace of a chief, whom Aidoo referred to as a great one indeed.

We returned to the highway, and farther along we observed mountains poking their heights above the clouds; we could see villages perched on the sides. Then we drove into a big, sprawling town located in a valley below a huge rocky bluff. Large groups of people, all dressed in their Sunday best, strolled about, conversing gaily. Aidoo slowed the car.

Ahead of us walked several young men who could only be described as warriors. The muscles on their bare shoulders and arms seemed to ripple; their heads were erect, their chests out. They were proud young men, and I thought to myself that colonialism had not left its mark on them. I did not know that they were but a sample of the proud Ashanti people I would live with and attempt to portray for the next few months.

Early in the afternoon we reached the College of Technology, four miles from Kumasi. Aidoo pulled off the highway to the left, and we entered the campus through a gate. On our left we saw dormitories, dining halls, and classroom buildings, and—beyond —steel girders representing skeletons of buildings to come. The road then curved slightly toward a group of brightly painted bungalows with wide screened-in porches, trimmed shrubbery, and neat gardens and lawns. This was faculty row. I felt at home.

We stopped in front of a five-room tropical bungalow, and Mr. Attefa, the registrar, led us inside. The house, which was to be ours, was spotless. Mr. Attefa introduced us to the cook and two stewards, and informed us that they went along with the house. Our luggage was brought in; we washed; then lunch was served. As we were getting up from the table Patrick Hulede, a member of the art faculty, came in. Beaming, he extended a hand and gave us a warm personal welcome.

Almost immediately he asked if we would like to observe a ceremony of drumming and dancing. I asked when this would be; I had not slept much for five days because of our crowded, exciting schedule.

"Now!" Patrick exclaimed, and I saw Hazel's eyes and shoulders drop.

"I'm ready to go," I answered, "but I think we'll have to let Hazel get some rest." The long drive through the forest, the acquisition of a new house with all those white-garmented servants, and the drowsing effect of a heavy lunch had almost finished her.

Patrick and I drove by for Miss Mary Kirby, a weaving instructor who never missed an opportunity to observe drumming and dancing; then we took to the highway. After traveling some distance we heard the drumming, faintly at first. Suddenly, from the crest of a hill, we saw a large crowd of people, all dressed in colorful garments. The sounds and the colors snapped me out of my drowsiness.

Patrick said that these were funeral rites which had been in progress for two months. But the mourning had ceased some time ago; this was the more cheerful part of the celebration. Money had been collected to pay off the debts of the deceased, and the amount left over was now being spent to buy drinks and food for friends who had participated in the rites. I remembered what the old people back home used to say: Cry when a child is born and be happy when he departs from this world.

The mourners—or celebrants, perhaps I should say—had formed a circle. Some were seated on stools. Others were standing. But all were singing and clapping, keeping time with the drums. Whenever a person felt moved to do so he entered the center of the ring and began dancing. The dancers were paired: two men, two women, or a man and a woman. Each dancer bent his body slightly forward from the waist, keeping his arms pointed toward the ground. His shoulders were in constant movement, backward and forward, as were his back and shoulder muscles, flexing and unflexing. Feet moved briskly, in time with the incessant drums. Each pair of dancers tried desperately to outdo the others, and when a couple became exhausted they would retire, dripping with perspiration. Others took their place. The rhythm was contagious, and we found it impossible to keep our own feet still.

After an hour or so we moved on to visit other groups farther down the road. The scene was the same: Colorfully dressed men and women clapped hands, sang, and danced. A leader—or sometimes several leaders—directed the groups by singing a phrase, which the group would repeat or answer. Then, as the music became more enchanting, couples responded by moving into the center of the circle and drowning themselves in syncopation. This was a familiar form of expression to me, and I remarked to Patrick and Mary that the similarity between these group expressions and those I had witnessed in night clubs and church meetings in America was startling.

We left the celebrants, and Patrick drove us through Kumasi, giving me a brief glance at the city—the railroad station, a new publishing house, the sprawling market, famous old Kumasi Fort, the public library and cultural center, the government house, and the main business street. Along a high grassy ridge overlooking the city stood roomy, palm-shaded houses once occupied by British civil servants. Africans lived there now.

We returned to the college about seven o'clock. I thanked Patrick for the outing, said goodnight, and retired immediately. I slept soundly until seven o'clock the next morning, Monday, when we were awakened by a knock on our bedroom door. It was one of the stewards, bringing hot coffee. I looked at Hazel rubbing her drowsy eyes and said, "You'd better wake up and enjoy this; it happens only once in a lifetime."

Later that morning Patrick showed us around the campus and the surrounding area. The tour began with a visit to the art department, where we saw students engaged in a variety of activities: sketching a live model, painting portraits, copying plaster casts made from European sculpture. In the pottery shop students operated a potter's wheel. Weaving classes made imitation *kente* cloth on broad looms; graphic arts students operated lithographic and etching presses. Finally we went to Patrick's bookbinding department, where he showed us something of his craft. He also introduced us to scores of his friends, being particularly thorough, I think, because he was soon to leave for Europe.

The tour was interesting, and I appreciated it. But I was thunderstruck. The department reminded me of a traditional art school in the United States. Not one piece of traditional African sculpture was to be seen, not one example of African jewelry. Here in the heart of West Africa—the fountainhead of African wood carving, of ivory and metal sculpture—there was scarcely a reference to African art, as if it should be ignored by college students and left to the illiterate people of the bush.

I felt that it was right for Africans to learn something about other traditions, other cultures, but that it was inexcusable for them not to be aware of their own. And these young Africans would be the teachers, the future leaders of Ghana! Women in the small villages made pots the size of barrels, pots that a grown man could climb into; and here were college men turning out pots the size of a drinking cup, as fragile as precious china and lacking its attractiveness. Moreover, copying plaster casts was no longer considered a good practice for an art student anywhere. But I was pleased to see that the traditional *kente* cloth had not been forgotten, and that many local weavers came to Mary Kirby to learn how to operate the broad loom.

We visited the administrative offices and met the president of the college, an Australian. We called on the registrar, the assistant registrar, and clerical workers. Then we visited many other departments—architecture and engineering, home economics, agriculture, music.

Visiting the music department afforded me some consolation after my earlier disappointment. There we met Ephraim Amu, department head, and found him greatly disturbed by an article in the local newspaper criticizing African music as being so primitive that it should be replaced by "civilized" music.

I soon discovered the reason for his concern: Mr. Amu had devoted his whole life to re-establishing African music and culture and to fighting the imposition of foreign traditions. He had lost his job in a Presbyterian college because of his conviction that African music should have a place in the schools and in national life. At Kumasi he had successfully led a drive to erect a campus tower housing a pair of talking drums. Classes changed by the language of the drums, not by bells. Still, Mr. Amu did not restrict his department to the teaching of African music. Later I was to hear his students give an exciting concert: During the first half of the program they played compositions of European masters on strings and brass, and during the second half they sang Negro spirituals and African songs and played traditional African instruments that he and his students had made themselves.

After telling us about the newspaper article Mr. Amu added, with considerable feeling, that he would have to take time off from his music and write the editor. It was important, because many people read the papers.

We left Mr. Amu then, and Patrick again drove through the town. There another surprise was in store for me: In Kumasi the city officials were building a zoo. Hazel and I, with our Hollywood outlook, had thought big game roamed all over Africa. We did not know that many American children are better acquainted with elephants, lions, and giraffes than are children in West Africa. (During our entire visit I saw only one monkey, a small snake crossing the highway, a few field rats—and many tropical birds. During some nights we heard the screams of small "tree bears," but we never saw them.)

These few days in Kumasi were pleasant and relaxing—and valuable as an orientation period. But I had come to see the country, and there was much more to it than Kumasi and Accra. The finance minister of Ghana, K. A. Gbedemah, loaned us his new Chevrolet sedan and a multilingual chauffeur, Kwasi. The administrative officer of the Ghana Vernacular Literature Bureau, Miss Ella Griffin, loaned us her cook, Kojo, and gave us some advice: visit French West Africa, to gain a broader view of the region. So in mid-July we left Kumasi, traveled to Accra, then journeyed eastward into French Togo and Dahomey. Ella Griffin herself joined us for the trip.

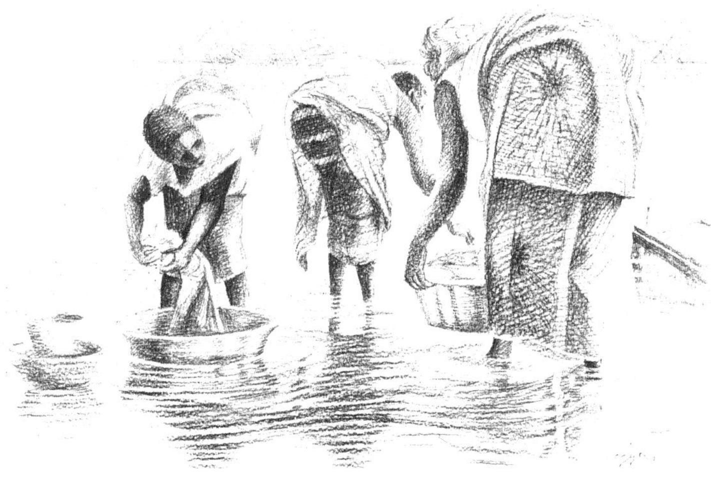

3

Kwasi and Kojo sat in the front seat, Ella, Hazel, and I in the back seat of Mr. Gbedemah's sedan. To our left we saw the campus of the University College of Ghana, situated on Lagoon Hill, and herds of cattle, spotted black and white, grazed upon the broad Accra plains. Far beyond loomed the Akwapim hills, providing an irregular, misty horizon. To our right was the cool blue Gulf of Guinea, its surf seeming to reach out for us. Clusters of fishing villages gave a human touch to the scene. For miles along the sandy shore stretched a succession of silvery nets. Women and children moved easily among palm shadows, adding softness and warmth to nature's boldness.

We rolled along at forty miles an hour, meeting lorries crowded with people or loaded with produce. Small European cars shot past us. Occasionally Kwasi was forced to slow down and pull over to the side to pass workers who were filling potholes in the highway. To the right of our asphalt road, men and machines moved tons of earth, laying the foundation for a new speedway. In the future this coastal wonderland would offer relaxation to the multitudes.

We had been traveling for about an hour when we saw, a few hundred yards ahead, a slow-moving line of cars, trucks, and buses; we were approaching the ferry landing on the mighty Volta River. Soon after arriving in Ghana we had heard of a project planned for this river—a dam that would transform the dry Accra plains into a fertile green area and provide electric power in abundance. We came up to the rear of the line of traffic and noticed, on the opposite bank of the mile-wide river, the town of Sogankope. But after a brief glance Hazel and Ella resumed an intensive discussion on a variety of topics ranging from the strategy used by the Convention People's Party for gaining votes to the clothing styles worn by market women. From venders who walked up and down the line of automobiles Kojo and Kwasi bought yellow ears of boiled corn on the cob and golden brown plantain cakes, and devoured them hungrily. But I peered out the car window, and as we slowly approached the river I could see displayed along its banks a symphony of motion. Scores of women were washing clothes at the water's edge; a few stood knee-deep, letting the river water slosh around them. The women paid no attention to a warm shower that had begun to fall. They kept up a rhythmical movement—up and down, slowly up and down. Big white enameled pans had been filled with sudsy water; the clothes were dipped into them, scrubbed, then rinsed in river water. But it was not all toil; the women conversed with each other with obvious friendliness and animation. They communicated with their voices, with their eyes, and even with their bodies.

One tall, elegant young woman caught my attention because of her striking beauty and graceful poise. I motioned to Hazel and Ella. Their chattering ceased, and we watched. After the woman had washed all the clothes in her bundle she began to remove, piece by piece, the garments she was wearing. First she removed her head cloth, revealing a braided hair style. She washed and rinsed the cloth, wrung it out, and carefully laid it with her other laundered clothes. Then she removed and washed her upper garment, revealing statuesque shoulders and well-formed breasts. Next she removed the cloth draped around her narrow waist, leaving only a wisp of a garment as a covering. Her dark, wet skin glistened with each graceful movement of her slender body. When the woman had completed her washing she strolled easily—on tiptoe, it seemed—to the top of a hill. There she hesitated for a moment, then entered her straw-roofed hut.

Never before had I witnessed such sensitive expression and delicate movement. To me her feminine form had no equal in its subtle beauty and its vitality, so suggestive was it of ripeness, fullness, firmness. She reflected tranquility and warmth, like the easy-moving, sun-heated river itself. But Kwasi and Kojo seemed not the least bit interested in the scene that I had found so fascinating, and later during our stay in Ghana I found out why: African men look the other way when a woman bares her body publicly for practical reasons like this.

The ferry whistle blasted; Kwasi started the engine and eased the car aboard. The boat chugged across the broad Volta, and it reminded me of crossing the Mississippi at New Orleans.

Leaving the river behind us, we sped forward toward the Togo border. There we encountered the usual customs and immigration formalities, first on the Ghana side, then on the French side. We were scrutinized carefully, and Kwasi had to answer many questions and to present a folder full of credentials. But Kojo never got out of the car. The officials seemed to ignore his presence. We also observed that residents of the area wandered to and fro through and around the gates on the beach side without being stopped.

Once past customs we eagerly resumed our journey. We drove through Lomé, then discovered to our delight that the shore drive from there to Cotonou is probably one of the most beautiful of its kind in the world. The showers had suddenly stopped; blue sky again predominated. Scattered powder-puff clouds drifted around the heavens. Sunlight splashed through the black-green palms lining the highway. The sand near the boiling surf could have been gold dust. In the distance, the horizon lay deep blue and silent.

The people who live along this shore had built their houses among clusters of rugged palms. These trees provided building material, food, and fuel. House sidings and fences were made of plaited palm fiber; roofs were constructed from the branches. Coconut meat provided a nourishing food, and coconut milk a thirst-quenching drink. Coconut shells, after drying, gave them good fuel. Along the shore fishermen mended nets while their women smoked fish.

Late that evening we arrived in Cotonou. We looked for rooms in several hotels without success; all were crowded. It was Bastille Day—July 14—and many people had come to Cotonou to celebrate. Hotel entrances were crowded with traders who sat with their wares of ebony sculpture, bronze figurines, textiles, ivory trinkets, and jewelry. We looked but did not buy.

We gave up, temporarily, the search for rooms and sought dinner at a hospitable hotel restaurant facing the beach. The soup, sizzling steaks, red wine, and French bread with butter made sumptuous fare—at one thousand francs each—but we still had no place to sleep. The restaurant manager telephoned a number of hotels, but without success.

The manager advised us to go on to the next town, Porto-Novo—the French capital of Dahomey. He felt sure we would be able to get hotel accommodations there. But our gasoline gauge registered empty, and since this was a holiday all petrol stations had closed early. We drove around town on the last few drops of gas, hoping to find some way out of our predicament.

Soon we met two men in a jeep, and I waved them over to the side of the road. They were good-natured Frenchmen. In their own language Ella explained to them what our plight was, and the driver of the jeep replied that he could help us. He invited us to come along to his house, where we could spend the night. He turned his jeep around, and we followed him for several blocks—turning right, then left, and finally pulling up to a white brick cottage surrounded by coconut palms. The Frenchman told us that he was married to an African woman and would be most happy to help "her people." It would not be inconvenient, he added, since his wife and children had gone to visit her parents, and he himself would be celebrating all night.

He struck matches to some kerosene lamps, and we entered the house. The living room and study looked comfortable enough. I forced some money on him, and he and his friend left. After the jeep had roared away we could hear, in the distance, dance music punctuated by firecracker blasts. We were not really satisfied with the accommodations but had no other choice. It had been a long day.

Examining the house again, more carefully this time, we discovered animal dung on the floors of the bathroom, the kitchen, and the two bedrooms. The Frenchman owned some goats, and he must have loved them enough to give them the run of the house. I was ready to leave, and so were the others, but a rainstorm hit, eliminating the only alternative—camping on the beach. We decided to clean the Frenchman's house, but even after scrubbing the floors we were not satisfied. An uncleanness lingered.

We moved a bed from the back room into the study and closed off the rear of the house. The mattress was in fair condition; so we put on clean linen, and Hazel and I lay down there. Kwasi and Kojo slept in the front room; Ella took the back seat of the car. Before I dropped off to sleep I saw a large rat enter the house through a hole in a screen. He wandered about, then left the same way he entered. I burned the kerosene lamps all night.

We rose at daybreak, drove to a petrol station, and waited for it to open. After filling the tank and checking the oil and water we drove to the beach, stripped, and bathed in the surf. The cool water and the crisp morning breeze gave us a clean feeling after our night's ordeal. Kojo started the kerosene stove and made coffee.

Then we dressed and called on a local official, to reserve a government resthouse near Abomey—or anywhere in the country to the north. We were determined to get out of Cotonou and away from the French atmosphere as soon as possible. The agent advised us not to go to Abomey; it was the rainy season, he said, and the roads would be washed out. He almost convinced us that the trip would be impossible.

We had two choices: to go on to Abomey against the agent's advice, or to go back to Lomé. We decided against taking his advice, and I did not like the look in his eyes. I felt that he thought we were snoopers. We were just that, in fact, because Africans of traditional culture lived in the country we had chosen to visit, and I wanted to know them. We went to a bank and changed our good English pound notes into almost worthless francs.

We began the journey northward and soon realized we had made the right decision. Ten or fifteen miles out of Cotonou the cultural atmosphere changed. Although the construction of the houses and the organization of the villages were similar to those along the shore and in the hill country of Ghana, I noticed certain differences. Near the doorways of houses, at the edges of yam farms, near the shoulders of the road, and sometimes in forest clearings a few yards back from the road, wooden and clay sculptures had been anchored in the ground. Many were weathered, but some were new. A few of the new clay sculptures had not even had time to dry. Over some of the sculptures, which were from one and a half to four feet tall, a libation had recently been poured.

I was filled with an emotion—an elation—that is difficult to describe. It was a joy to see art thus serving an important function in human life. But the people generally ignored our curiosity and enthusiasm; they went about their chores. Whenever I stopped to make photographs or sketches some of them would occasionally glance up and stare with eyes that seemed to look through me. Then they would often shake their heads and frown indignantly, as if to say, "There's another tourist fool on the prowl among us."

Most sculptures along the road were conceived in human form, but some combined human and animal features. One impressive clay sculpture, four feet tall, stood protected under a four-post construction topped by a conical grass roof. The sculpture was round at the base, which was about thirty inches in diameter, and rose in a cone shape to the shoulders. From the shoulders grew a cylindrical neck and a large egg-shaped head. To the head were attached cow horns and large eyes, of some kind of glass. The nose and the mouth were modeled.

Later I learned that clay sculptures like this one were protected from the weather for only one season. When new crops were planted new sculptures were erected. The builders had no intention of making them permanent; the idea was to create anew—each year, during planting time—a new vitality, to bring forth an abundant harvest. When the harvest season was over, the clay sculptures were left to disintegrate; they had served their purpose. I felt that this was indeed a dynamic and an unusually creative approach.

All the way to Abomey the road was in fairly good condition, even though we drove through several downpours. The rain made the clay roadbed slippery at times, but we had no serious trouble. I had, in fact, driven over red-clay roads much worse than these in my native North Carolina.

We rode for miles over gently undulating plains covered with tall elephant grass. We studied the countryside constantly, hoping eventually to see some big game. But during the trip from Cotonou to Dahomey only a field rat obliged us with an appearance, scurrying across the road a few yards ahead of the car.

Nearing Abomey, we found the roads fringed with tall palm trees. Villages were no longer far apart. Plots of cultivated land lay between houses and compounds; people in large numbers walked along the road. We began meeting many automobiles and trucks, and shortly after noon we arrived in Abomey.

We found a crowded, bustling city. There were many fine homes with columns, porches, and upstairs balconies; the homes were painted chrome yellow, salmon-pink, pale-green, lavender. We passed petrol stations and market places; everywhere there was congestion. Numberless people dressed in a myriad of colors moved in all directions, carrying bundles atop heads. We pulled over to the side and waved to a khaki-garbed policeman who was directing traffic. He was a tall black man with sharp features, and he was brisk—but friendly. We introduced ourselves with friendly handshaking, and he expressed pleasure at meeting Americans. Ella requested directions to a hotel or a resthouse, and I asked where we could find the craftsmen—weavers, wood carvers, potters, and metalsmiths. The policeman listened respectfully, then called to a small boy, about nine, and told him to take us to a hotel and guide us around Abomey. The lad climbed in the front seat with Kojo and Kwasi and directed us to a rambling, cream-colored hotel where we could have dinner. Broad concrete steps led up to a wide porch framed by dingy white columns.

The proprietor, a fat, smiling, brown-skinned man, gave us a grand welcome. Not only was he delighted to have our business; he seemed genuinely happy to have Negro Americans as guests. He directed Hazel and Ella to a washroom, then called his cooks enthusiastically. Spirited activity in the kitchen followed, and our young guide said he would wait outside until after the meal; then he would take us to the craftsmen.

The proprietor pushed two tables together and over them spread a long white tablecloth. We all sat down to a bountiful meal—guinea fowl soup with okra, roast pork, barbecued chicken, fried tomatoes, boiled yams dripping with butter, and red wine. Ella asked Kojo his opinion of the food, and he answered, "It is proper chop, madame." His jaws were full and his eyes were smiling—just like mine. We ate entirely too much—the meats were tender and succulent—and drank two bottles of that delicious red wine.

Our host pulled up a chair, and we had a lively conversation with our meal. Through Ella I fired a hundred questions at him. He was an African Nationalist, and though he respected De Gaulle and the French he believed that Dahomey must have self-rule. During our conversation he also told us something about the craftsmen of Abomey and offered to guide us to them, but our nine-year-old friend was waiting to do that. Then, having finished our meal, we found our young friend.

We drove into the heart of the city, and our little guide pointed out interesting sights with intelligence and insight. After easing through a sea of humanity and passing many blocks with row after row of mud houses we finally stopped before a tall wooden gate leading to a very large, high-walled compound; the clay walls must have been twelve feet tall and three feet thick. We drove through the gate and found that the walls enclosed a lawn as large as a football field. To our left, built into the wall, stood a massive mud house, twenty feet tall, topped by a thatched roof. On the opposite side of the grassy field stood a similar house facing us. It was open; several columns supported the roof. We drove across the compound to this building, a weaving center, and found two teen-age boys operating looms. Hanging on the back wall and laid out on tables were samples of their weaving: black and red geometric patterns woven into backgrounds of lemon yellow and cream white; textiles made of a coarse, strong cloth into which had been woven cubistic animal and fowl forms. Hazel and Ella made purchases, and I took photographs—with the weavers' permission.

Across the compound was a third house, much smaller than the others. Inside we saw a man spreading out a colorful checkered cloth about the size of a bedspread. We examined it, and I saw the piece had been made in much the same way that my mother made patchwork quilts back home in Gastonia. This one was decorated with symbolic figures of human beings, animals, and plants; it was indeed a work with charm.

I asked Ella to find out if there were wood carvings for sale too, but all her inquiries concerning sculpture were passed off in a manner which I soon learned was an African way of saying, "I'm not interested in that subject." Why should a person ask for sculpture when weaving was displayed for sale? We paid several thousand francs for some of the textiles; then I demanded to know where I could locate sculptures.

The master weaver, exasperated now, sent one of the boys away with an impatient hand motion. When the boy reappeared a few minutes later he was holding a sculpture carved out of mahogany; it was covered with dirt and obviously had been buried. The boy handed it to me quickly, as if it were burning his hand, then stepped backward a few paces and demanded five hundred francs. I gave him the money and deposited my purchase in the automobile. The sculpture I had bought is called Asu, a fertility deity that at the same time possesses maleficent qualities. The eyes are dominant; they are spherical—all-seeing, all-knowing. The hands support a gourd-like breast, reminding me of the Ashanti proverb: "If the King's breast is full of milk, it belongs to all the world." The sculpture is neither male nor female; it simply symbolizes fertility.

Our little guide suggested that we now visit the King, whose palace was near Abomey, for the King could direct us to wood carvers and other craftsmen if we wished. We thanked the master weaver and left.

Our guide directed us along ten miles of twisting, but smooth, dirt roads, all lined with towering palm trees. Then we made an abrupt turn to the right, drove alongside a plot of farm land, and—at our guide's insistence—stopped near a farmer who was hoeing vigorously. His huge shoulders and chest and his powerful arms oozed perspiration. Our guide asked for directions to the King's residence, and the farmer stopped hoeing just long enough to wave us on straight ahead.

A quarter of a mile farther the road ended abruptly at a heavy wooden gate. Thick, high walls extended to each side. The gate was weather-worn, but patterns carved in low relief were still evident. Through our guide we explained our mission to the gateman, and he allowed us to enter. Immediately I noticed brilliantly painted murals covering the outside walls of the building facing us; the form concept was similar to that decorating the appliqué cloth mural that we had seen on the wall of the weavers' compound.

A thin old man, probably about seventy-five, stepped toward us, slowly but proudly. Again our mission was explained, and the old man invited us to enter the center building. This we did, and we were delighted to find the interior cool and clean. Six or eight cushioned chairs lined a wall, and the man asked us to be seated. Then he left by a side door which led to the open courtyard. We waited a few minutes, and a small boy about the age of our guide came in to ask the nature of our visit. Our guide told him, and the royal inquirer left by the side door. Another boy came in, asked the same questions, and left; then a third lad entered, repeated the questions, and departed. After another wait a sturdily built elderly woman clothed in deep purple appeared and questioned our guide, this time at length. For the sixth time since we arrived at the gate our young friend explained our mission. He looked over at us with large brown eyes that were clear and patient, but that held a hint of excitement in them. Finally the woman left, and we waited another twenty minutes. Suddenly another woman appeared, dressed in silver-gray garments and wearing gold earrings, and announced that the King would greet us. Our little guide asked us to stand, and we did.

Through the open side door we could see two figures in brilliant array—a rather small woman and a man of great bulk—walking through the sunny courtyard. The woman was trying desperately to hold an umbrella above their heads and at the same time bestow tender, embracing care on her corpulent companion. But doing both of these things simultaneously was an impossibility, for the man was of such huge proportions that as he lumbered along his feet seemed too delicate and fragile to support his bulky weight. Getting through the door was an even greater struggle for them.

I looked at our little guide and saw that he was trembling with respectfulness. Each of us was allowed to shake the King's hand, which was extended as a numb appendage without feeling. Then the King spoke to his woman companion, obviously one of his wives, who had by now succeeded in closing the umbrella. She motioned for us to sit; then the King plopped his massive weight into his chair with what must have been relief. We saw that he wore a gold crown studded with jewels, gold armlets that cut into his fleshy arms and gold rings that squeezed his stubby fingers, sandals with gold nuggets attached, and a silk robe of green and gold. His flesh was the color of the mud houses of that area—burnt sienna—and reflected an oily smoothness. The woman sat beside him, on his left, continually adjusting his robe as a mother would look after a child. Her hands and eyes were completely attentive to him. Our little guide sat on a floor mat directly across from the King and never once gave an indication of any feeling but awe.

Suddenly eight or ten small children, ranging in age from two to seven, bounced into the room, sat on the floor near the King's feet, and created a clamor with their frolicking—laughing, shouting, rolling, and wrestling. The King uttered a command in a gruff, guttural voice and gave a harsh wave of his flat little hands, and the children scampered to the door as if to leave the room. But they lingered there, then one by one they returned to their place on the floor and the riot of play began all over. The King repeated his command often, but it became a game for the children.

Despite these interruptions we were able to communicate, through a complex system of translation and interpretation. I would speak to Ella in English, and she would relay my message in French to our little guide, who would translate the message into the African language to the King's interpreter for final relaying to the King. The King's answers and his questions came back in reverse order. I thus told him that my wife and I were of African origin and that we had come all the way from America to visit him—a statement which he did not believe. I added the information that I was a university art teacher in Texas and that I wanted to understand the culture of my forefathers.

The King listened attentively; an expression of genuine sympathy and understanding spread across his face, which now displayed a sensitivity that had not been so noticeable before. But he told us to come back at a later date and to write him a week before our return. He would then gather his craftsmen together and have them prepare an exhibit of their work. We thanked him for his hospitality, and as we were leaving he told us that his secretary was in the United States studying at Columbia University, that upon his return he was to teach the King the English language.

The King, his wives, and his many children walked to the gate with us. Again one of his wives tried to hold the umbrella and at the same time bestow tender personal care. We took our places in the automobile, and the entire royal family waved goodbye to us.

In Abomey we left our little guide, but I believe that Ella seriously wanted to adopt him. We gave him a wad of hundred-franc notes. He was thrilled with the payment and shook our hands gratefully. Ella and Hazel kissed him goodbye; then we drove off. But we looked back once and saw that he was still standing in the middle of the dusty road, waving to us.

Our trip to Abomey had been rewarding, and we were pleased that we had made up our minds to chance the road against the government agent's advice. We had sampled the remnants of a sturdy culture that had attained a peak ages ago; we had met a descendant of once-powerful monarchs who had ruled West Africa for centuries. The splendor of the past was now dim and obscure—only scattered sparks glowed—but its brilliance of long ago could be imagined.

We began the trip southward to Lomé in the late afternoon, while the sun was sliding down the western horizon. As we drove through rolling, palm-crowned hills we met long lines of people coming home from the fields. I felt flowing over me that feeling of love and serenity experienced in every land when mothers, fathers, and children return home in the evening, after a day's toil, to comfort each other, to relax, to laugh and play.

Especially were the African women impressive. They walked in single file—hundreds of them—their heads crowned with hand-woven baskets loaded with produce from the earth: yams, cassavas, corn, pineapples, groundnuts, peppers, and paw-paws. They walked quickly, gracefully, determinedly—bringing food and warmth to their families.

Many of them were stripped to the waist, their bosoms embracing the evening glow. Young maidens, mature women, old matriarchs—all walked up from the valley of pregnant earth, breasts protruding with green-gourd firmness, or gently dropping with melon fullness, or sagging with time-wrinkled service and sacrifice. But they all held their backs and shoulders erect, these earthly goddesses of fertility, as they walked without hesitation upon life's sacrificial altar.

The burnished-gold sun burst upon them and glorified them. Gold shot from their bodies and ricocheted from the fertile black earth; the light blinded us. And out of the same valley—the valley of the morning, it seemed—came more black silhouettes, like columns of marching soldier ants—growing into bold contours of human flesh and cloth fiber as they approached us—passing us by, as time does, for we could embrace them for only a moment —then leaving us behind, marching onward across the plain in silhouettes of tomorrow—vanishing into the night. These African women are daughters of the moon, queens of the fertile earth, mothers of toil and sorrow, descendants of Eve tramping through life's Garden of Eden, as countless generations before them had tramped and were trampled on, bearing their burdens and their gifts with pride. As I watched this magnificent procession of warm, red sorrow march into the cool blue of the northern skies it seemed to me that the leafy crowns of the tall palm trees grew still, that the evening no longer moved, that the nugget of gold fire hesitated in its downward plunge. But flocks of black crows cried out, startling me, and I realized that darkness was upon us.

This had been a golden day in our own time; Mother Africa had embraced me. Deep emotion, carried within me from early childhood, rose like a flood tide as I reflected on Africa's ageless drama, on her continuing human tragedy, on her quiet evening beauty.

As we drove southward toward the sea we continued to meet women returning home in a never-ending stream of life. We drove, slowly, through many villages, and in one of them we stopped. Children gathered around us; then came young women and young men who leaned on the car doors and peered through the windows. Their freshly bathed bodies were in harmony with the subtle fragrance of the evening, and we were delighted to accept from them corn balls, yams, and gourds, forced upon us by warm, clean hands.

We were exchanging knowing greetings: greetings between strangers who look deep into one another and know they are not strangers, for in each other they see their own image, and that image is good. We could hear drums beating, could feel them deep inside, throbbing with our heartbeats, with our laughter and communication. We were discovering all over again that which is good and human in man. We were finding roots.

We drove on then and reached Lomé about ten o'clock that night. We bathed quickly and sank into soft beds. Not far away a furious surf thundered, but distance softened the roar. Winds from the Gulf of Guinea rippled the window curtains, and we fell asleep easily.

The next few days were instructive, with visits to the Lomé market and to the shops of master craftsmen—goldsmiths, carpenters, wood carvers, cabinetmakers—but I had been overwhelmed by the atmosphere which had evoked such deep emotion during the preceding days. The time had come for me to portray the fountain of African life. We drove to Accra, returned the Chevrolet sedan to Mr. Gbedemah, and went on to Kumasi in another automobile. There I struggled for days to portray the African woman—"*maame,*" which means mother—in her golden glory.

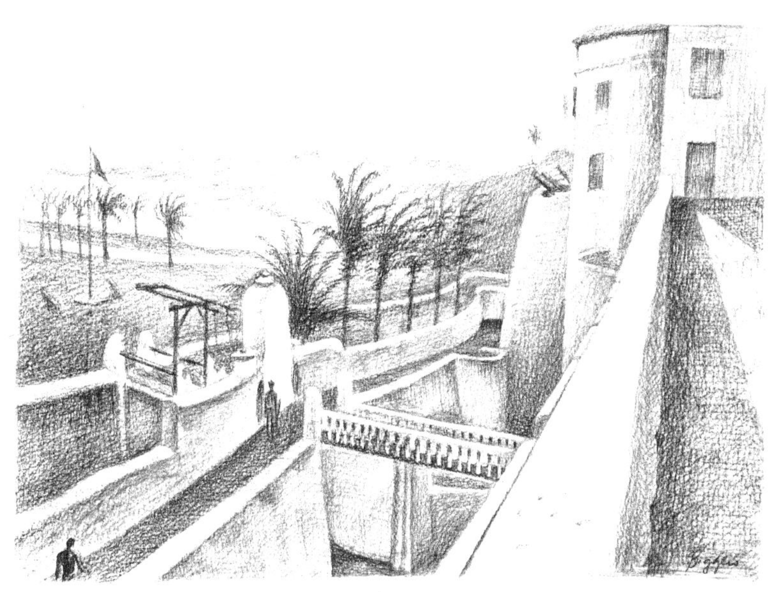

4

PATRICK HULEDE was responsible for our going to Cape Coast and to Elmina, neighboring towns on the Gulf of Guinea about one hundred miles southwest of Accra. Patrick was a staunch Catholic, a hard-working layman, and he had been chosen to represent Ghana Catholics at an international convention in Rome. He was making a trip to Cape Coast to receive instructions from an archbishop, an old Englishman who was returning home soon, and from the young African bishop Amissah, who was replacing the Englishman. We were delighted to accept Patrick's invitation to accompany him to a part of Ghana we had not visited; there were some historical sites along the coast that we could not afford to miss.

From Kumasi we took the Cape Coast highway through Bekwai, a town thirty miles south that is the site of some recent excavations resulting in important archeological finds—terra-cotta sculpture, pottery, and other relics. But more immediately exciting was the scenery; we drove around treacherous curves, through steep mountain country, and under a green canopy of a majestic rain forest similar to the one between Accra and Kumasi.

Along the highway we saw abundant crops of plantain, banana, paw-paw, and cocoa—all growing in the forest. At first I wondered at such unusual farming methods, but then I learned that many of the plants could not thrive under a hot African sun; so cocoa seedlings had been planted in the cool shadows of towering vegetation, and other plants had been similarly protected. Thus the crops grew beneath and among forest growth—and towering above all were the giant Bombax trees, sometimes more than two hundred feet tall.

Along the highway we also saw bamboo clusters, thirty to sixty feet tall, that spread out like ribs of a giant umbrella. I noticed that bamboo was used for fences, house sidings, and roofs, and that bamboo fiber went into baskets and fishing traps. All over West Africa, however, corrugated metal is swiftly replacing bamboo and thatch in roof construction because of its durability—but not because of its coolness on a hot day or its aesthetic appearance. When the metal roofs rust an African mud village takes on the appearance of an American slum. I thought to myself as we drove along that a tile made from the red African clay would be superior to corrugated metal as a roofing material, both aesthetically and functionally. And clay is a native material, to be had in abundance only for the digging.

About thirty miles from the coast the landscape changed, and I had something else to think about besides West African roofing. The tall, luxuriant growth and the overhanging foliage gave way to abbreviated vegetation—to pineapple farms and coconut palms. The land became undulating; sharp turns in the highway became fewer; and in the distance there appeared a distinct horizon. We noticed more sunlight and a cooler, lighter atmosphere, and we speculated on the ways the great forest, so dominant and overpowering, might affect the lives of its human inhabitants. But our discussion was cut short by our arrival at Cape Coast, a beautiful old city nestling among a series of rolling green hills that drop off sharply at the edge of the sea.

History surrounded us as we cut through narrow winding streets and passed buildings stained with time. In the city itself the steeples of protestant and Catholic churches and missions, centuries old, stood out boldly, while the green hills to the north were crowned by newly constructed schools and ancient castles. The scene vaguely reminded us of Lisbon, but only for a few minutes, for farther down the narrow street we saw the graceful, colorful figures of African women. And not far away was the sprawling market with its women—hundreds of women, babies rocking on their backs, heavy loads of produce atop their heads.

But most Cape Coasters declare with pride that their produce is education. For generations the town has provided many leaders of the country. There are parochial schools, mission schools, and government schools—both elementary and secondary—and the government gives financial support to every one of them. Children from all parts of Ghana attend Cape Coast schools.

We had looked around the city only a short time when Patrick suggested we go on to Elmina, fifteen miles westward down the coast, while plenty of daylight remained; so we breezed down a highway that paralleled the beach. To our right we saw open green fields with trees and scrub bush growing sparsely; to our left, acres of palm trees. The trunks curved like huge bows, from the point where they poked out of the sandy earth to the top of their waving, bushy heads. Among the trees were villages constructed entirely from palm fiber, and lingering in every village was a blue haze, a pungent reminder of smoking fish.

These sea people live for hundreds of miles along the coast—far beyond the boundaries of Ghana: northwest to Liberia and southeast to Angola. For centuries they have sailed across the Gulf of Guinea and parts of the South Atlantic in sturdy boats brilliantly decorated from bow to stern with crescent moons, stars, sea-life symbols, proverbs, symbols from mythology. Many of the oars are carved to resemble web-fingered claws; they scoop through the water effectively and propel the boats with slicing swiftness.

Now on the distant horizon loomed Elmina Castle, a chunk of brutal brilliance against a background of soft sea and sky. We saw that it was surrounded by palm trees whose leafy heads danced to the tune of the breakers. But this peaceful scene belied a ghastly history, for in Elmina Castle thousands and thousands of slaves were held for shipment across the Atlantic to Spanish-conquered lands.

We crossed a bridge spanning a lagoon, parked near the castle, and got out of the car. Before the great white stone walls we stood like ants, with our egos as shriveled as they had been in the rain forest. This old landmark is kept brilliantly whitewashed and spotlessly clean, for it now serves as a Ghana police post. But my mind was not in the present; I had been swept off into history. I had the feeling that this structure was a gigantic magnet, that it had pulled me back through space and time—back to the stone prison which had held my forebears in countless numbers, held them until the ships were ready to haul them, as so much cargo, on their voyage of terror.

So I stood silently for a few moments, caught up in the hands of time. Then I said to Patrick and Hazel, "Let's go! Let's see the insides of this monster." To Patrick I added, "where your forefathers helped to put my forefathers some generations ago." I laughed, at first with irony. Patrick held his sides and laughed his African laugh. We three held each other and shook. We were still laughing as we crossed the first drawbridge, passed a rigid African guard dressed in crisp khaki, and crossed the second drawbridge. This castle had two moats separated by a wall at least six feet thick.

Then we entered the castle itself and saw that we were in a small reception room. We introduced ourselves to the captain of the guard, who ordered a man to guide us through the interior. He led us out into the compound, an open area of about 100 by 150 feet surrounded by two-tiered stone cells. To our left, stone steps led up to a platform, then to the chief officer's quarters. On this platform, centuries ago, captains of slave ships stood to inspect the multitudes and to decide their fate.

The guide, a very courteous fellow, took the lead, and we followed him in single file down through low, arched tunnels that led below into darkness. We were forced to walk slowly at first, but then our eyes became adjusted and we could see that a little light from far above filtered in through small slit openings. We walked slowly, with bent heads and hunched shoulders, down steps and descending passageways. Again we had trouble seeing, and breathing seemed to become exceedingly difficult. Finally we arrived at the "women's dormitory," and I silently shook hands with Dante. A concrete gully bisected the floor of the women's room; fifteen feet above the floor was a small opening that slanted upward through tons and tons of stone, providing the only light and fresh air for this foul hole. Ghosts of my ancestors writhed before me, laughing insanely and rattling their chains, and a stench from that open gutter seemed to become unbearable. "Good God!" I exclaimed. "Let's move on."

We visited many other cells, and the torture of the dark past overwhelmed us. We looked at the "men's dormitory" and the "dormitory for the insane"—many souls evidently had not been able to make the psychological adjustment that their chains required. Then, with profound relief, we began the ascent, winding our way to the main compound again. The fresh air and bright sunshine actually made us dizzy, or perhaps our giddiness stemmed from joy—the kind of absolute joy one experiences when he wakes from some especially horrible nightmare and realizes he has been dreaming. We climbed a winding stairway on the right side of the compound and entered the quarters where the healthy women slaves were inspected and sorted out. We almost forgot history here; many windows allowed a cross ventilation in which we reveled, after our sickening experience of a few minutes earlier. On the wall at the far end of the room still hung a picture of the Queen of England. Around the room were several other photographs of distinguished Britons and Africans, and it was difficult now not to associate these photographs with the terrible past.

From this room we went to one which had a sign reading, "Prempeh's Room." I learned that Prempeh was an Ashanti king who had been captured in the last war with the British, near the turn of the century. We walked in, and from a corner of the room facing the Gulf of Guinea we peered through iron-barred windows. A stiff breeze from the sea slapped against our faces as we studied the watery turbulence far below: A breaker would pull itself up to a magnificent height, then hurl its whole force at some huge rocks jutting out into the water. After a few moments the rocks would re-emerge, towering once more over their antagonist, and another breaker would try. The guide told us that centuries ago slaves were marched out on those rocks, when the water was not so rough, to be loaded into small boats for transfer to waiting schooners lying nearby.

We retraced our steps, now going down the winding stairway, and returned to the compound. There the guide swung open a large door in the floor of the compound and told us to look in. Below us, at a distance of some fifteen feet, we saw water—sea water. Through this opening the slavers floated the dead out to sea. Not far away was another opening we peered into and saw more water—this time fresh water, for drinking.

Back in the small reception room we signed the guest book, and the captain of the guard showed us Adlai Stevenson's signature. The captain wished us a pleasant journey and said that we were welcome to come back for a longer visit any time. I shot Patrick a glance; he read my thoughts and laughed infectiously. I laughed too, and so did Hazel.

So we departed the same way we entered—across the drawbridges, through the opening in the six-foot wall, past the rigid African guard dressed in crisp khaki. And we were laughing—laughing instead of crying. But all three of us soon became solemn again, and I found myself once more being swept off into history.

The massive construction of Elmina Castle certainly was a manifestation that the Portuguese had come to West Africa to stay. But in the seventeenth century the Dutch captured it and continued to use it in the slave trade, fighting off many attacks by Africans and by the English, who had established a fort of their own at nearby Cape Coast. Finally Elmina was sold to the English—sold, as had been most of its occupants during hundreds of years. Gold, a timeless symbol of the life-giving rays of the sun, had brought sorrow and death to untold thousands here at Elmina, to untold millions all over the world.

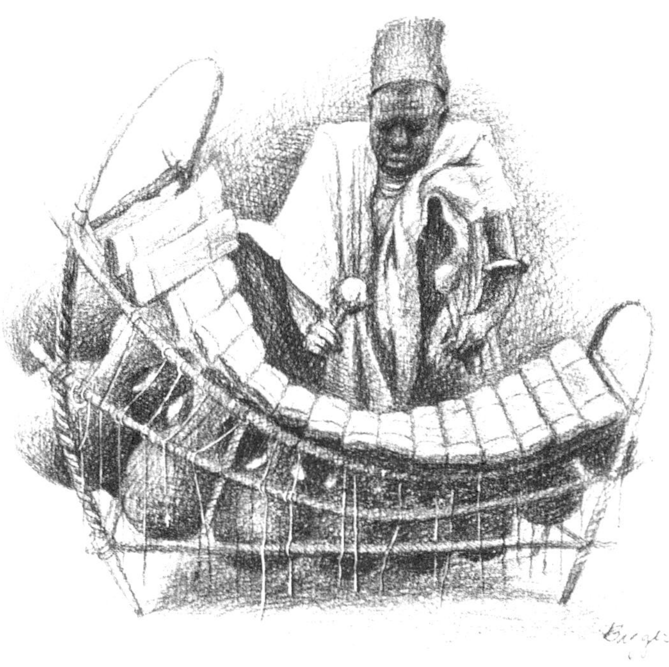

5

Early in the morning of September 3, 1957, we rose, gulped hot coffee, and departed on our last extended automobile trip into Ghana, this time to the Northern Territories.

We had been living in Patrick Hulede's residence on the campus of the Kumasi College of Technology since August 8—shortly after our return from Cape Coast and Elmina—when Patrick had left for Rome, entrusting us with his house, his servants, and his automobile. The night before our departure we had loaded the car trunk with cooking gear, food, linen, and a five-gallon can of gasoline. Now, with the drowsiness gone from us, we piled into the car—our cook Kwame Bonny and I in the front seat, Hazel and Mary Mensah, who taught in a Kumasi elementary school, in the back—and sped northward up an asphalt highway in a pre-dawn gloom.

From Kumasi we drove through some of the most

picturesque mountain country in Ghana, along a highway that cut through luxuriant growth, that snaked sharply around mountain cliffs and up steep grades. After an hour we came to the famous old craft center of Mampong, where we saw carvers busy turning out stools of many sizes and designs.

On the other side of town the hills leveled off into gently undulating plains; the tall trees of the forest thinned out; elephant grass and stump bush covered the ground as far as we could see. After several more hours we reached the Upper Volta at Yeji, a village where potters made attractive egg-shaped water jugs with deep-brown glazes. We crossed the river on a ferry.

Along the way the design of the houses changed, becoming round structures with conical thatched roofs. We passed many heavy trailer trucks and lorries loaded with cattle, sheep, and goats that thrive on the northern plains. Many times we had to slow down and pull off the highway for herders and their animals. Seeking to avoid shipping costs, they were driving their herds to market; some drove them almost five hundred miles across mountains and through forests to Accra. We also passed numerous lorries loaded with giant yams and saw in the towns along the road women stacking these vegetables in piles; some yams must have been three feet long. Scattered in intriguing patterns across the plains were giant baobab trees, beneath whose limbs, in deep-green splotches of shade, grazed bunches of cattle. Flocks of guinea fowl and chickens roamed aimlessly along the road, frequently causing me to jam on the brakes and to swing wide in order to miss them.

The vast plains began to remind me of parts of Texas, but the towns certainly did not. We passed villages from which arose gleaming white minarets, indicating the extent of the Moslem influence in the Northern Territories. Early in the afternoon we arrived at Tamale, about 225 miles north of Kumasi, and found it to be an orderly city with paved streets, impressive stores, a modern airport, a secondary school, and a university under construction. Comprising the residential area, a most exciting one, were groups of screened-in, round houses built of brick and reinforced concrete and roofed with thatch, tile, or corrugated metal. Each group of houses was surrounded by broad green lawns, shrubs, and flowers.

The government resthouse, where we stayed three days, was composed of a cluster of round, brick-walled rooms fronted by a wide flagstone porch. Covered, screened-in passageways connected the kitchen, bedrooms, dining rooms, living rooms, and bathrooms. The beds were enclosed by freshly laundered mosquito netting.

The next day we visited the official in charge of the government publication office and the Vernacular Literature Bureau. He was also editor of the local newspaper, in which his poetry regularly appeared—in English and in several vernaculars. We were pleased when he consented to read to us several of his poems. Standing tall and handsome in his flowing, embroidered toga, he read slowly and distinctly pieces concerning age-old battles, wedding feasts, and games of children and adults in a pastoral land. I made several photographs of him, and this seemed to delight him.

Each night during our visit to Tamale we heard drumming. The resthouse keeper told us that it came from a neighboring village and that it announced a wedding soon to take place. The drums sounded like mellow, tender calls—at first vibrating softly, then gradually increasing in volume and tempo, next diminishing to a haunting decrescendo, and finally dying away to silence. With slight variations the drumming continued at intervals throughout the night, and I imagined the chosen young couple listening in rapturous anticipation.

In such an enchanting atmosphere we found that time passed too quickly; we had to leave. With thundering smoothness our little MG glided over a grassy sea toward Navrongo, 150 miles north. The vastness of the open plains, which covered thousands of square miles from the Ashanti forest region to the fringes of the Sahara, seemed to soak up our sounds, spongelike, and we fancied ourselves as ants, with numbed antenna, crawling across the earth. We noticed the deep green of the forest of grass gradually change to an ocherous green, then to desert yellow. Humidity vanished; the atmosphere became dry and invigorating. Every few hundred yards stood a great baobab tree, a lonesome reminder of the ravages of time. Each great trunk was twisted as if in a tortured writhing, seemingly with the intention of cautioning us that nature is not always at peace. Some trunks exhibited a thick, wrinkled bark resembling elephant skin, others a bark like uneven concrete, and still others a bark with a greenish-gray metallic sheen. Among the awesome baobabs rose huge smooth-backed boulders, looking like great whales suddenly surfacing in a silent sea.

In this land of extravagant space there were startling contrasts. Meandering streams occasionally watered the land, and along their green fringes naked boys wearing conical hats tended quiet herds of grazing sheep and gentle cattle that responded individually to names. And from these streams there rose, like the dawn, regal female figures crowned with earthen jugs and clad only in Eve's ancient attire of leaves. These tall, graceful women seemed oblivious of our presence, and all four of us—Kwame, Mary, Hazel, and I, children of this land of burnt faces—were stricken with a feeling of insignificance. I recalled an Akan proverb: "The stranger who came says he did not see anybody in town, and the people he met also say, 'We did not see anyone come'." Somehow we felt that we were treading on hallowed ground, but in this ageless region I called up no historical references. It seemed to me that this land and its people could have been here long before a Garden of Eden existed, before the Pillars of Hercules rose from the sea, even before the moon swung into orbit to govern earthly tides. Here man was truly one with nature; he walked upon the land without shame for his nakedness, so much was he a part of the surroundings—the same as the trees, the birds, the lower animals that moved on four feet. These people possessed an obvious pride, but it could not be associated with conceit, selfishness, pretentiousness; it was instead a pride born simply of being, of sharing in nature's immensity. Upon this land man lived with the rhythm of the seasons.

After our arrival at Navrongo I lost no time in plunging into this intriguing atmosphere with an enthusiasm equal to that of a bather who seeks the cool spring waters on a hot day. We were introduced to the Chief of Navrongo, who treated us with kindness, with refreshing millet beer—and with enlightenment. I asked him why the crocodile was so important to many people of the Northern Territories, and in good English he told me: Many centuries ago his people migrated from the ancient desert kingdoms of the north and northeast, fleeing from hordes of invaders who came to force upon them a foreign way of life. In their southward flight they came upon "the river of waters" (which I presumed was the Niger), and there giant crocodiles lay quietly side by side, from bank to bank, forming a bridge over which the people could pass. But when the enemy sought to cross, the crocodiles submerged, drowning the invaders to the last man.

The Chief granted permission for me to make photographs and drawings of the magnificently conceived mud villages surrounding his walled, two-story palace, and from a second-story balcony we observed them: clay buildings in the form of cones, spheres, half-spheres, obelisks, and pyramids. To me these did not look like the houses and barns that they were, but like gigantic ceramic sculptures and exquisite earthen vessels produced by a master sculptor who used delicate, abstract patterns to enhance the beauty of his product. We were told that each man built his own house and decorated it according to his own taste, utilizing an intuitive philosophy based upon an understanding of organic form and function as related to the limitations of his material, and upon an understanding of coherent relationship to the rest of the village and of the needs of the people who lived there. Later we visited some of the houses and observed that the builders knew their business inside and out: We felt a coolness produced by downdrafts that gave excellent ventilation and circulation of air currents.

We also visited the Catholic university, where we saw a magnificent arts-and-crafts collection that included ancient artifacts; old weapons and other war gear of iron, stone, brass, and wood; sculpture of clay, stone, and wood; beautiful textiles; and cooking and ceremonial ware. Teachers and priests at the university had spent years accumulating this collection.

Later we enjoyed the hospitality of the government agent at Navrongo, an Englishman who had stayed over from the colonial period to make Ghana his home. His African wife directed the servants in preparing a sumptuous dinner of groundnut soup, mutton, and yams. As a memento of the visit our host gave me, from his personal collection, several old clay pipes fashioned after animal and human figures; the craftsmen of Navrongo were noted for their pipe-making. Then over good Scotch we talked late into the night about the revolutionary changes that were producing a new Ghana and a new Africa.

We spent several fascinating days in the Navrongo area, making photographs and drawings of the people, the animals, the yam farms, the architecture. Then, too soon again, it was time to return to Kumasi, this time to gather up our belongings and to arrange for transportation to the United States. As we sped over the highway leading south a large yellow monkey—one of the few wild animals I saw—crossed the road fifty yards ahead of us, crawled into a roadside bush, and watched us with inquisitive eyes until we had passed.

Our last day in Kumasi was tinged with the sadness that partings always evoke. It was hard to say goodbye to so many friends who had accepted us so graciously into their lives. Mary Kirby, Mary Mensah, Ella Griffin, Patrick Hulede's students and many others filled our luggage with art objects and embraced us with family warmth. We went to Accra, then to Lagos, Nigeria, where we arrived December 23, 1957, for a last sight-seeing fling. Donald W. MacRow, an Englishman who edits *Nigeria Magazine,* planned for us a tour through sections of western Nigeria.

We motored from Lagos to Ibadan, visited the impressive university there, then drove on to Ede, where we were unable to find accommodations in the resthouse. But Mr. MacRow had previously communicated with His Highness the Timi of Ede, informing him of our mission and of our interest in studying the Yoruba culture, which over the years had remained harmoniously intact. So we drove directly to the Timi's palace, where we were received graciously. The Timi made arrangements for us to live in his brother's house and to take our meals with the Timi himself. And he personally conducted us on a tour of his province, showing us the craftsmen at work and taking us into many shrines never before exhibited to outsiders.

Then we returned to Lagos, and on January 1, 1958, flew to the ancient city of Kano, more than one thousand years old. Characteristic of twentieth-century Africa, there were two cities: medieval Kano, with its resplendent mosque, its equestrian soldiers, and its camel and donkey trains; and modern Kano, with railroads, air transportation, paved roads, and luxurious hotels. The dry desert air filled us with a new vigor for our return trip home, and the immigration officials were friendly and courteous, wanting to know if we had enjoyed our sojourn in the land of our forefathers.

That caused me to recall, with a smile, how the Timi of Ede had welcomed us a few days earlier. When we drove through the palace gates the drums, those eternal African drums, announced our arrival. Almost immediately the Timi appeared with his retinue, greeted us, then spoke in Yoruba to the people gathered in the courtyard. When he finished they laughed and applauded.

Addressing us again, the Timi said, "The drums announced that two foreigners had arrived through the palace gates. I have just told my people that you are not foreigners, but brothers who have returned home after an absence of three hundred years."

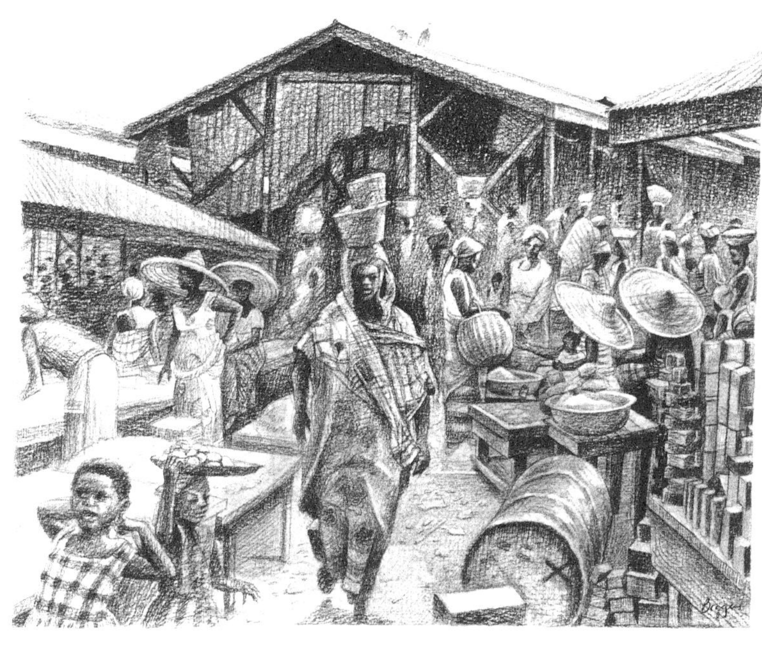

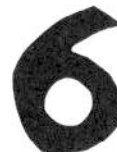

SETTLING DOWN to interpreting African life was the most difficult task I had encountered during my eighteen years of painting and drawing. The impact of Africa almost paralyzed my creative efforts; the drama and the poetic beauty were devastating. Until I was able to reorient myself I was literally broken; I felt unequal to the task.

"How can I portray this overwhelming country?" I asked myself. "Six months isn't long enough. I need two years, ten years—perhaps a lifetime—to mine the gold of her being."

I was filled with fresh, poignant odors, tastes, sounds, visual images; and the vigor of these new experiences aroused in me deep emotion and thought. How could I produce a convincing image of *maame* —the fountain of life, the mother of all men? How could I show her divine origin, how depict her divine son, the king, symbol of the resplendent sun? And how could I capture convincingly the magnificent procession of black-gold children—stars moving on their course, sometimes in contradictory patterns but always forward and always with dignity, pride, and sensitivity.

I had witnessed grand spectacles, solemn rites, and an unbelievable abundance of human vitality. I had been held spellbound by the harvest symphony glorified in the gold of evening, had been delighted by the warmth of washerwomen on the banks of rivers and streams, had been filled with wonder by the beauty of naked truth—of mind and body—that I had observed on the tranquil, grassy northern plains of Ghana. But to grasp a more fundamental and complete image of Mother Africa I consulted history—especially Eva Meyerowitz's *The Sacred State of the Akan*—because I believe individuals reflect not only contemporary personal images but also images, both physical and spiritual, of their historical roots. Meyerowitz aided me in understanding the Akan concept of creation: The Akan people of Ghana—the Fanti and Ashanti—believe in male and female entities of God—Nyame. The female entity is personified in Ohemmaa—the female king or the queen mother—who created the universe by giving birth to the sun. She is looked upon as the creator and owner of the state and the mother of everyone in it, including the king. She is regarded as the daughter of the moon, and her body—as well as the body of every other woman—is thought of as being as delicate and beautiful as the full moon. Silver, representing moonlight, is her color—just as gold, the color of the sun, represents her son, the king. During ceremonials the minstrels sing, "The queen mother is the moon; the king is the sun." The queen mother's stool is plated with silver, and the king's stool is plated with gold. The African woman, in her divine creative capacity, motivated within me a desire to paint murals on creation from a matriarchal point of view; whereas European artists had been motivated to paint creation from a patriarchal point of view.

The African philosopher Dr. J. B. Danquah offered to me in his *Akan Doctrine of God* the concept that all men are descendants of the first progenitor—the ultimate ancestor and creative force. An Akan proverb declares, "All men are the offspring of God"; and the Akan people believe that all men should share in the beneficence of God, that to be excluded from the family of man is to be treated as a beast.

The four thousand proverbs of the Akan people, so universal and so similar in meaning to the Hebrew proverbs, were spiritually stabilizing to me. And when I realized how the African so often speaks in proverbs of basic life forces—birth, love, death—a gap was bridged, and I identified spiritually when I heard and read African poetry—such as the following stanza of an African funeral dirge, taken from Meyerowitz's book:

Thou speeding bird tell father,
Tell father where he left me,
Thou speeding bird tell father
That he left me on the other
side of the River (of life).

I also identified spiritually with Yoruba poetry. H. U. Beier's *The Story of Sacred Wood Carvings From One Small Yoruba Town* contains a poem that Yoruba women in Nigeria sing when they greet the shrine of Erinle, a mighty warrior who is always depicted on horseback:

He is firm and strong like a rock.
He is clear like the eye of God that
does not grow grass.
Like the earth he will never change.
He puts out the lamp and lets his eyes
sparkle like fire.
He will turn the barren woman into
one who carries child.
He is the father of our King; he is
the one who looks after my child.

When I heard the talking drums I identified with the tonal, musical languages of Africa, and I understood something of the important role played by the poet-drummer-historian in the traditional society. R. S. Rattray's *Ashanti* gives a passage from the language of the talking drums in regard to creation:

The stream crosses the path,
The path crosses the stream;
Which of them is the elder?

Did we not cut a path
to meet the stream?
The stream has its origin long,
long ago,
The stream has its origin in
the Creator. . . .

One of the most arresting and meaningful concepts which I encountered—one which helped me to a fuller understanding of the land and its people—is the concept of "Ananse."

Ananse is the spider, a heroic character in African folklore. Like Br'er Fox, he outwits all the other creatures of the forest. He depicts every kind of hero. There is an Ananse story for every situation in life.

God gave Ananse the meaning of order. He taught him architecture, the structure of dwellings, and the structure of life and society. This is symbolized by his web, which stands also for the sun and its rays, and the sun personifies God.

For the first time I was able to identify with African art—with its spiritual as well as its aesthetic values. I found that it is basically religious. In western Nigeria, for example, Orisa shrines utilize wood sculptures stimulating religious feeling: The sculptures are symbolic of tribal ancestors, each personifying some aspect of divine power, who made outstanding contributions to the preservation of the race in times of war, during pestilences, and in times of social upheaval. Sango symbolizes God's vitality; Ifa, his omniscience. Obatala symbolizes God's creativeness; Esu, his cleverness. The Ibeji, twin figures, are symbolic of good fortune. Art thus serves the African just as it has served all people everywhere: glorifying an image of man and linking that image with the universe. This spiritual identification with art and with the African made physical and visual identification much easier for me.

The African's unwavering belief in the brotherhood of man and his praise for the unseen power that controls all things convinced me that it was no mere coincidence that his offspring who were brought as slaves to America created songs and poetry of great beauty and pathos. They were simply restating their ancient belief in the universal deity, but in a new form which was organically changed to meet spiritual needs in a new and different environment. While I was in Africa I became convinced that the "promised land" American Negroes had sung about and prayed for during centuries of slavery was only a historical memory handed down from the golden past of Africa.

Another interesting link concerns woman. Had not this same *maame* who was, and is, the cradle of African life become the cradle of American life also—for both white and Negro people? The word "mammy" is only a vulgarization of *maame*. The role of the African woman as a leader has been personified not only in thousands of "mammies" who reared white children as well as their own, but also in such women as Harriet Tubman, Sojourner Truth, and Mary M. Bethune.

Some authorities might think I present scant evidence to bridge a historical gap, but to me these culture patterns are real—real enough to make it possible for me to see my being and fate reflected in the African and his struggle. When I addressed African women as *maame* and heard them respond with a warm "my child" or "my son" I rejoiced with a wonderful feeling of belonging.

Having acquired this feeling of belonging, I attempted to embrace the people of Africa. I was captivated by the craftsmen as they worked: I loved to see the wood chips fly as the carvers swung their adzes with rhythm and precision; I enjoyed walking along Kumasi streets where the goldsmiths were and smelling the wax melting from the molds and hearing the hoarse breathing of the bellows; I loved to hear the singing treadles of the looms as brilliant threads of many colors were woven into the luxuriant designs of *kente* cloth.

But though we had been fascinated by Africa, Hazel and I had arrived woefully ignorant and misinformed about the continent—its history, culture, prevailing conditions. Ninety-nine per cent of the books and articles we had read before leaving the United States were out of date or slanted; so in Kumasi we visited the public and college libraries once or twice a week, bringing home stacks of books on African history, anthropology, art, and culture. We compiled more than one thousand research cards with information from sources we believed were unavailable in America.

This reading, supplemented by our own observations, emphasized one point above all: that Africa is undergoing a rapid transition. Not all of the changes are praiseworthy, I contend, and mentioning some of them here is pertinent, because the depression that stemmed from the awareness of their harmful effects was one reason for my difficulty in settling down to interpreting African life.

Most important, in my opinion, is a tendency of some Africans to accept the white man's images indiscriminately, for in the process the African belittles himself. This practice I know well; it has also thwarted the cultural development of the American Negro. In Africa I was disheartened to see a vacuum created by the force of Christianity displacing certain ethnic values—and providing in their stead only superficialities. While visiting West Africa I observed with horror a grotesque image of man in a number of religious services in Catholic and protestant churches: multitudes of black women, men, and children kneeling and mumbling prayers in African dialects before paintings and sculptures of a Caucasian Christ and Caucasian apostles, turned out by Africans who were imitating European artists. I also saw Catholic ceremonies in which there was an obvious attempt to imitate—to surpass, in fact—the spectacle and splendor of the African *durbars* and other pagan festivals. Catholic priests walked under great umbrellas of satin and silk—symbols of the pagan chiefs—carrying crucifixes embellished with African designs. Behind the priests came Africans dancing their syncopated rhythms to the music of brass bands.

I was saddened to learn that the ancient pottery center of Mampong, near Kumasi, no longer flourished. The women potters told me gloomily that they now sold cloth—cheap imported cloth—because there was no longer a demand for their pottery; imported ceramics were much cheaper and more plentiful. I felt that if a modern ceramics factory were built in Mampong it would not only utilize native clays and native talents, but would also preserve Mampong pottery traditions.

In Nigeria I found a similar situation: The village chemists—old, wrinkled women who made soaps and dyes—knew that their usefulness had run its course. Imported soaps and dyes were cheap and plentiful, and no new apprentices were coming in. These old women reminded me of the washerwomen back home who made soap by boiling hog fat, lye, and ashes in big black, metal, wash pots.

Finally, I was sickened to see traditional European art taught in some of the schools and colleges at the expense of the rich African art heritage. It was particularly shocking to realize that the tremendous Ashanti culture—art forms, techniques, and aesthetic philosophy—was being ignored in the very heart of the Ashanti region.

But the positive outweighed the negative. We saw Christians, Moslems, and pagans living together in harmony, which is certainly a primary consideration today anywhere in this strife-torn world. I found the pagan to be a man of culture, a refined listener and speaker. He is not inhibited, but he has restraint—and a dignity that I had rarely encountered before going to Africa, for I had been accustomed to living with inhibited people and people with warped personalities all my life. I admired the African's straightforwardness, a characteristic that contrasted sharply—and much in his favor—with the slippery maneuverings of our culture. And when I heard the great drums call the people, when I saw the people respond with an enthusiasm unequaled by any other call of man or God, I rejoiced; I knew that many of these intrinsic African values would never be lost in the dehumanizing scientific age—just as they were not lost during the dark centuries of slavery.

Slowly I reoriented. The problem of portraying my impressions of Africa became, if not less difficult, at least soluble. It came into focus now: My intention was to discover and to portray what was intrinsically African. I was not interested in showing the degree to which Africans measured up to American or European standards in materialistic acquisitions; I was solely interested in capturing something universal in the many Kojos, Kwasis, Kwames—the many Abenas, Amas, Afuas—the washerwomen, farming women, fishermen, lumber workers, market women, mothers, fathers, and children.

I envisioned three general geographical areas that offered contrasts: life near the sea, life in the forest region, and life on the open plains. Yet I wanted to show in these contrasting areas a thread of homogeneity that held the people together, that linked them in their struggle, in their destiny. The eighty-nine drawings in this book represent my effort.

The journey to Africa was the most significant of my life's experiences. Living intimately with the African and understanding something of his problems enabled me to better understand my own. Thus strengthened, I gained a new confidence for the future.

At the beginning of our tour I had experienced the discomfort, the uneasiness that an outsider always feels. I did not know from which tribal culture my forefathers were torn; I did not possess linguistic ability for communication. I soon realized, however, that having to identify with all Africans could be an asset instead of a liability, for the future of Africa depends to a great extent on dissolving intertribal dissensions. I also realized that I was probably a composite of all West African tribes anyway, because economic and sociological pressures in America during past centuries had eliminated the many tribal factions and had solidified the Negro into a common group.

But now let the dead past take care of itself. A new dawn challenges this world and demands the salt of every one of us. There can be no doubt of our sodality, for in each of us we reflect one another's image, and our composite image mirrors the tragedy and the comedy of the whole human race.

PLATES

Carved from a single tree trunk, the Fanti fishing boat is roughed out in the forest, then transported to the coast and given a smooth finish and made seaworthy.

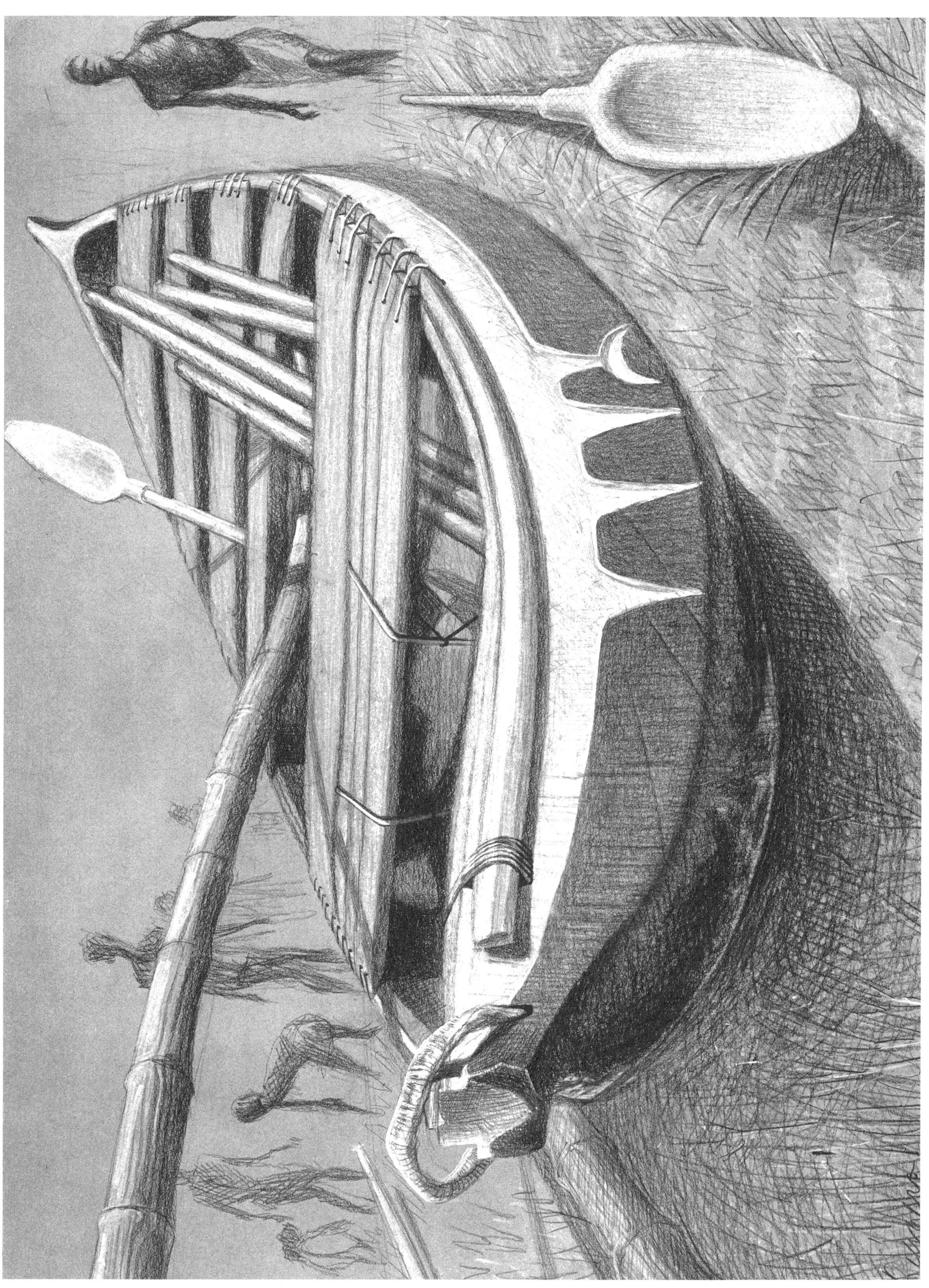

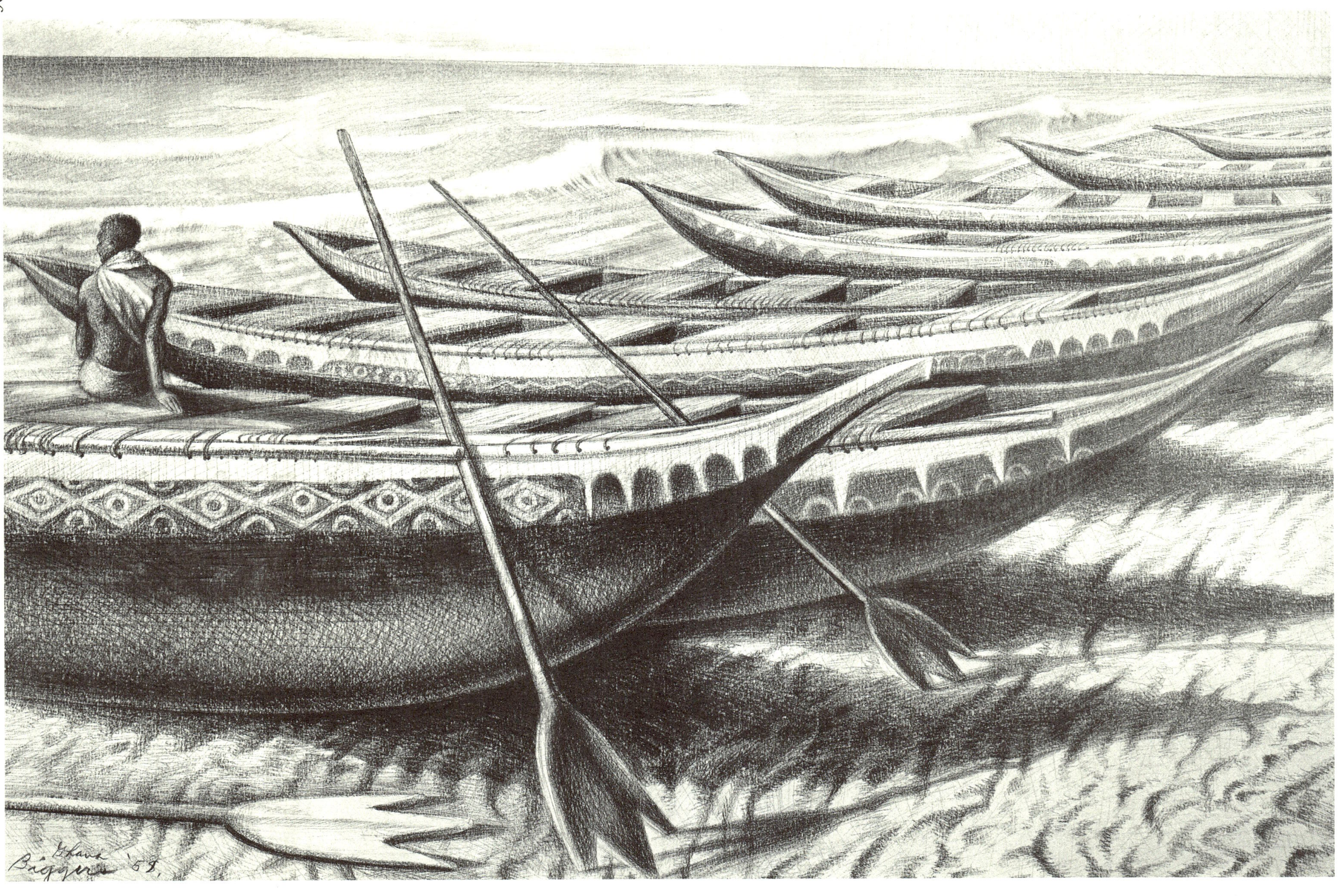

Proverbs and symbols expressing the philosophy of each boat crew adorn the sides. Delicately carved in low relief, they are painted in bright reds, brilliant yellows, and deep greens. The hull is black.

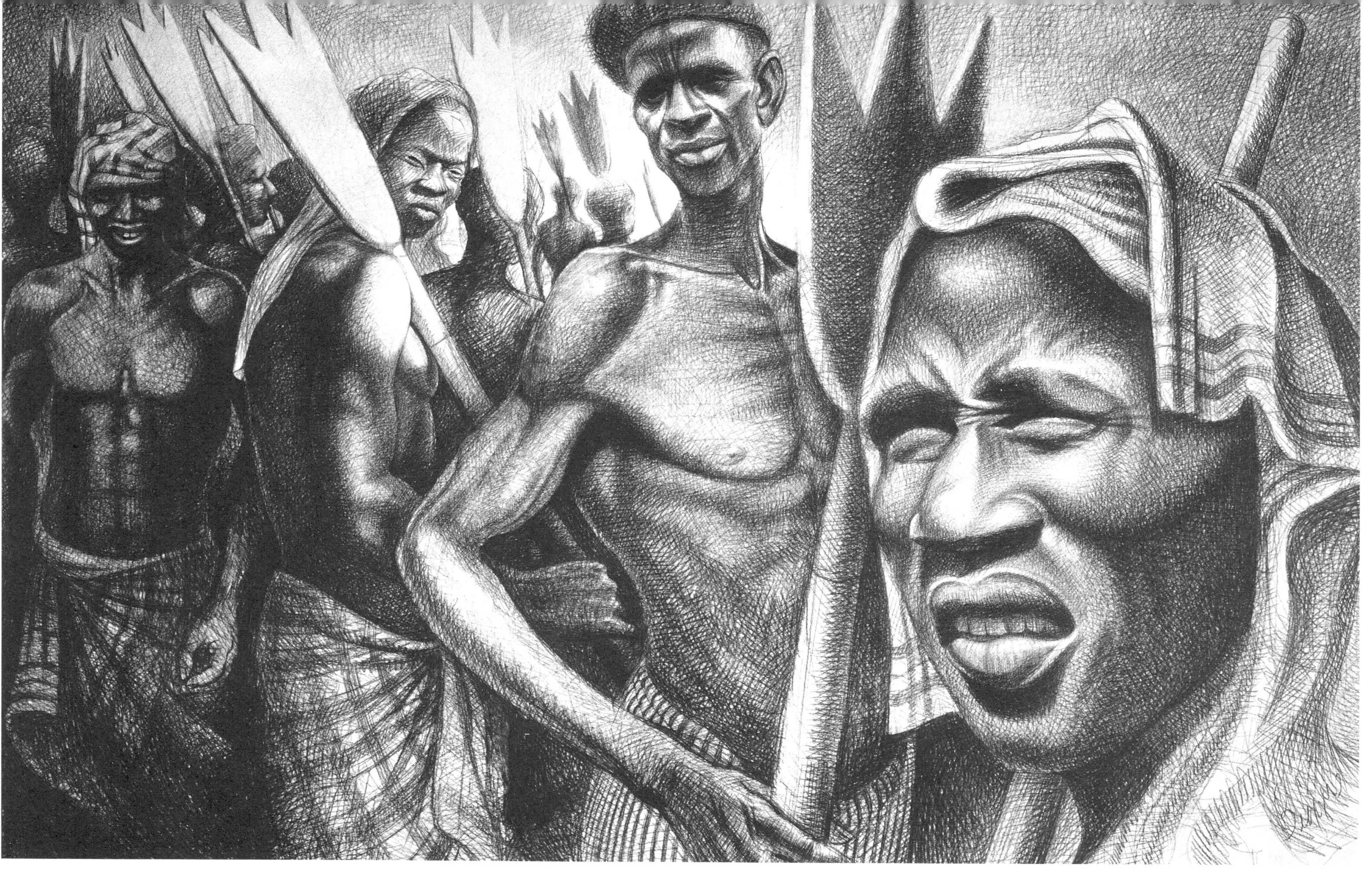

Men of great physical strength and courage are the surfboatmen of Accra. To the cadence of rhythmical chants they plop web-fingered oars into foaming water and pull between vessels anchored offshore and the beach, ferrying goods ranging from automobiles to safety pins.

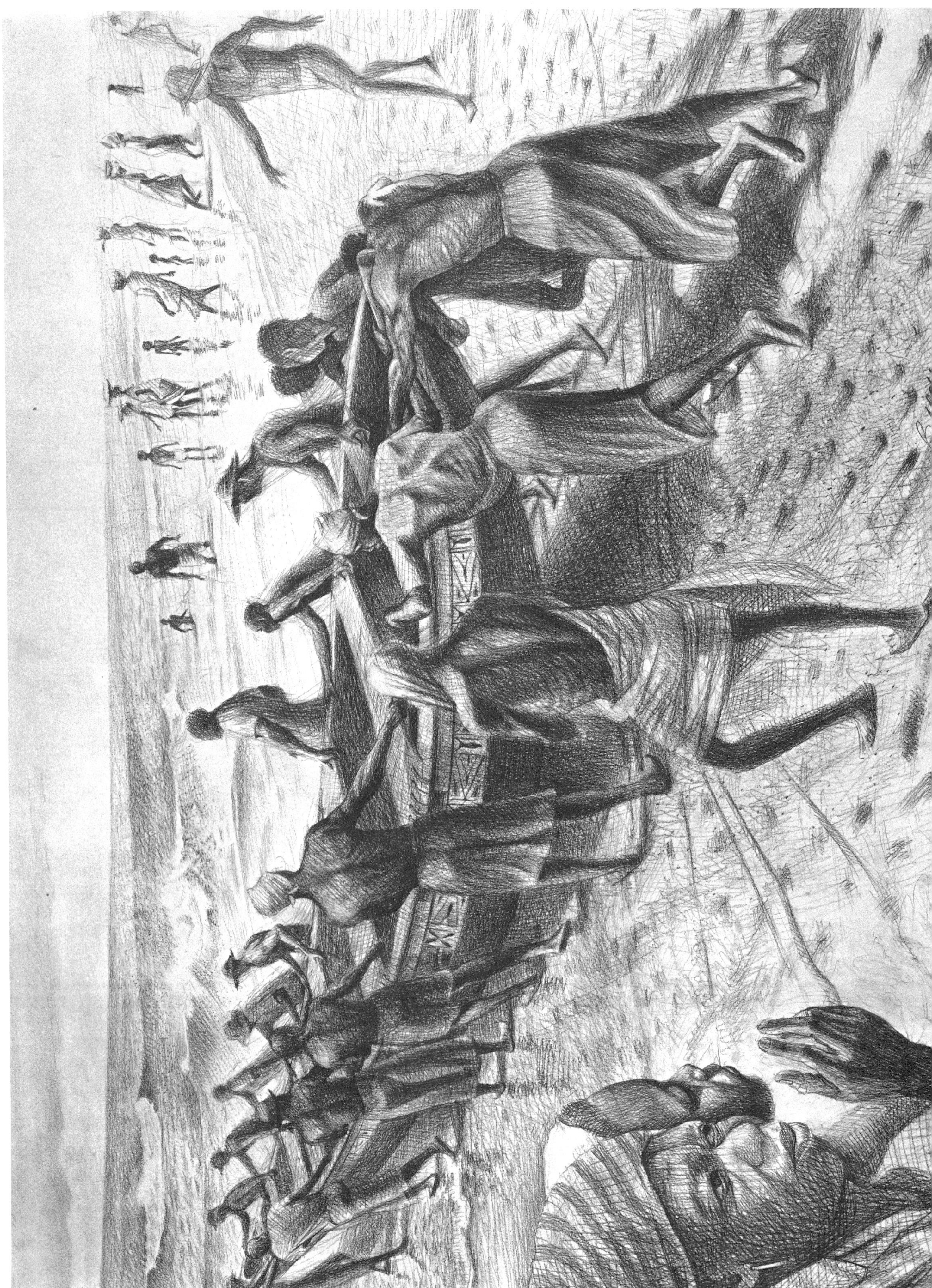

Across cream-colored sand fishermen push their boat into the boiling surf. When the vessel becomes water-borne the nimble, muscled men will leap into it and paddle furiously for deeper water, where they will raise bamboo poles and set sail for the fishing grounds.

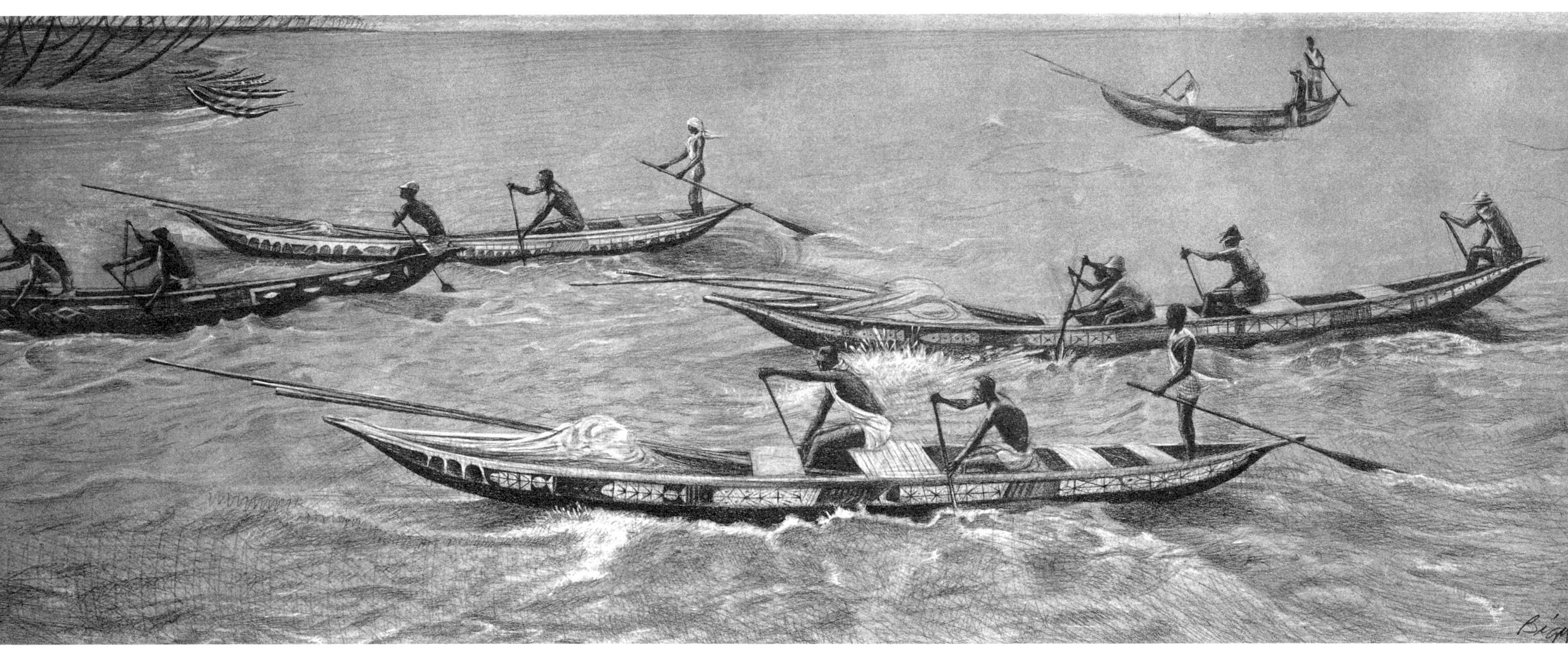

First appear pink dots of sail on the late-afternoon horizon; the fishermen are returning from several days at sea. As the boats near land the crews lower sails and poles. Now, with a final burst of energy, they pull for shore and home.

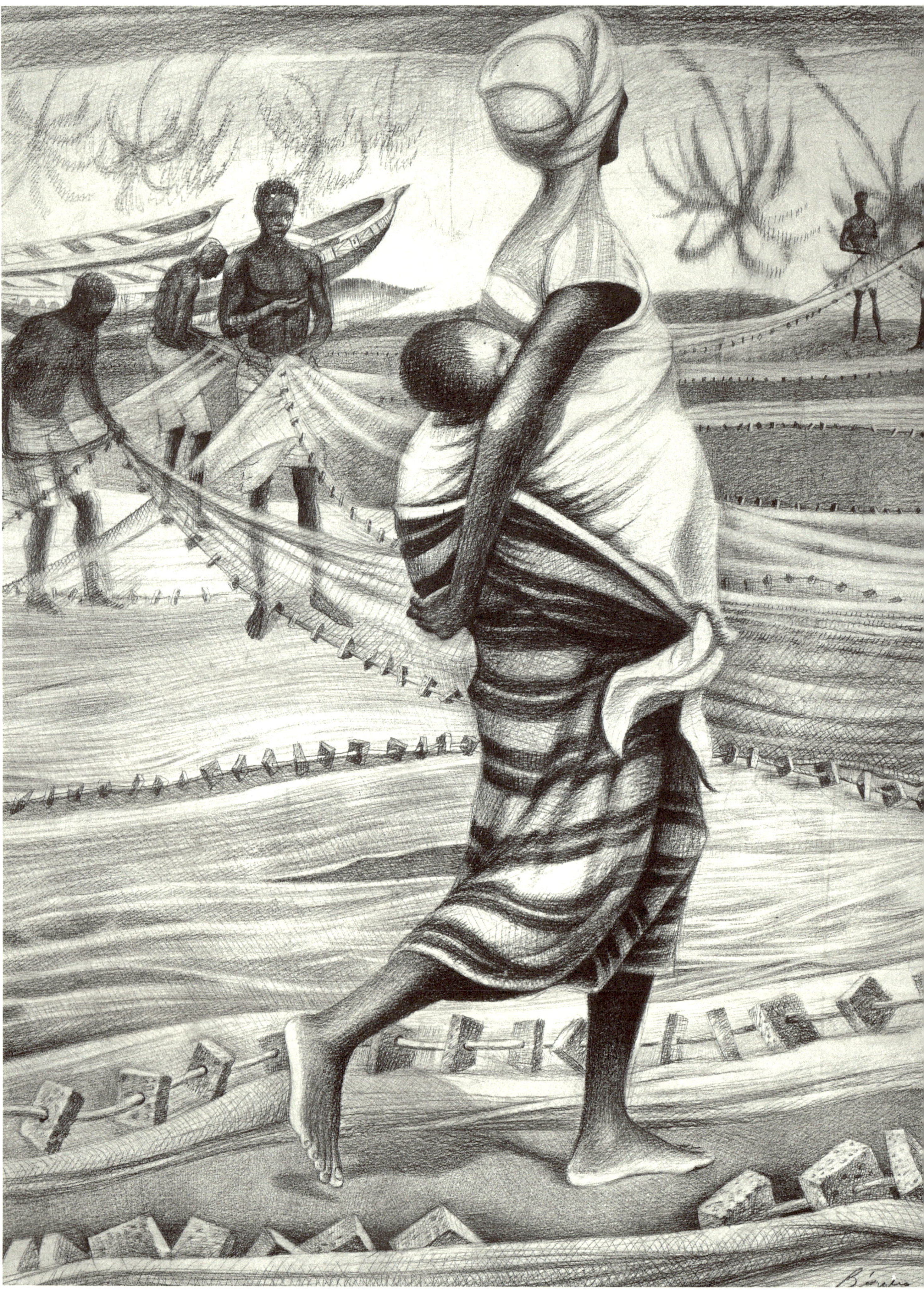

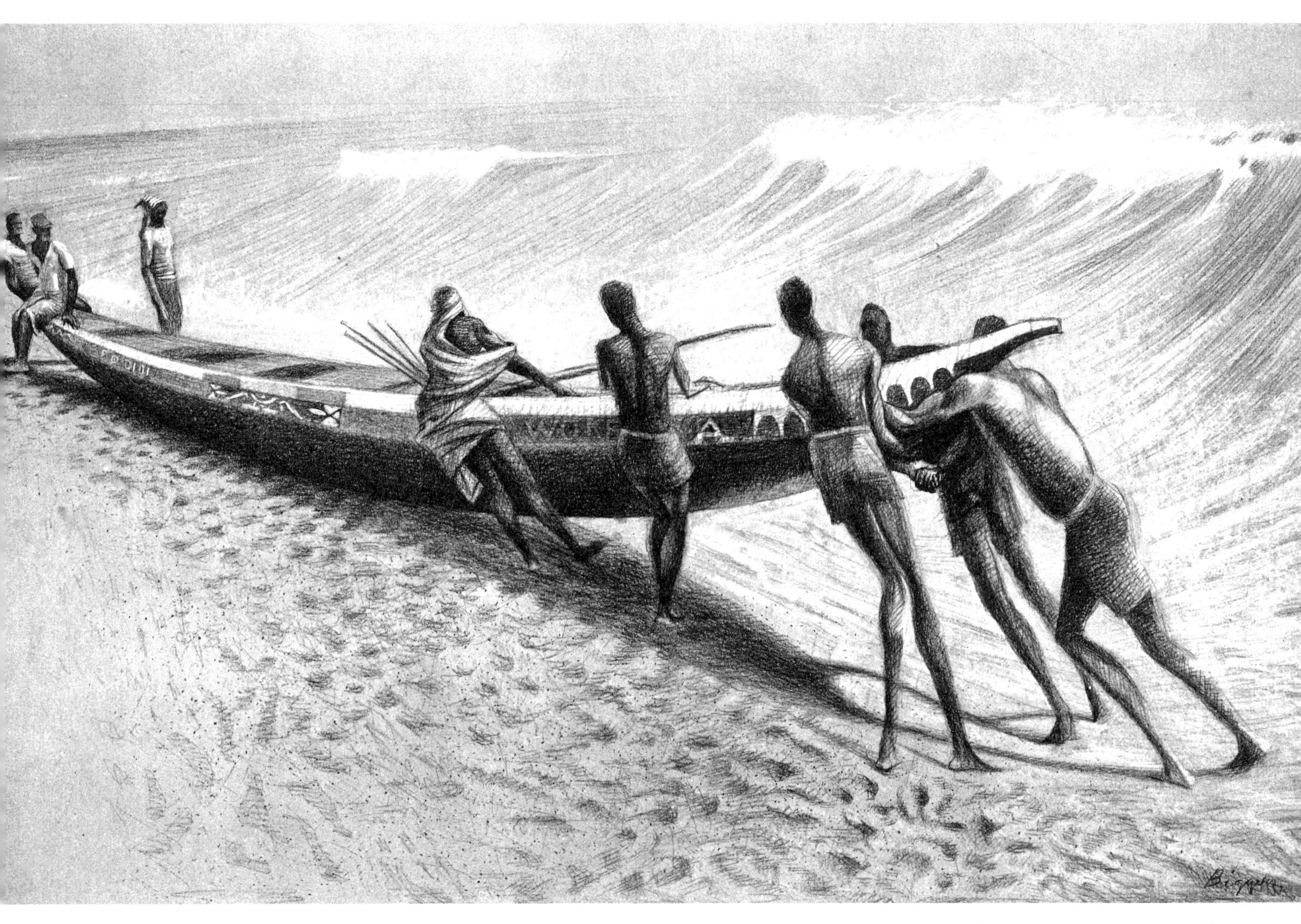

Through milky foam the fishermen nose their boat onto the ground, then spring over the sides into shallow water. Now five men lift the stern, pivot the boat on its bow, and leave it resting safely on the sandy shore.

The fishermen's songs, carried by the wind, tell this young mother that her man is returning. With quick, graceful steps she treads through the cobwebs of nets being mended, on her joyful way to the landing.

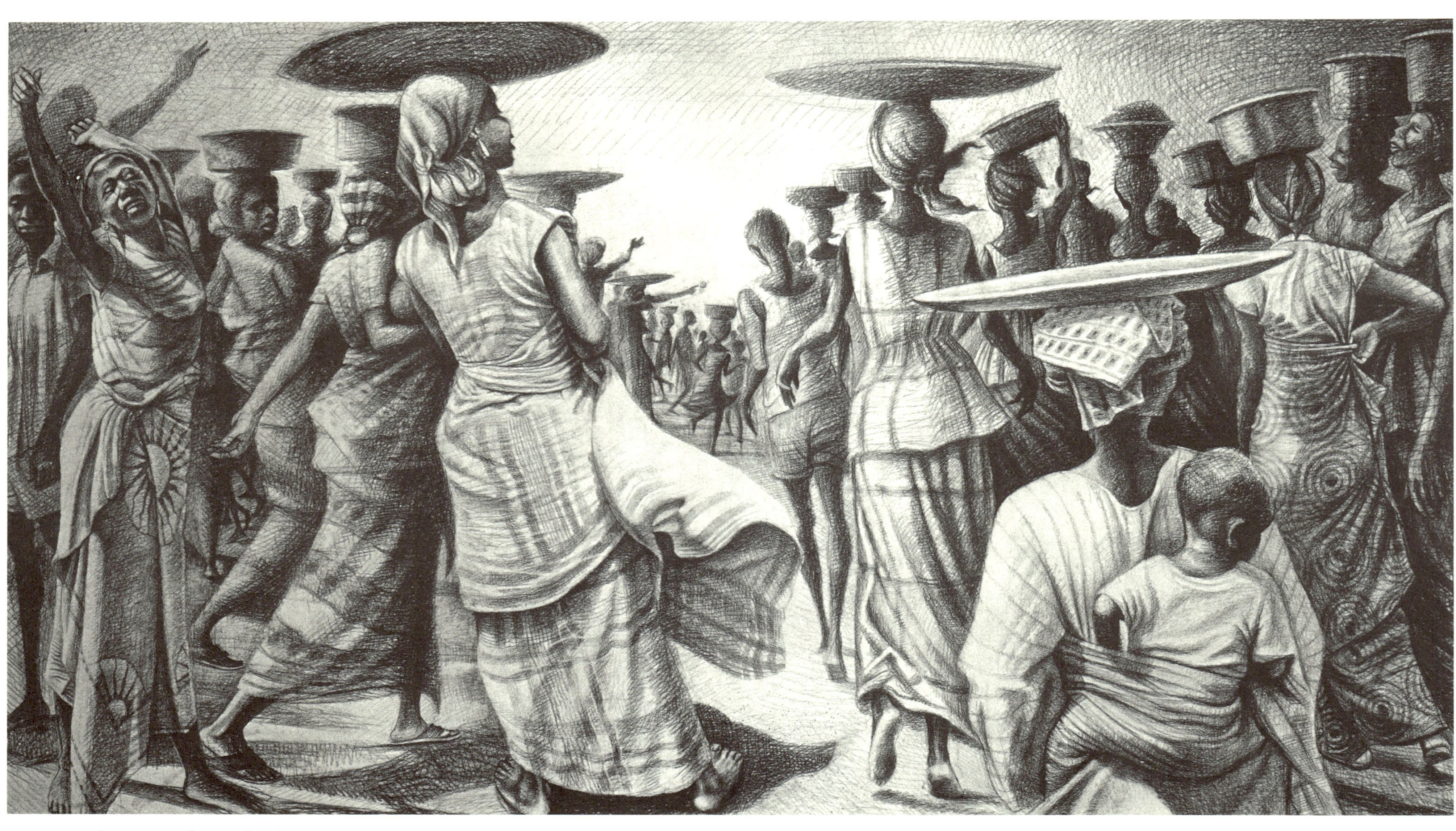

A growing hum of voices broadcasts the news: a bountiful catch! It sparks an awakening, a bustling, a scurrying toward the place where the harvest will be spread. But joy is tempered with anxiety. Sometimes the sea takes as well as gives.

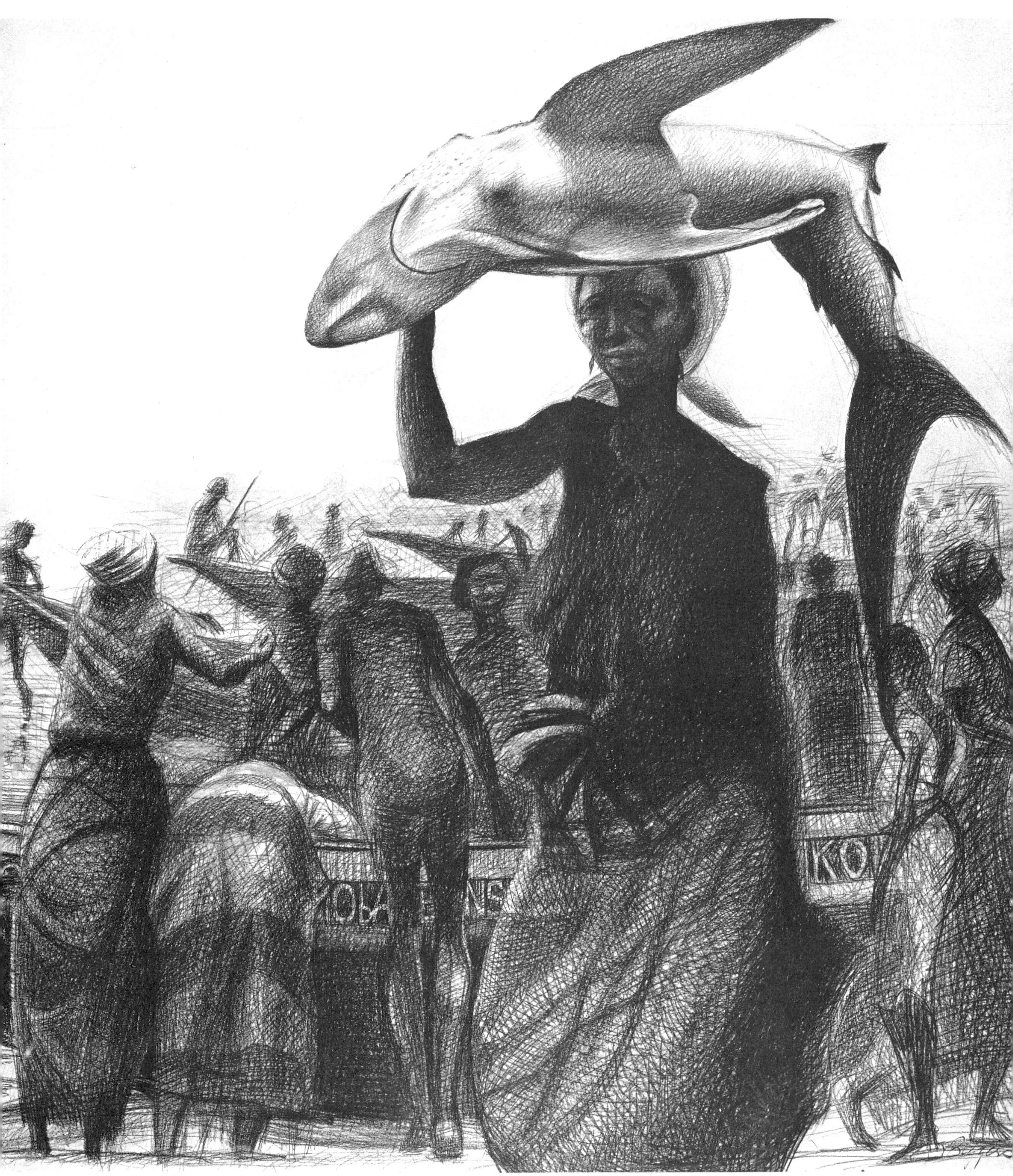

From the boisterous crowd of eager bargainers emerges, with native composure, a queen of the sea harvest. Nearby, but unseen, black pigs and mongrel dogs scrap for morsels of fish thrown their way, adding their unsatisfied grunts and snorts to the din.

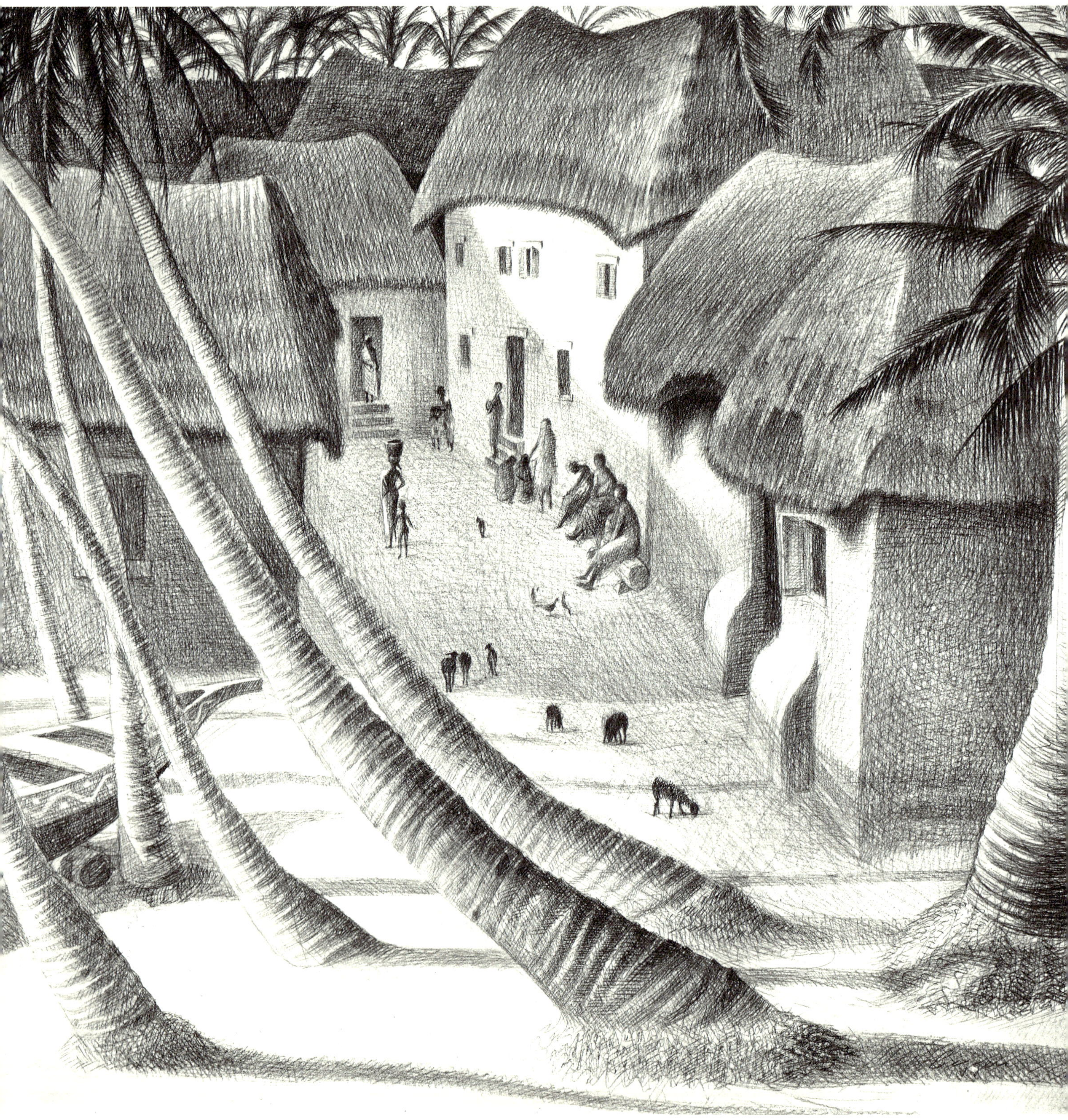

In warm, neighborly clusters stand the fishermen's houses, surrounded by rugged palms whose trunks have been twisted and bent by the furious ocean wind. In all such villages lingers a persistent blue haze, a pungent reminder of smoking fish.

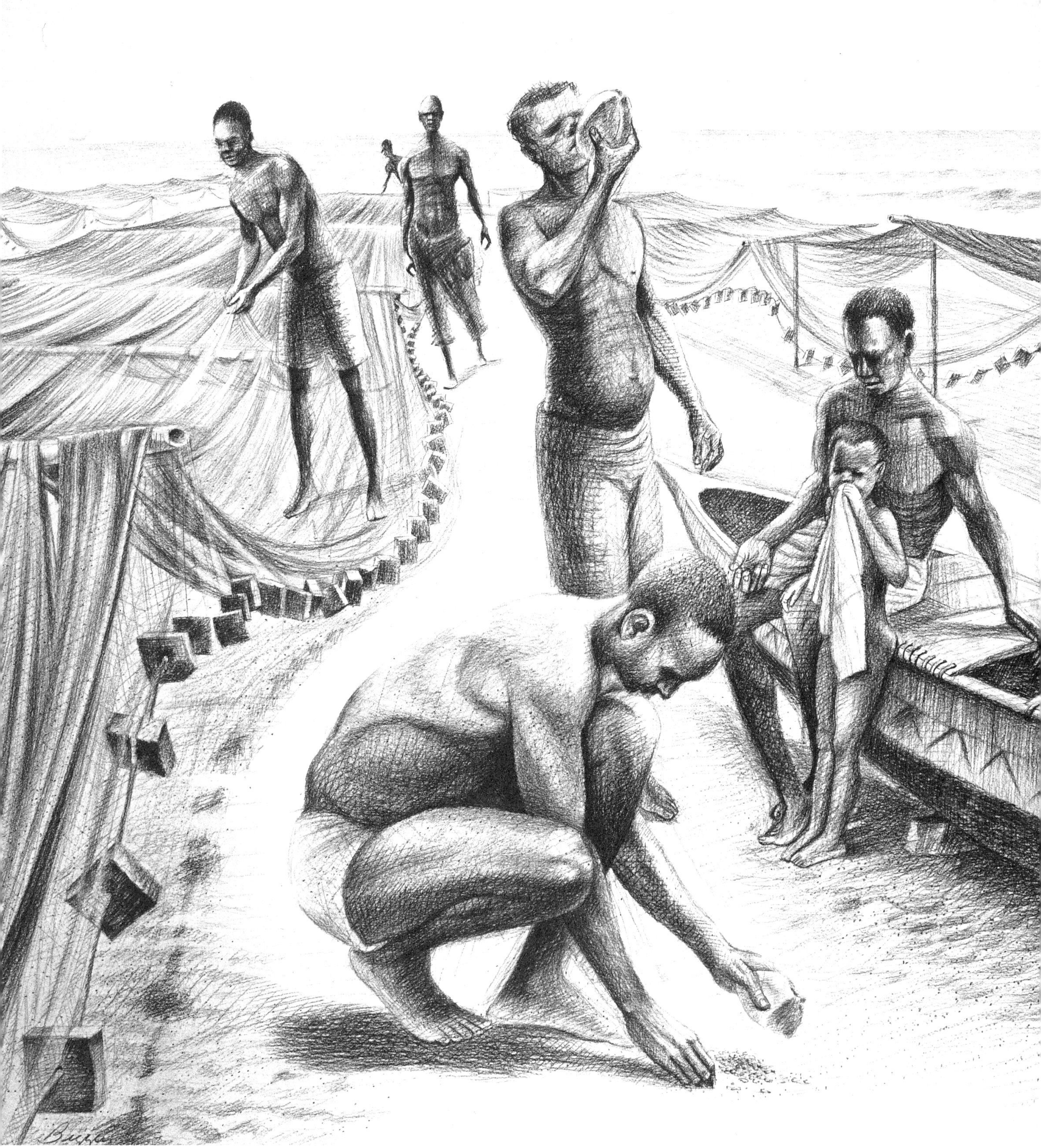

Draped over bamboo poles, the nets are exposed for drying and for repairs. Occasionally the sea breeze ripples the mesh in rhythmical waves, giving it the appearance of the surf which lies just beyond.

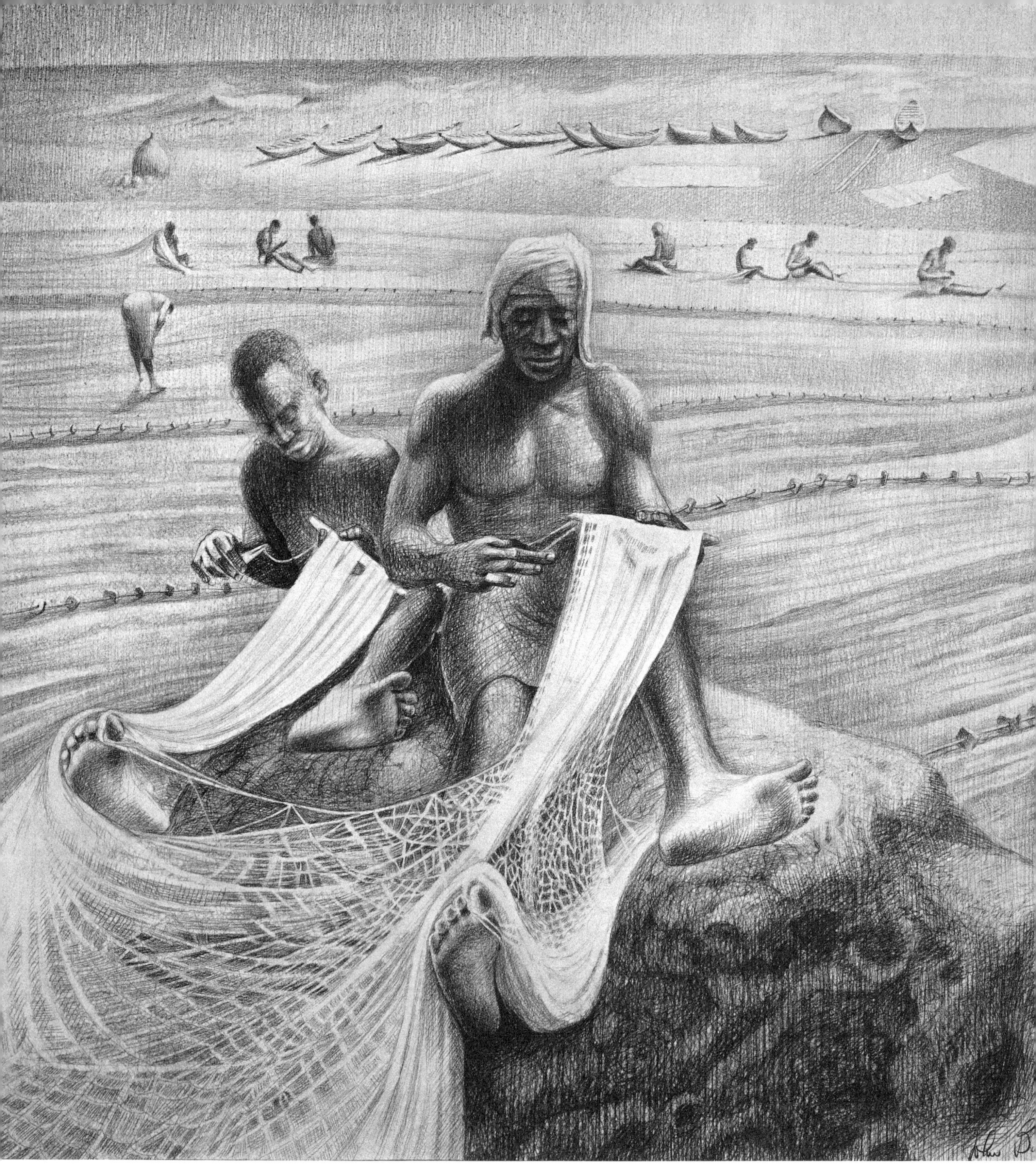

A silvery veil of fishing nets stretches for miles along the Ghana coast. Watching the busy fishermen, I was struck by the feeling that, with the new threads, they were weaving into the nets the meaning of time itself.

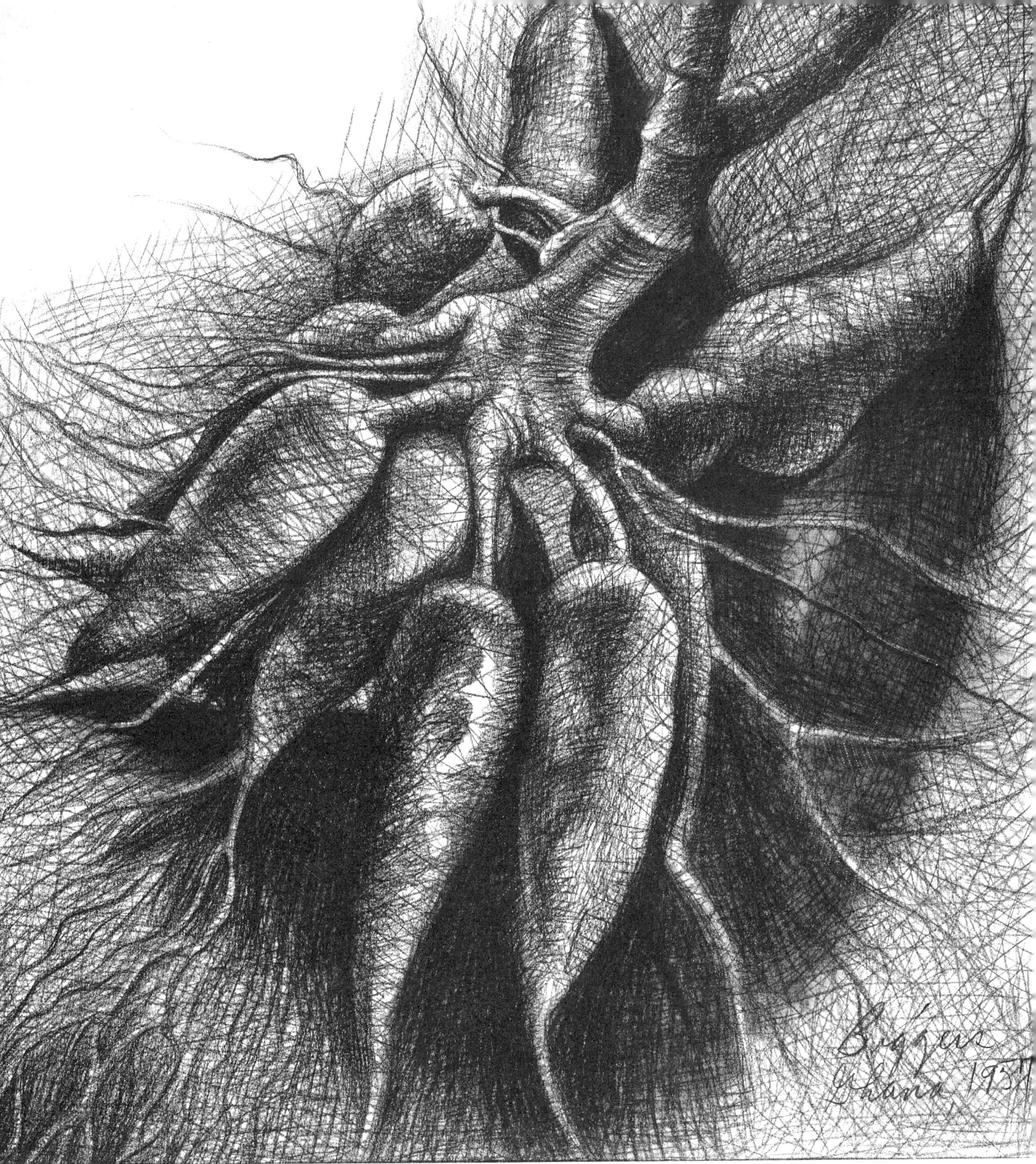

A staple food in Ghana is the cassava plant, whose rootstocks are peeled, boiled, and pounded into a food resembling mashed potatoes. It thrives along the coastal plains and throughout the forest region of West Africa, usually yielding two crops a year.

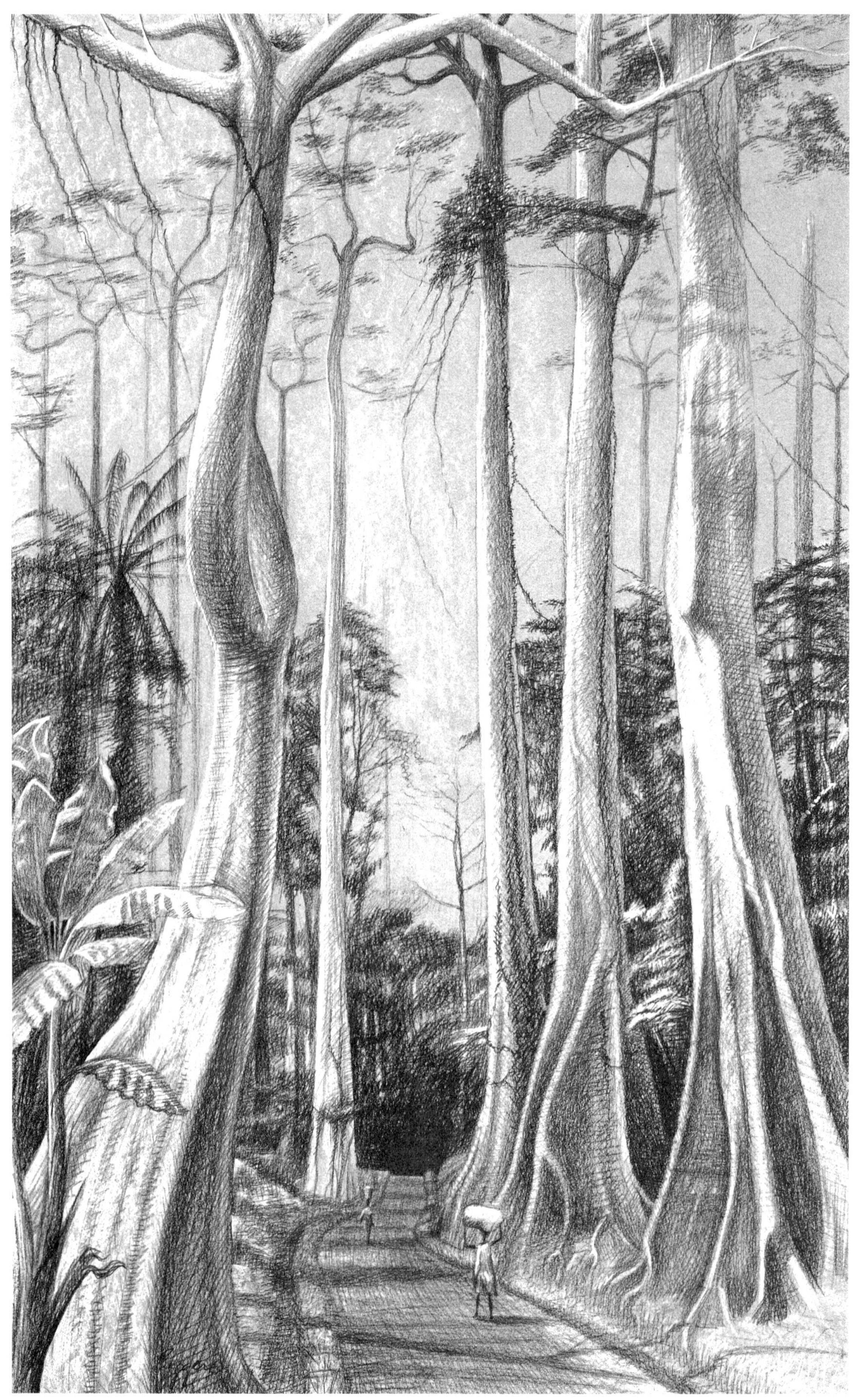

Lining the road like titanic sentinels are ancient Bombax trees, their smooth bark coated with silver lichen and their long branches, two hundred feet overhead, sometimes covered with orchids.

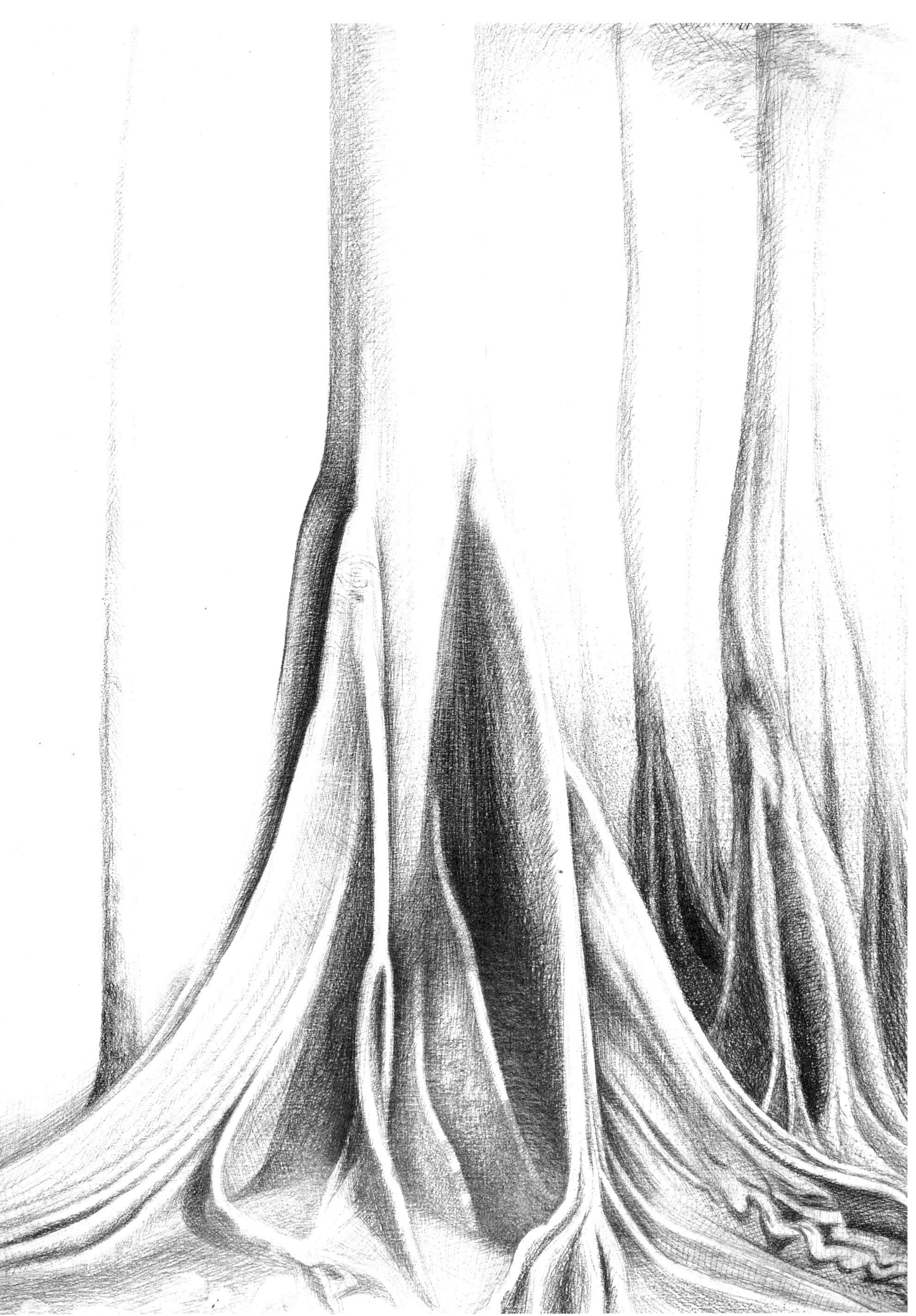

After traveling for some time among the giants of the forest one becomes subdued by nature's architecture. Great trunks writhe upward defiantly; yet they still reflect a serene, eternal majesty.

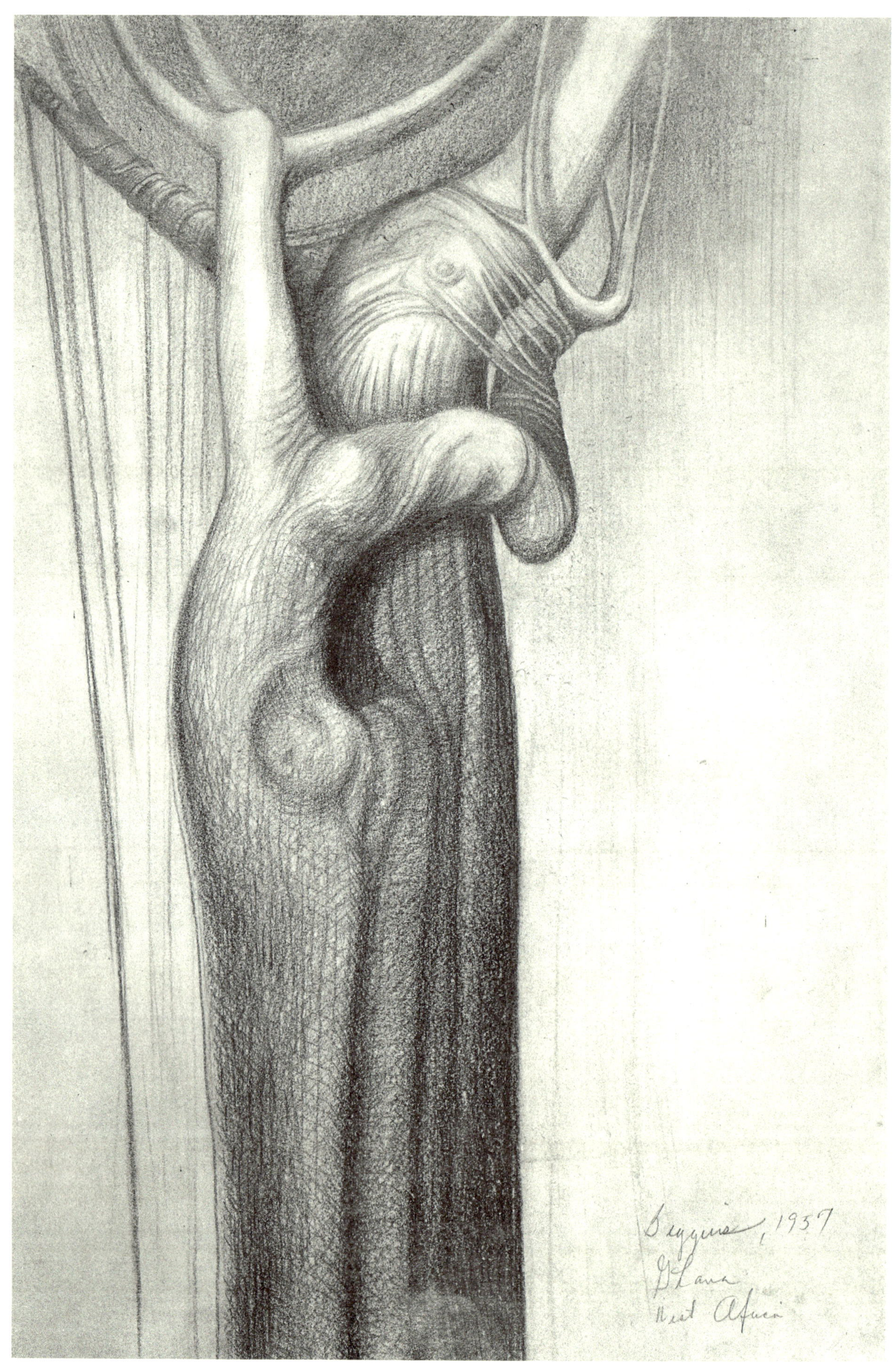

Some trees in the forests of Ghana have an almost human quality. The Creator must have relished his role, for he obviously enjoyed testing his ability as a maker of new form.

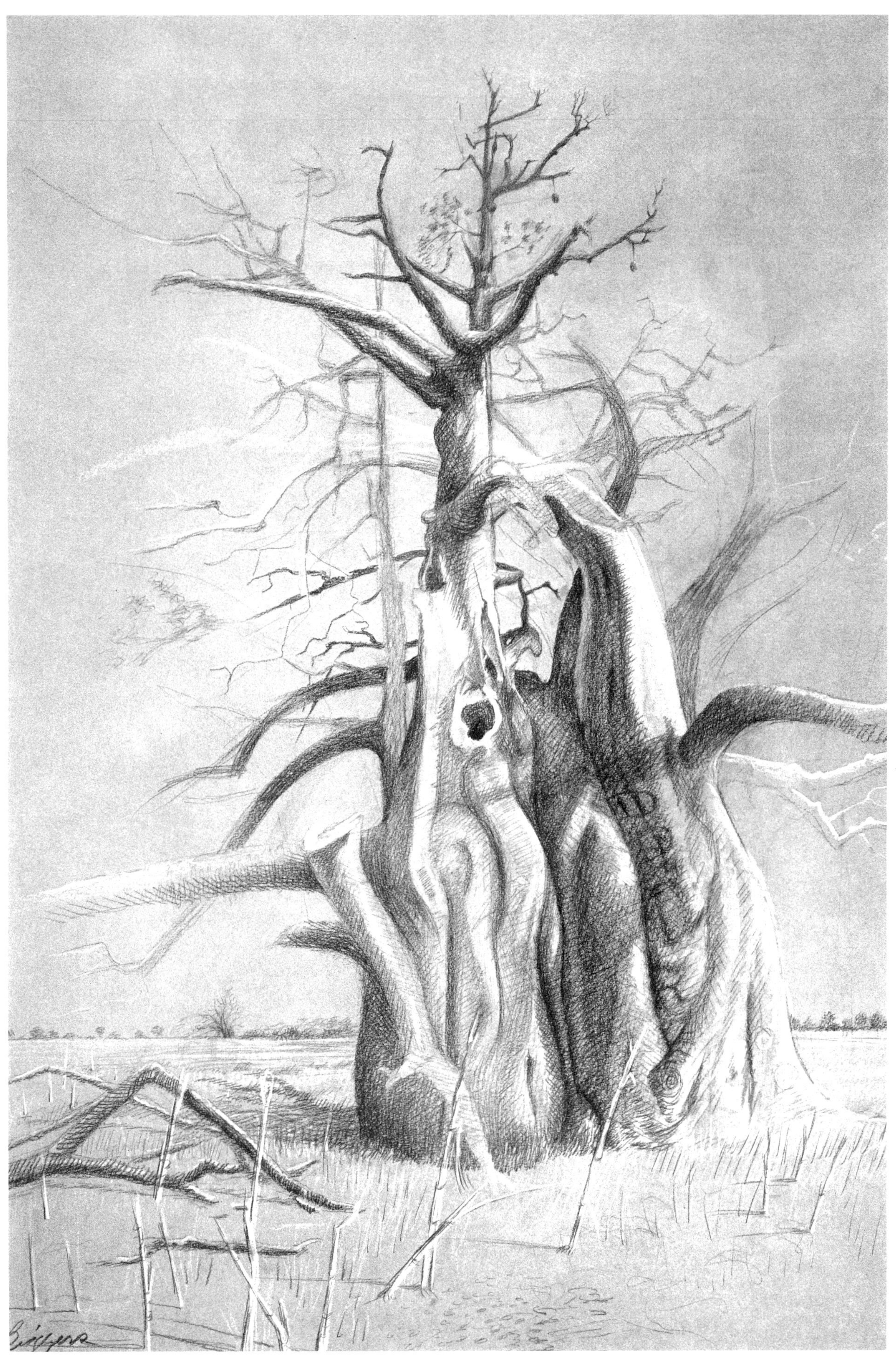

Dominating the northern plains of Ghana are the giant baobab trees, but they, in turn, can be dominated by an unseen, revengeful hand: In their struggle to live and to grow some seem to have consumed themselves.

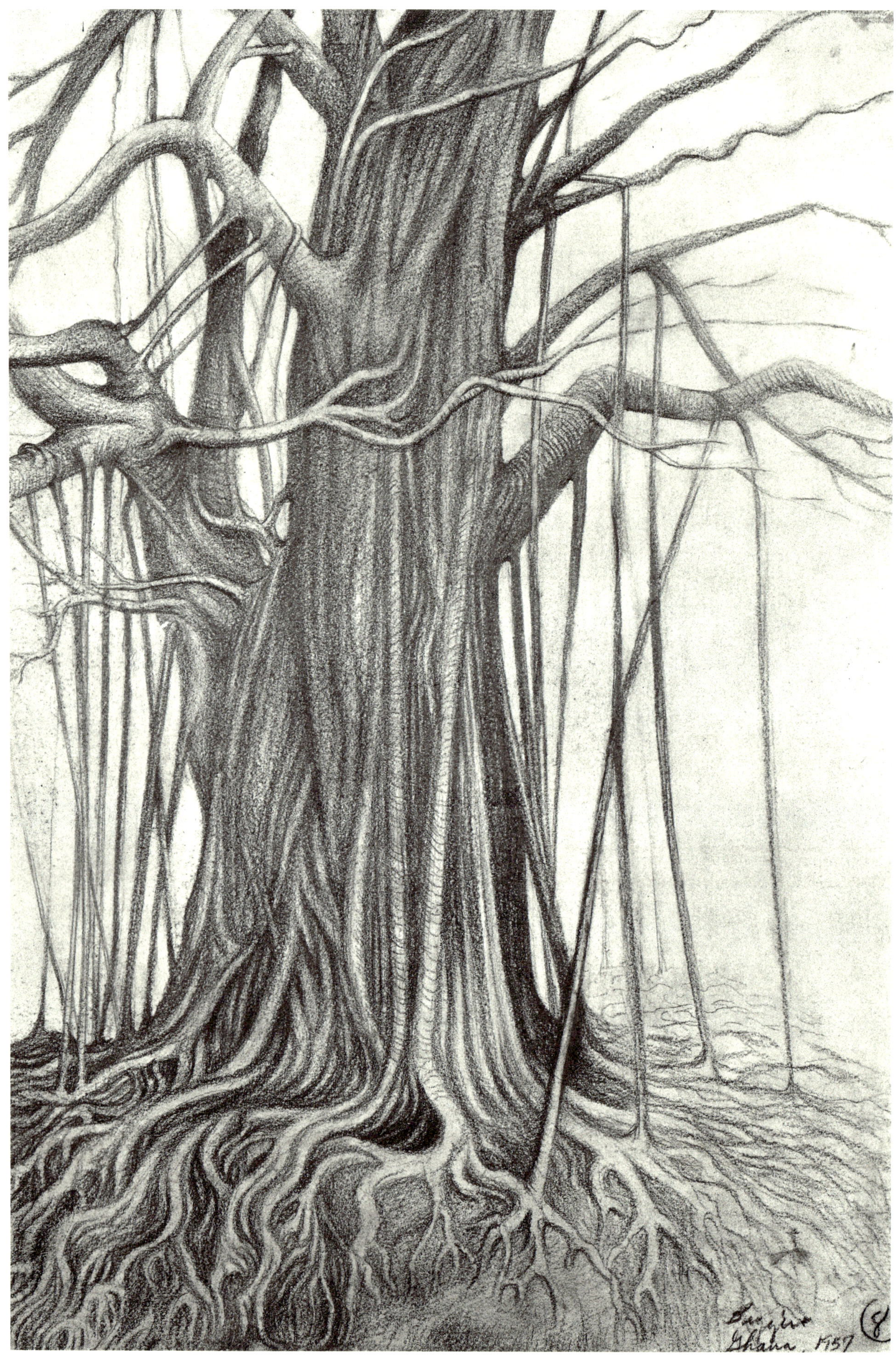

Roots of the *kuma* tree weave an awesome pattern as they interlace over the ground, grasp at the trunk, and sometimes climb up the tree. Aerial roots plunge downward from overhanging branches.

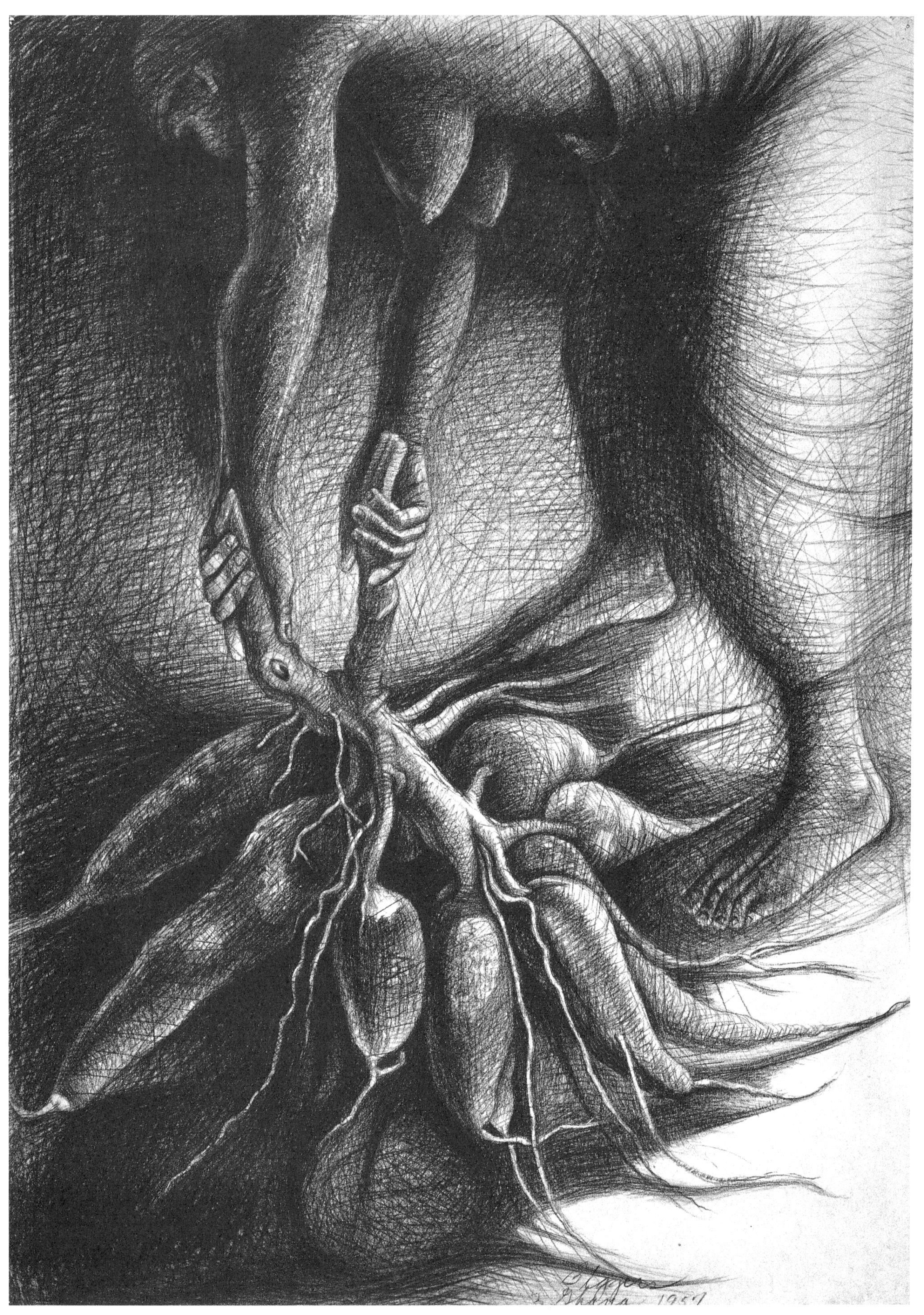

A depiction of a creative, life-sustaining entity—woman and the cassava root. A man can survive on cassava alone, and because of this many Africans speak of it with profound respect. Their name for cassava: "It is life."

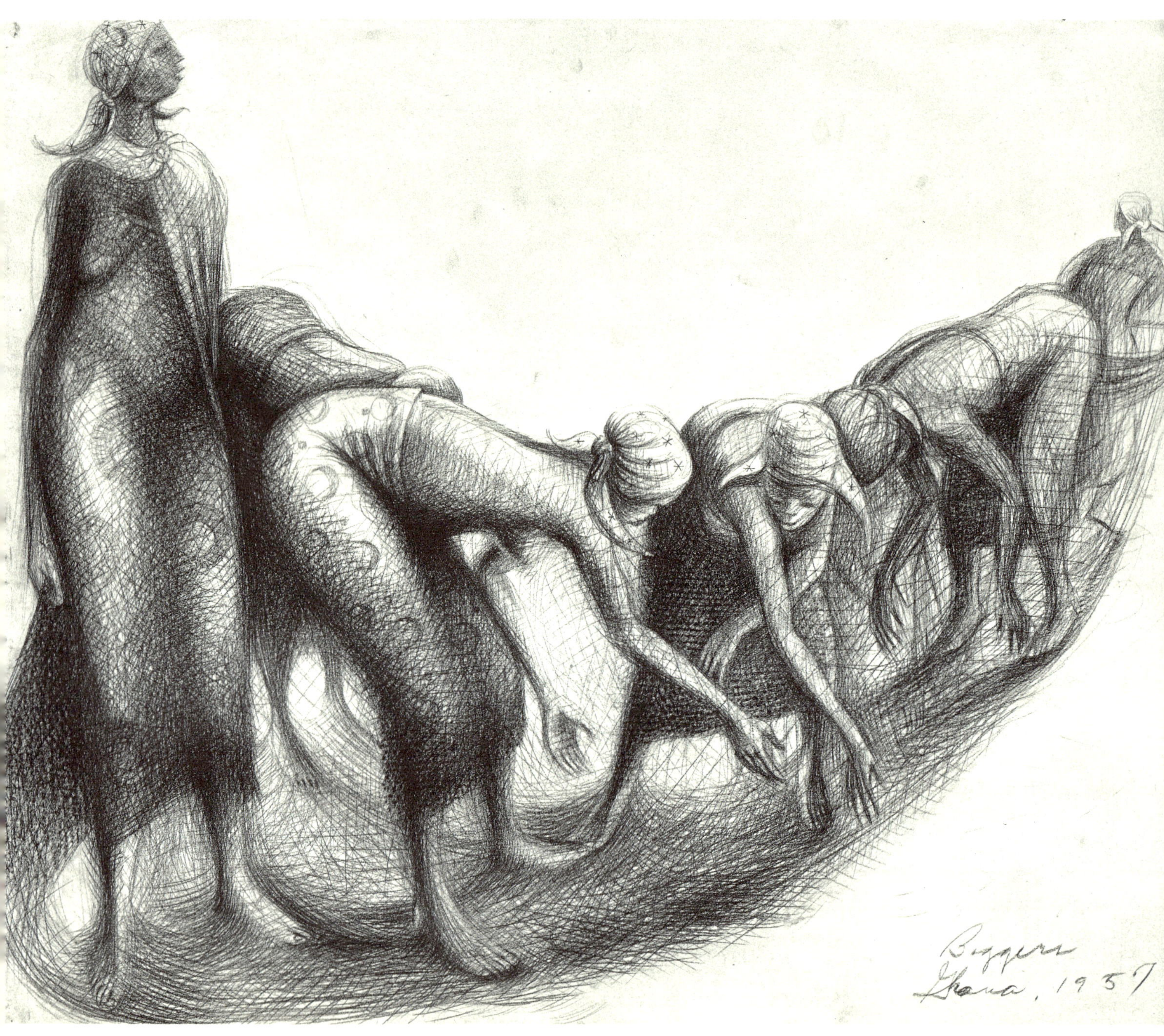

A splendid example of good human relations and cooperation is offered by Ghana village life. These womenfolk, working together, reveal to the senses a satisfying rhythm of life. Man is one with nature, integrated with himself and with the earth.

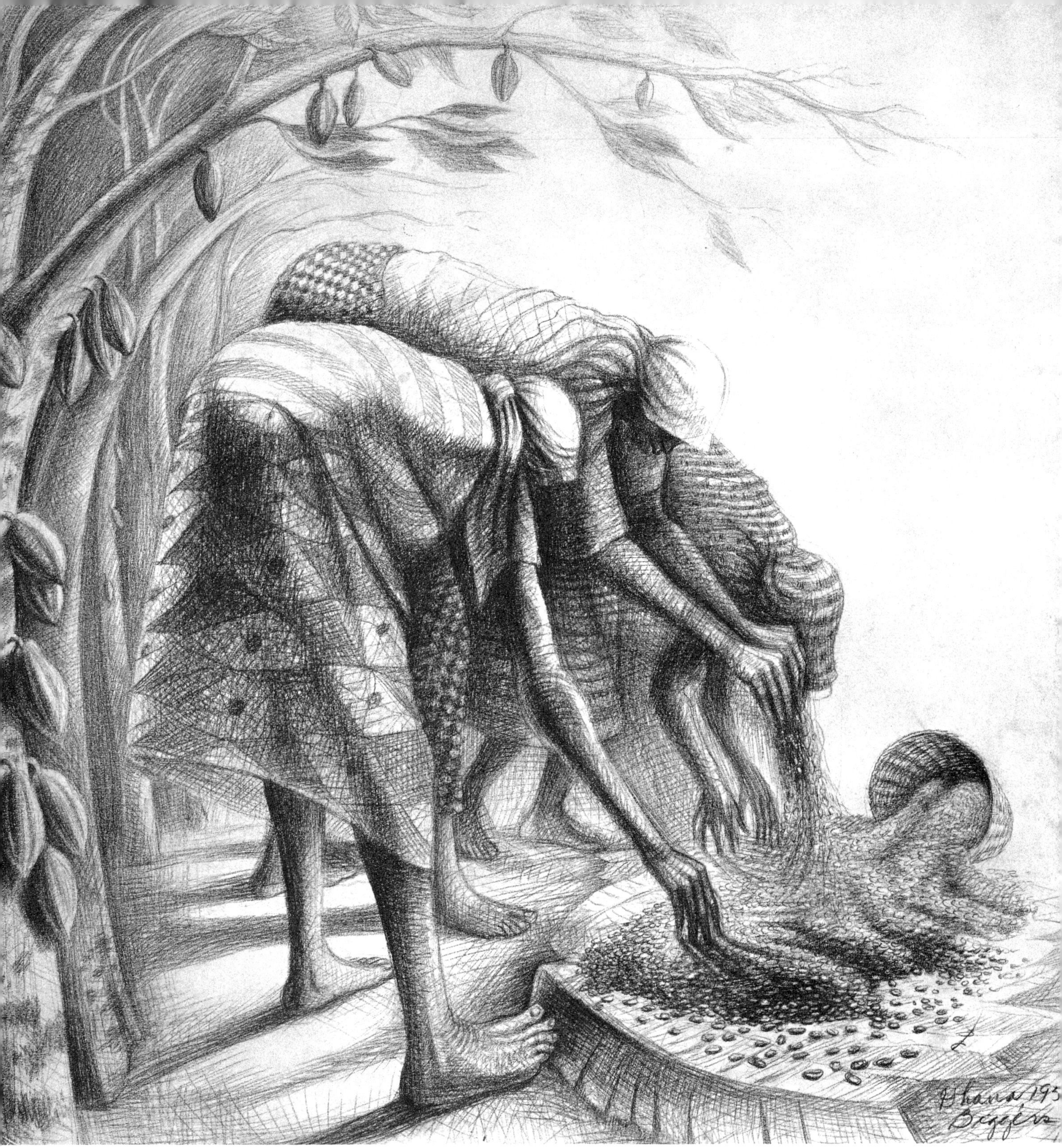

The pod that grows from the trunk and main branches of the cocoa tree provides the main cash crop for Ghana. From it the seeds are removed and spread out to dry, then ground into fine powder.

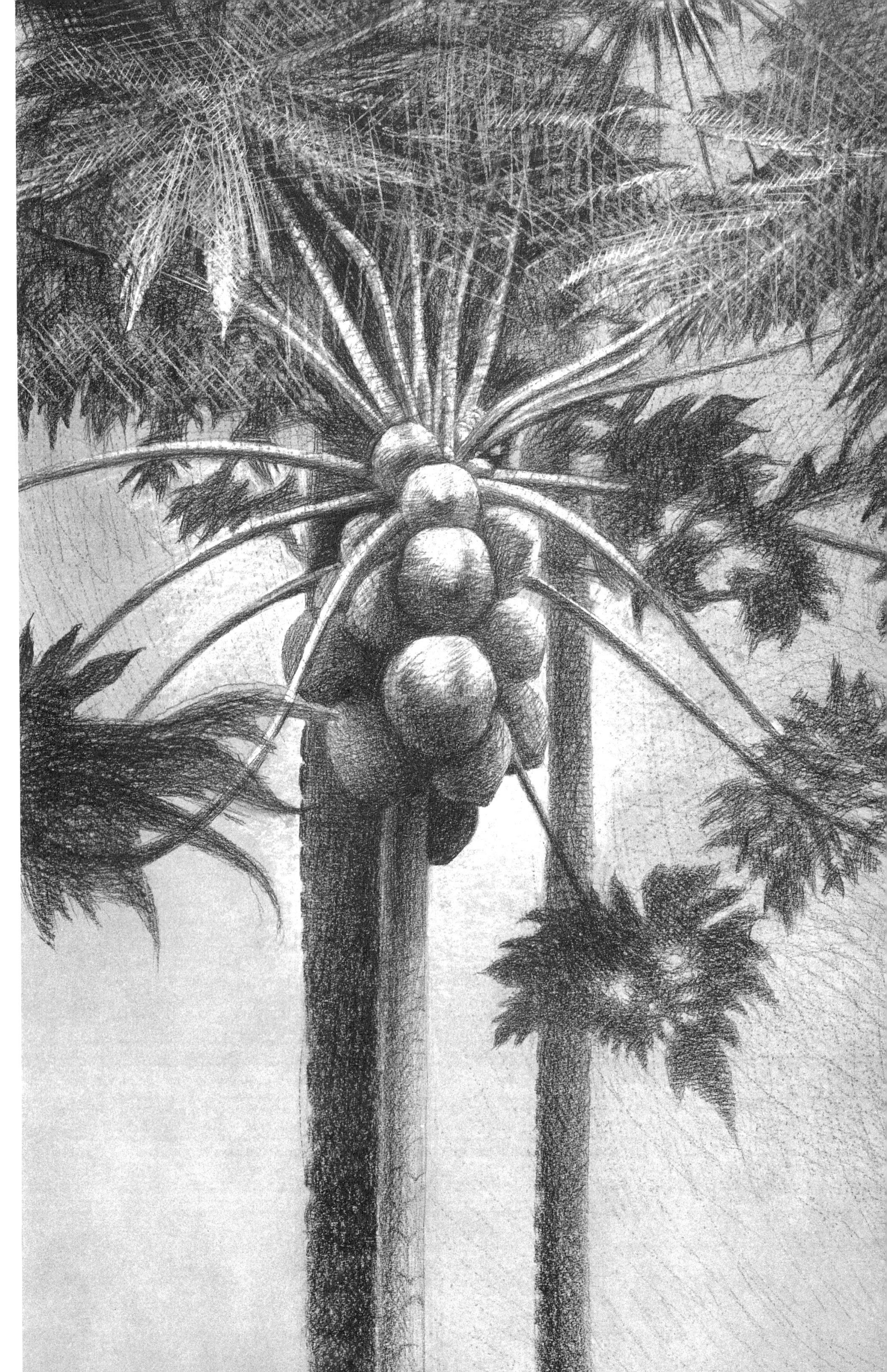

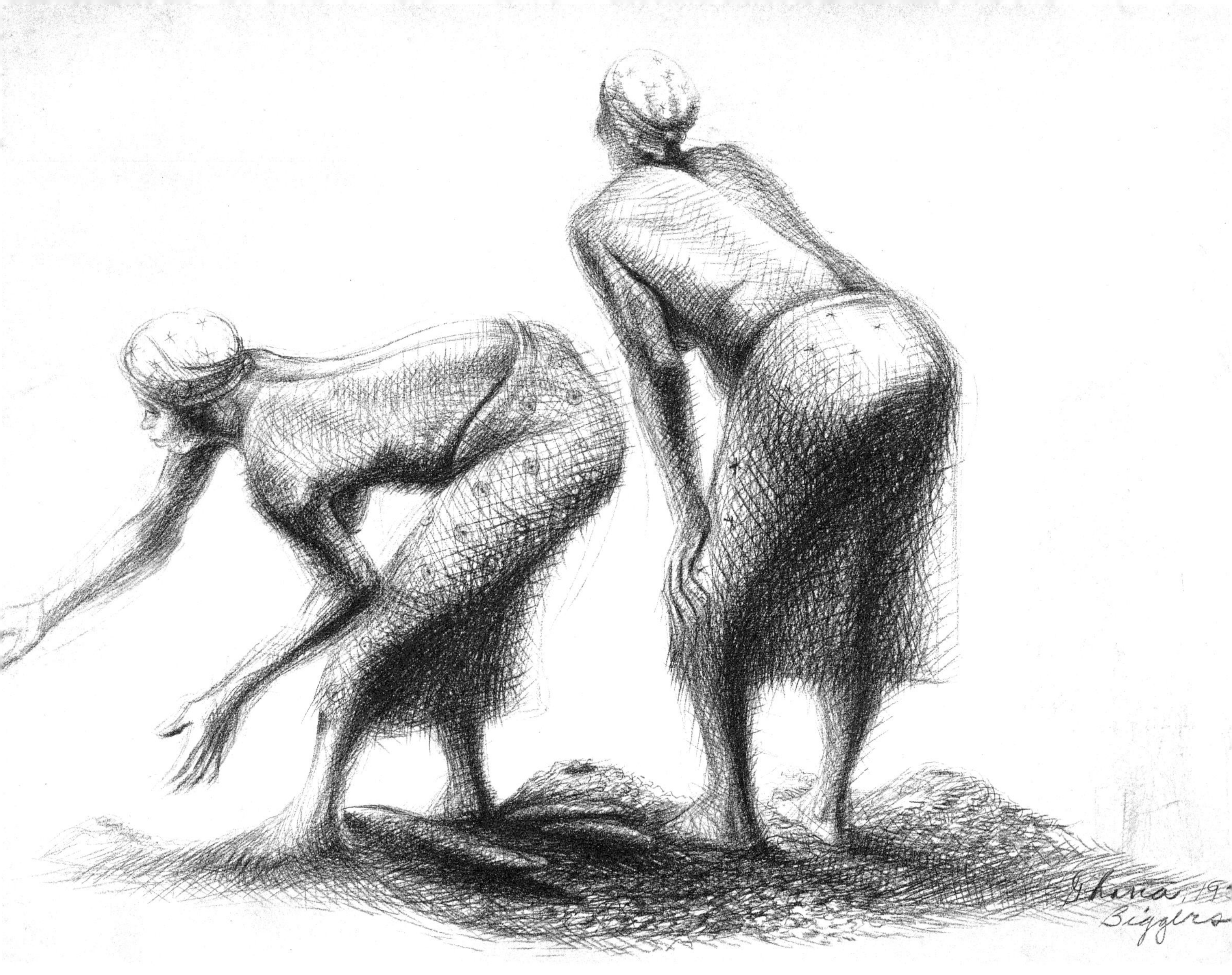

Bare to the waist, two glistening, sun-splashed bodies moist from the day's toil mirror man's eternal struggle for existence.

High atop the paw-paw tree grows a pregnant cluster of fruit. Single-leaved branches shooting outward emphasize that it is plucking time, that the fruit is ripe and tender.

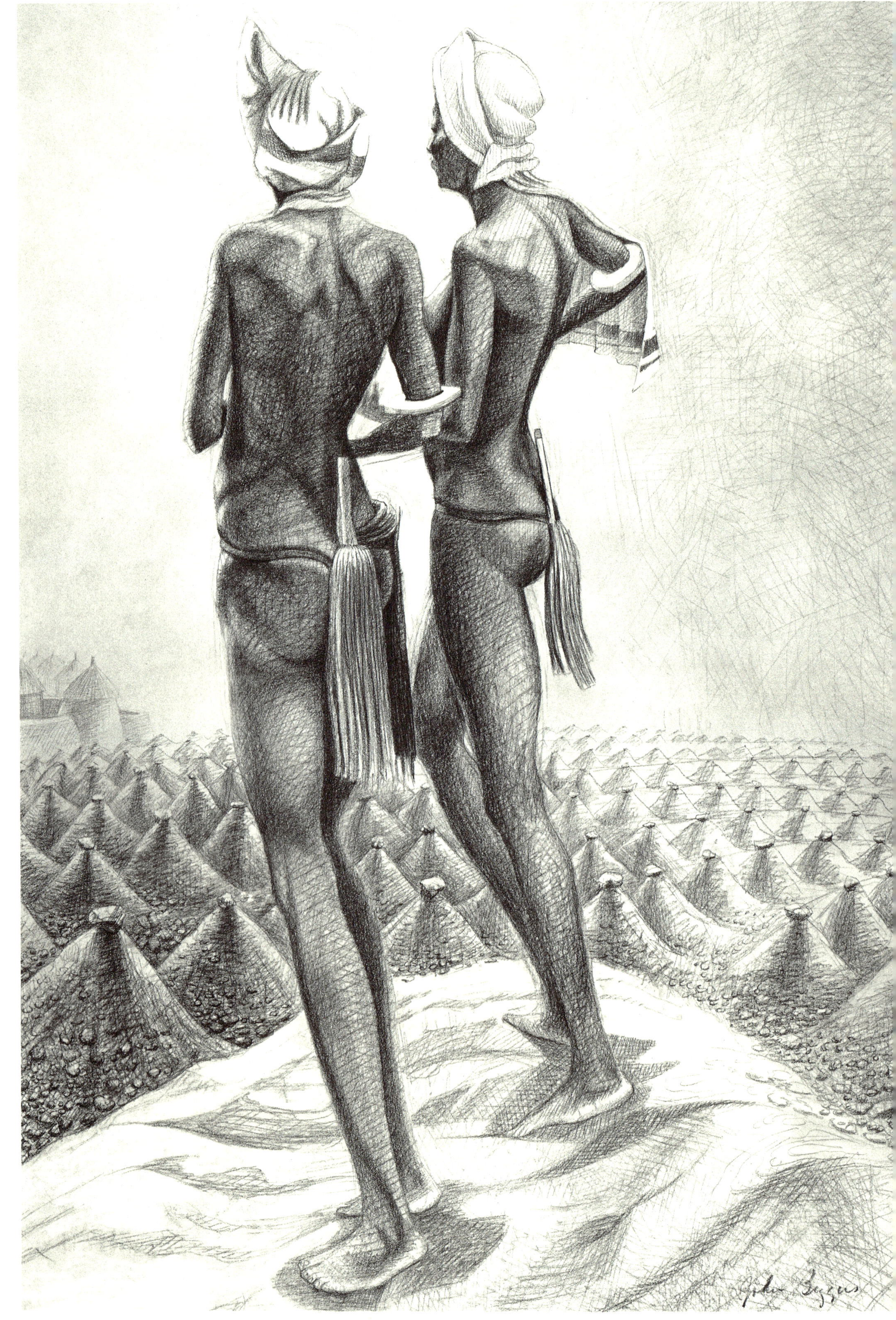

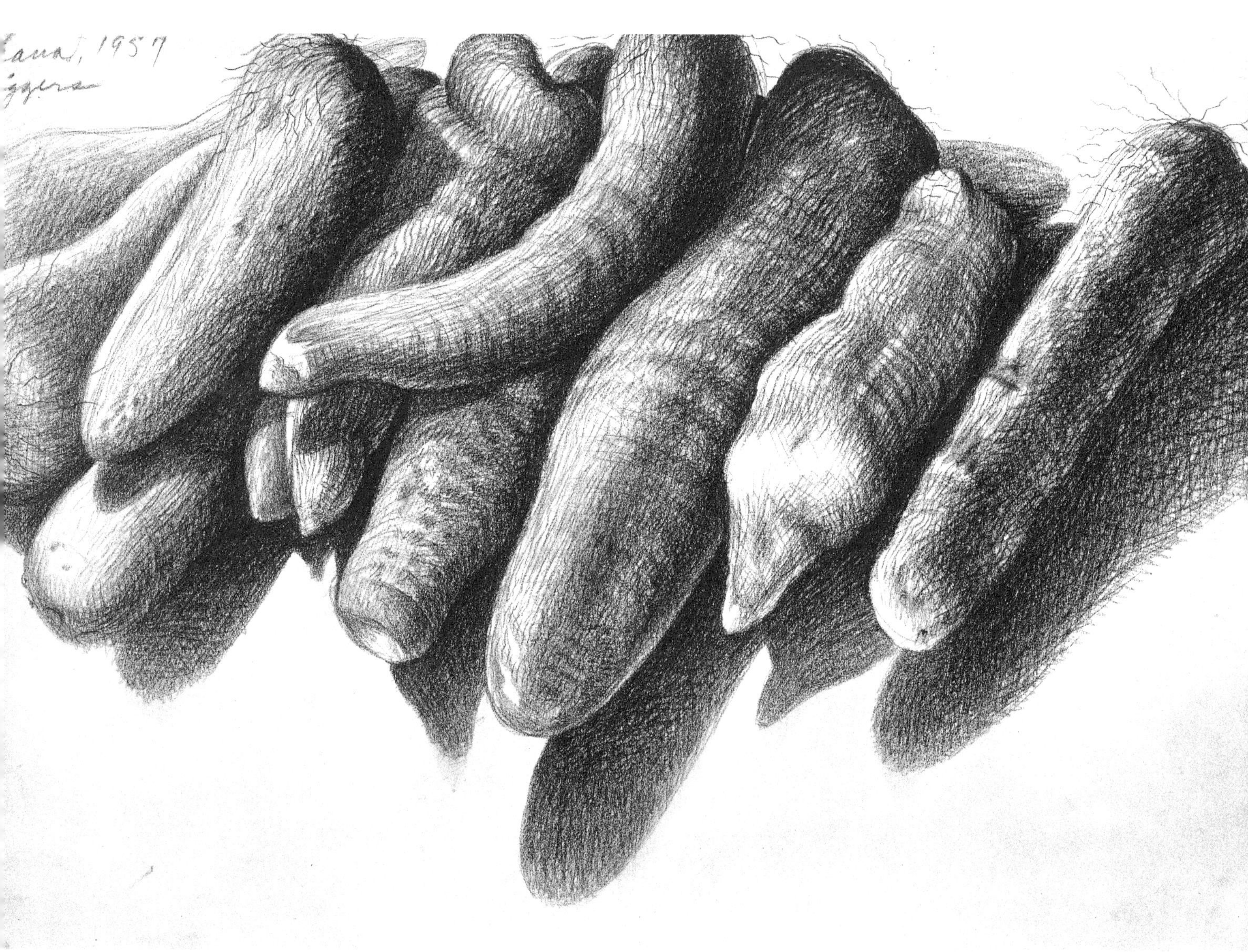

Yams are peeled, boiled, and smashed into a doughy mass for making *fu-fu,* a delicious, popular meal in West Africa. To this base, meat and vegetable soups are added.

Before a field of yam hills stand two royal daughters of the Northern Territories. Each wears only a headdress, a loin cloth, and an ivory armlet, all marks of spiritual perfection and ideal physical form.

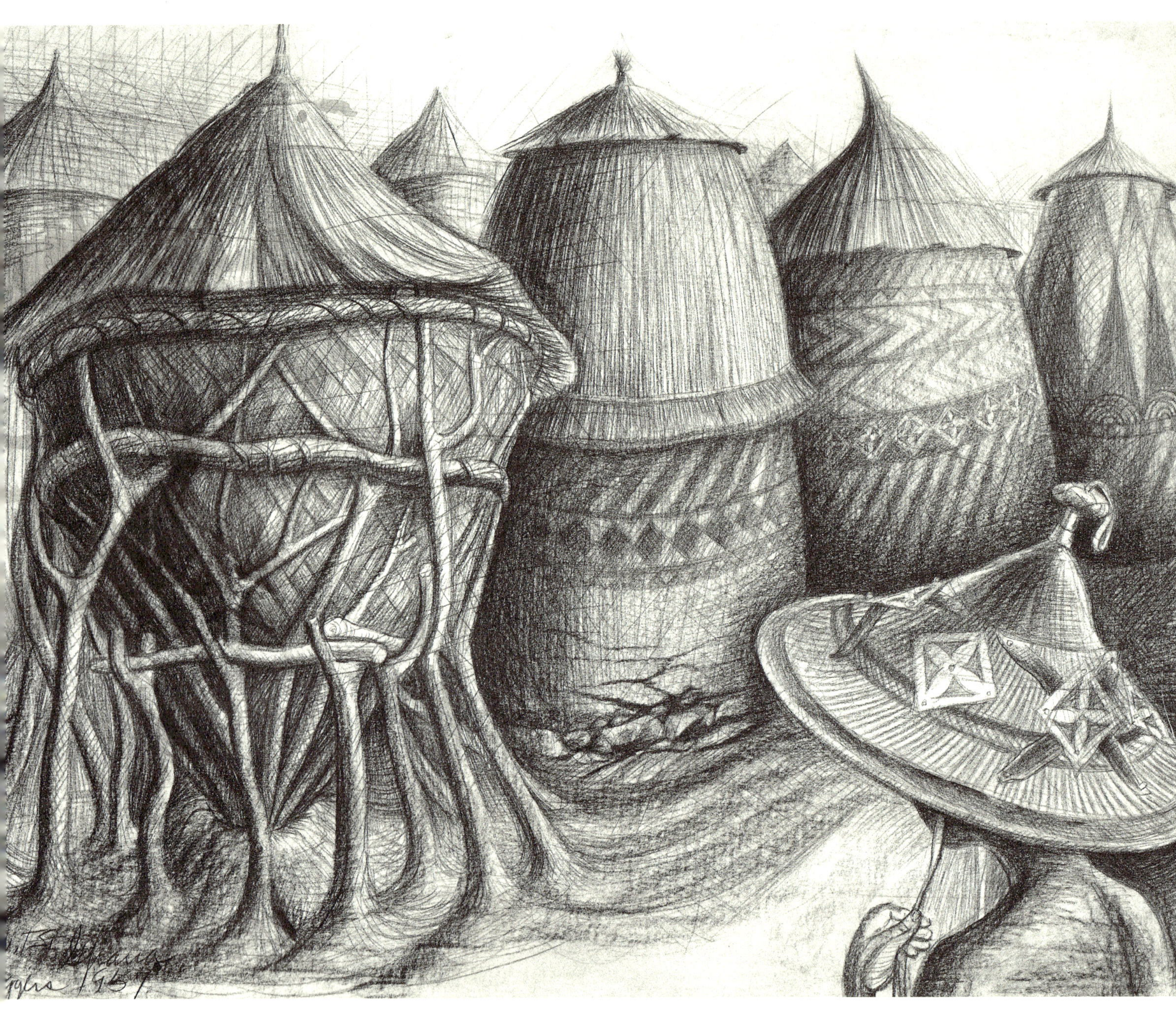

Storehouses for yams, millet, groundnuts, and grain are made of earth called "swish," then embellished with colorful, abstract symbols and patterns. The thatched roofs resemble in design the hats worn by men.

For freedom of movement and for coolness women remove their upper garments when engaged in farm work or other heavy chores. When a woman's bosom is thus bare, African men usually look in another direction, even while carrying on conversation.

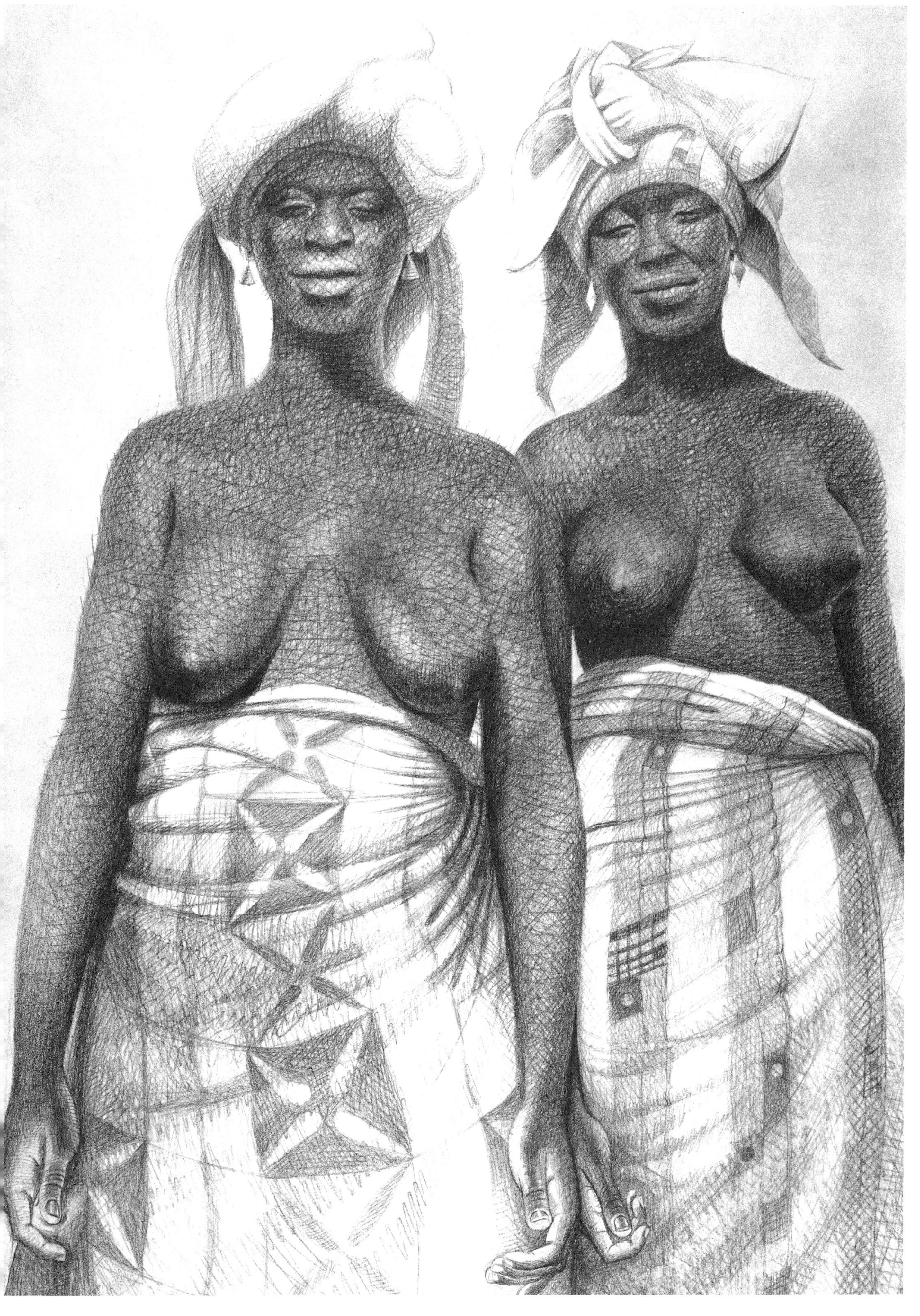

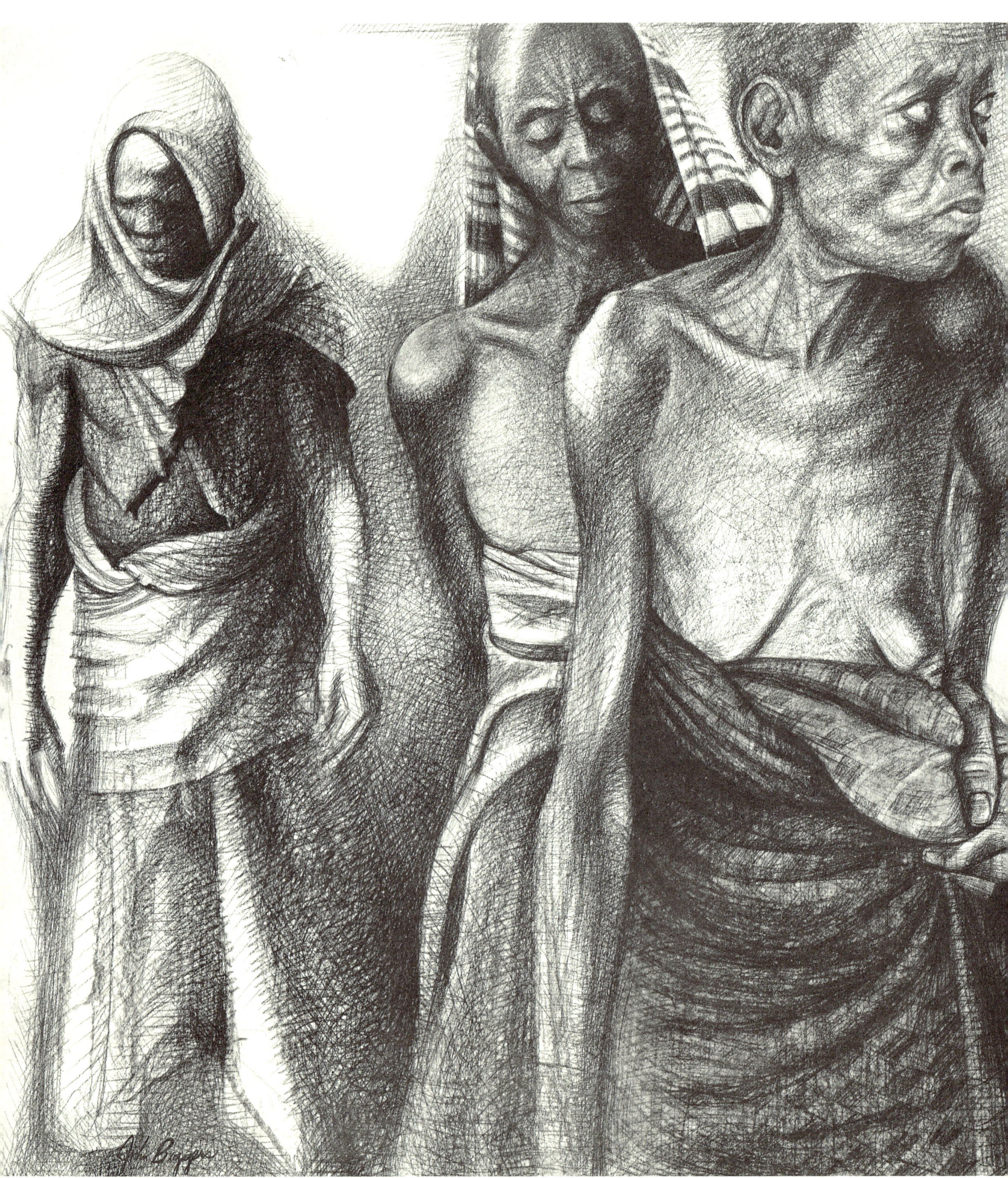

For many years these old women have served as village chemists, but when they die the secrets of their craft probably will be lost. Imported dyes and soaps are plentiful and cheap, and young apprentices are scarce.

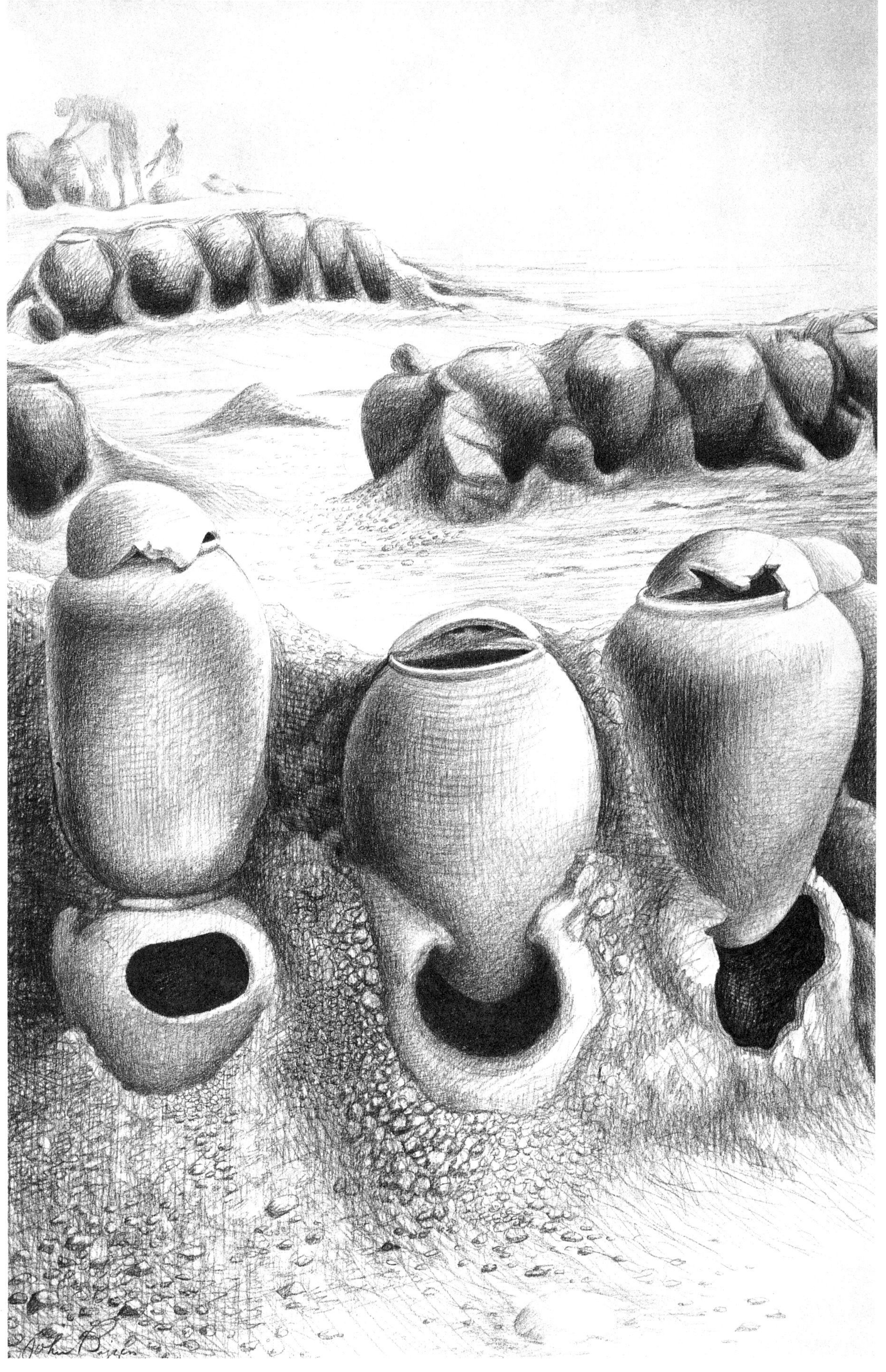

Women potters made these earthenware vats, and in them women chemists distill dye and make soap for their village. Gravel is piled around the vessels to provide support.

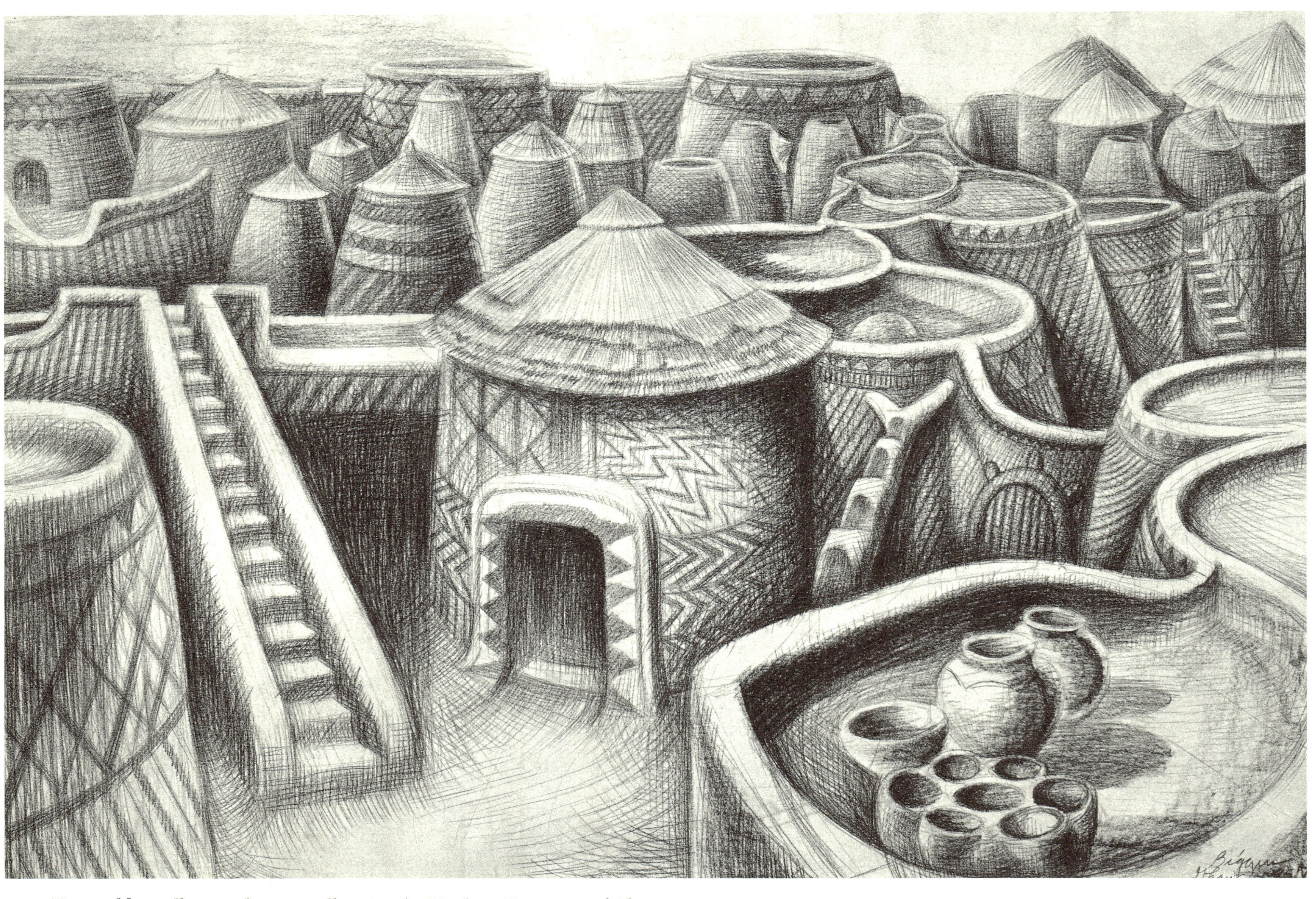

Fortresslike walls encircle many villages in the Northern Territories of Ghana. With the exception of the cone-shaped, thatched roofs, the buildings are made entirely of clay. A century or so ago, when this construction was begun, warfare raged and wild animals roamed the plains.

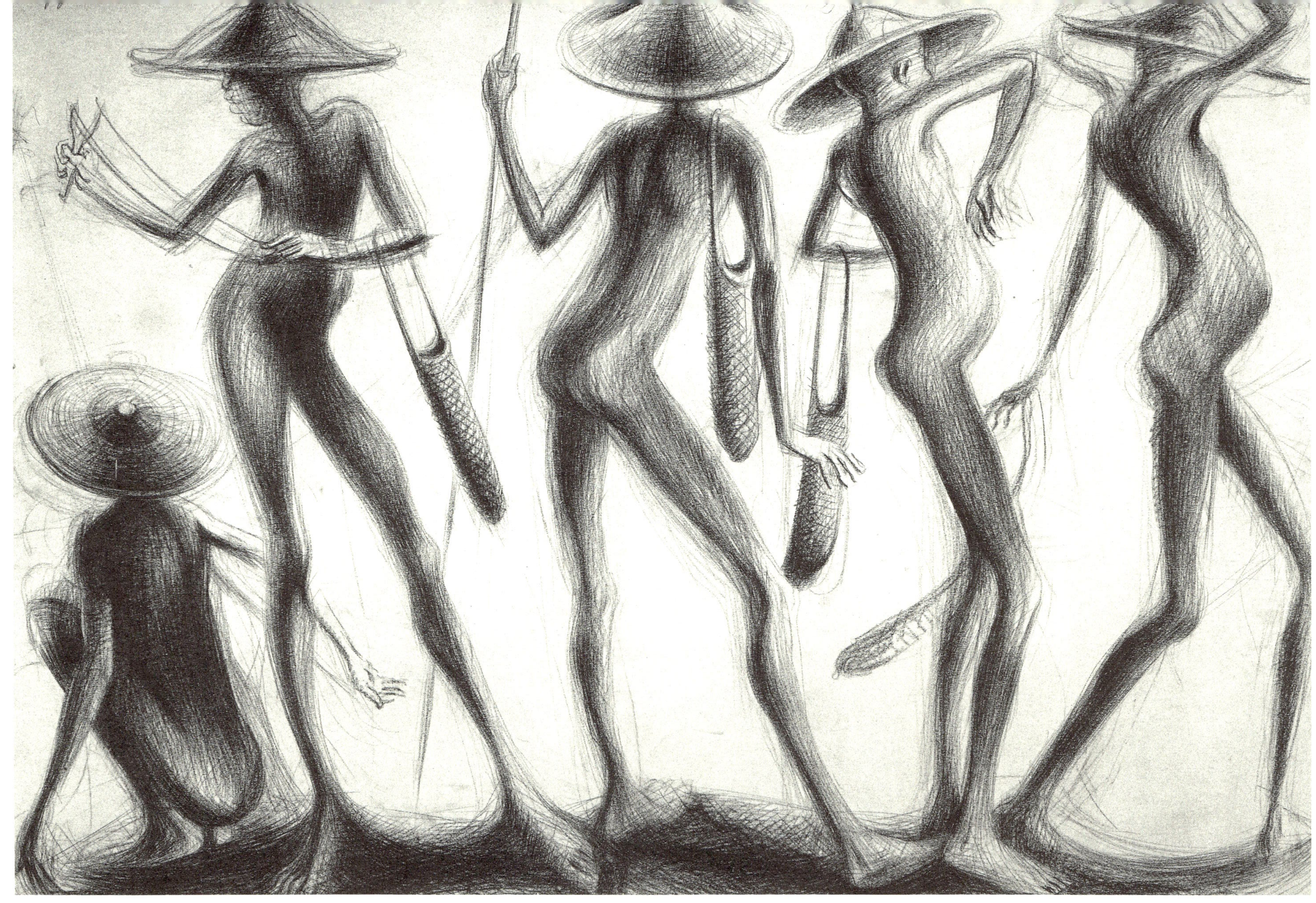

Youth of the Northern Territories are nimble and robust. Along highways and pathways they play games, climb trees, and ride the backs of cattle and donkeys—only slightly protected from the fierce sunshine by conical hats.

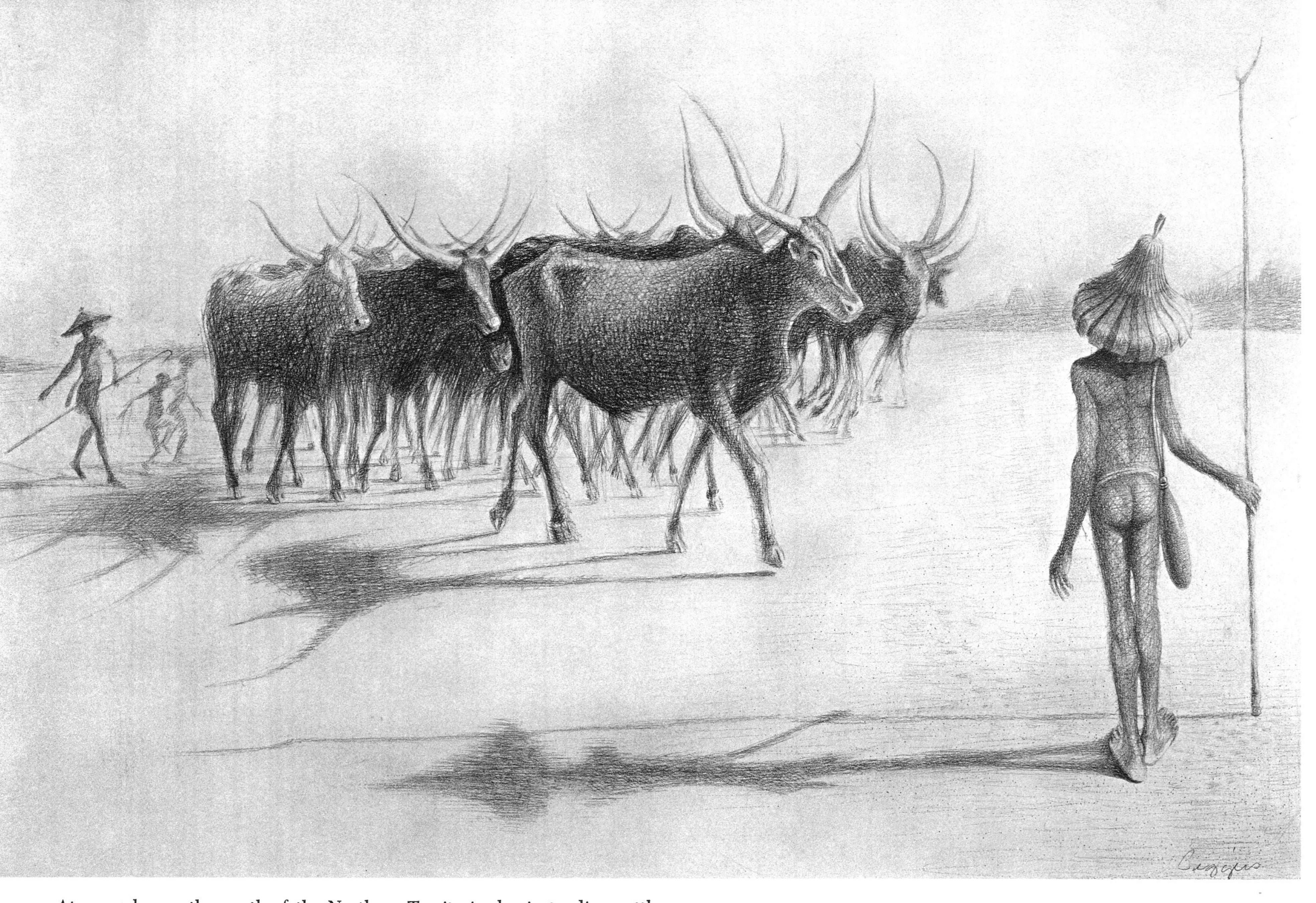

At an early age the youth of the Northern Territories begin tending cattle, sheep, and goats. From youthful shoulders hang hand-woven fiber bags filled with snacks of groundnuts and grain, and handsome gourds containing water. The animals have names and respond individually when called.

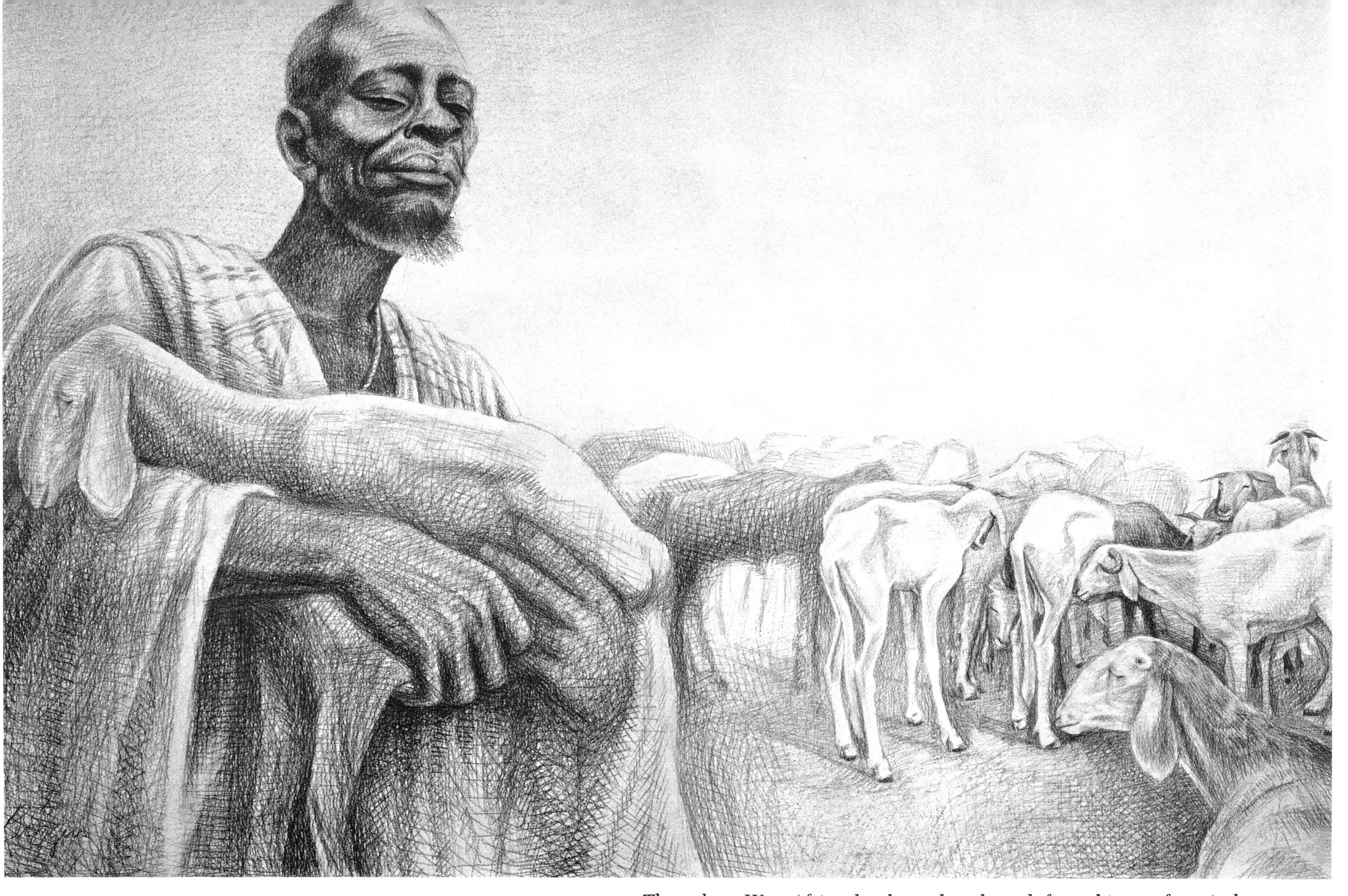

Throughout West Africa the sheep—long-legged, from thirty to forty inches tall—are used for sacrificial offerings as well as for the food and wool they provide.

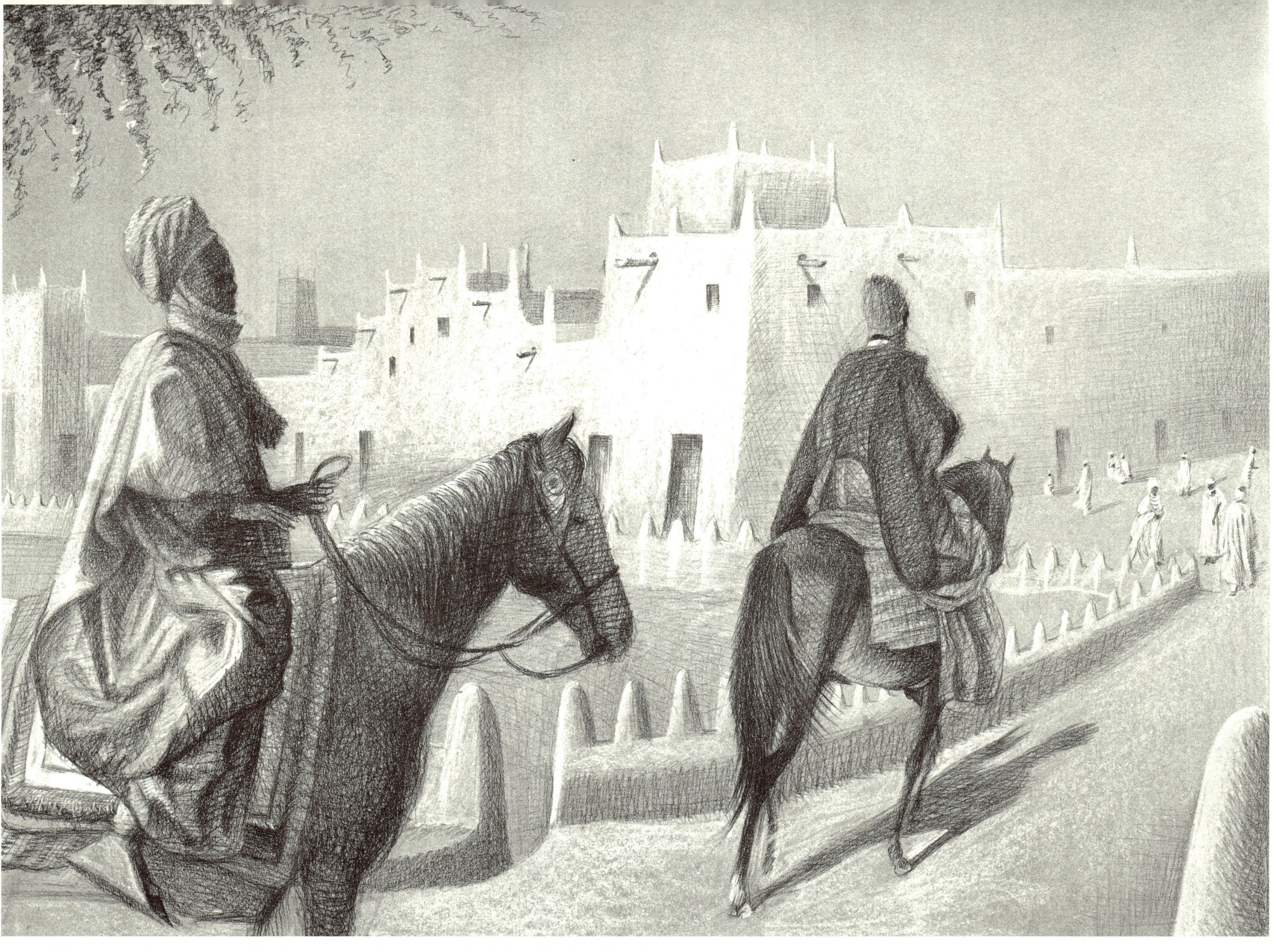

Horsemen of the ancient Moslem city of Kano are called, locally, "Big Men," a name made especially fitting by their dress and manner. Wearing colorful, flowing robes, they ride their war stallions arrogantly.

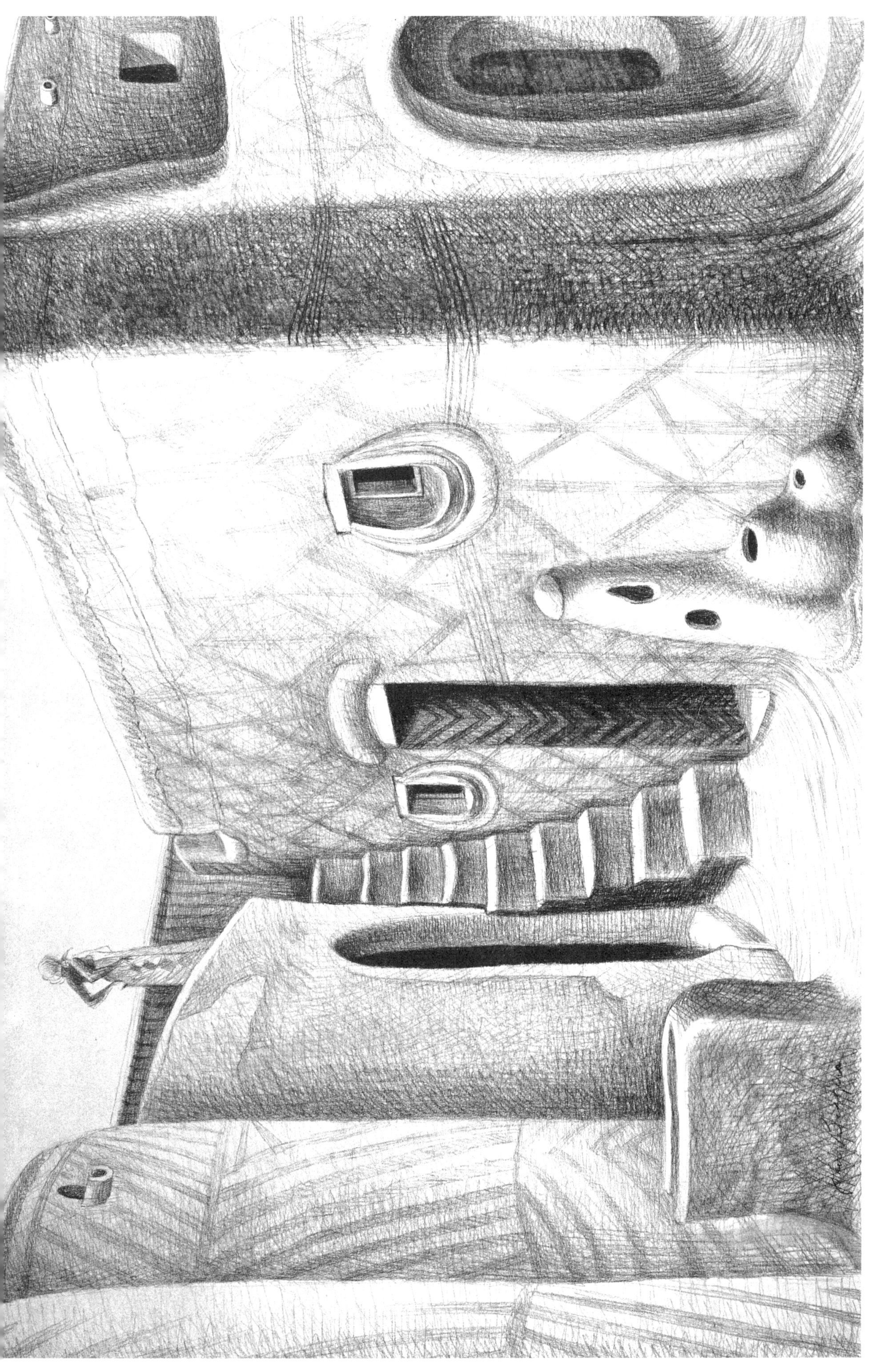

Individual expression and innovation are recognizable in these clay houses found on the arid plains between Kano and Navrongo. This one manifests the builder's individuality in window and door design, outside ornamentation, and the addition of storage bins that look like giant wasps' nests attached to the wall.

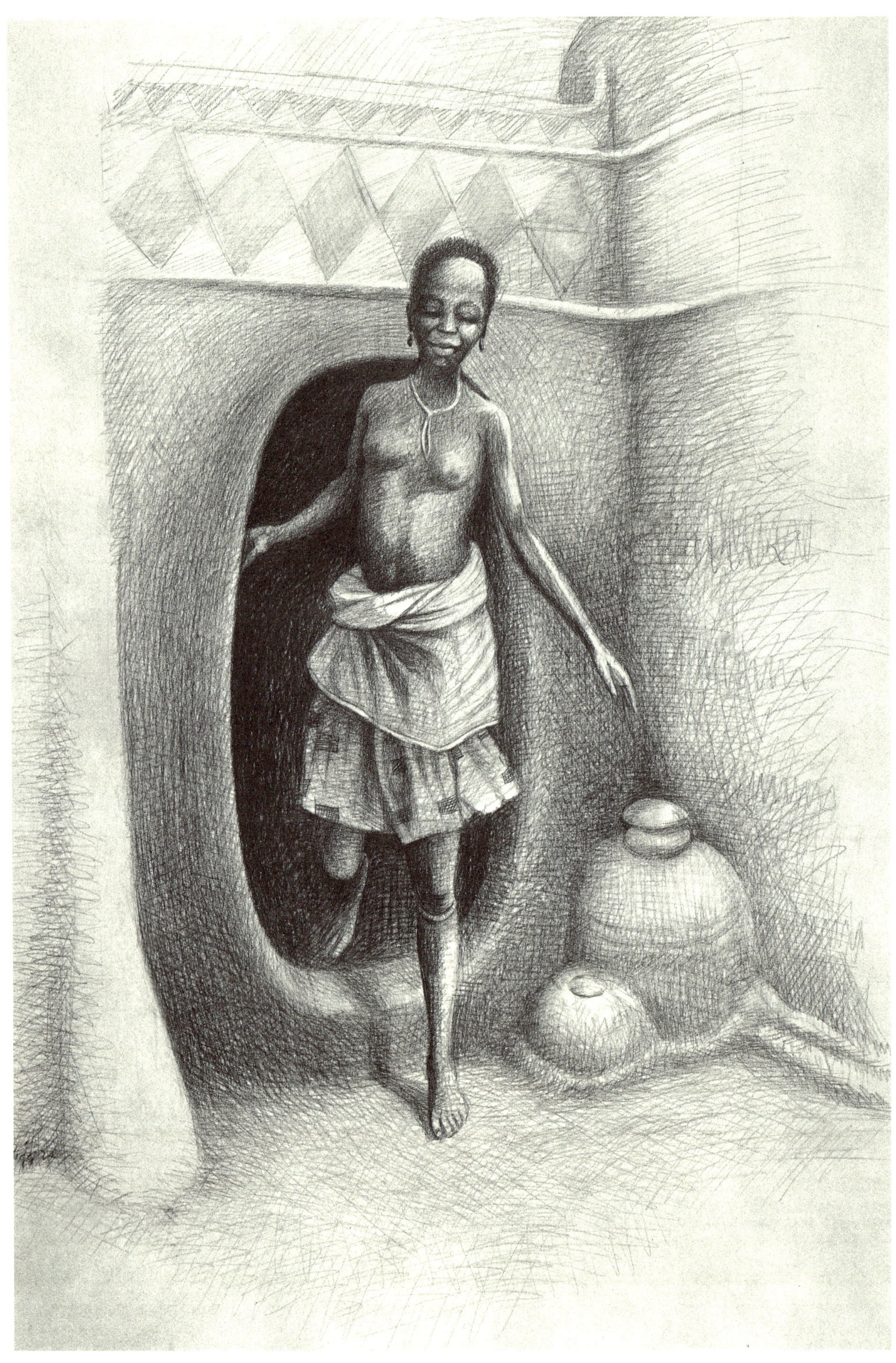

In Navrongo this young woman emerges from her cocoonlike dwelling to greet us. Later her husband will give us satisfying, stimulating millet beer, served in gourds adorned with stripes, moons, and stars.

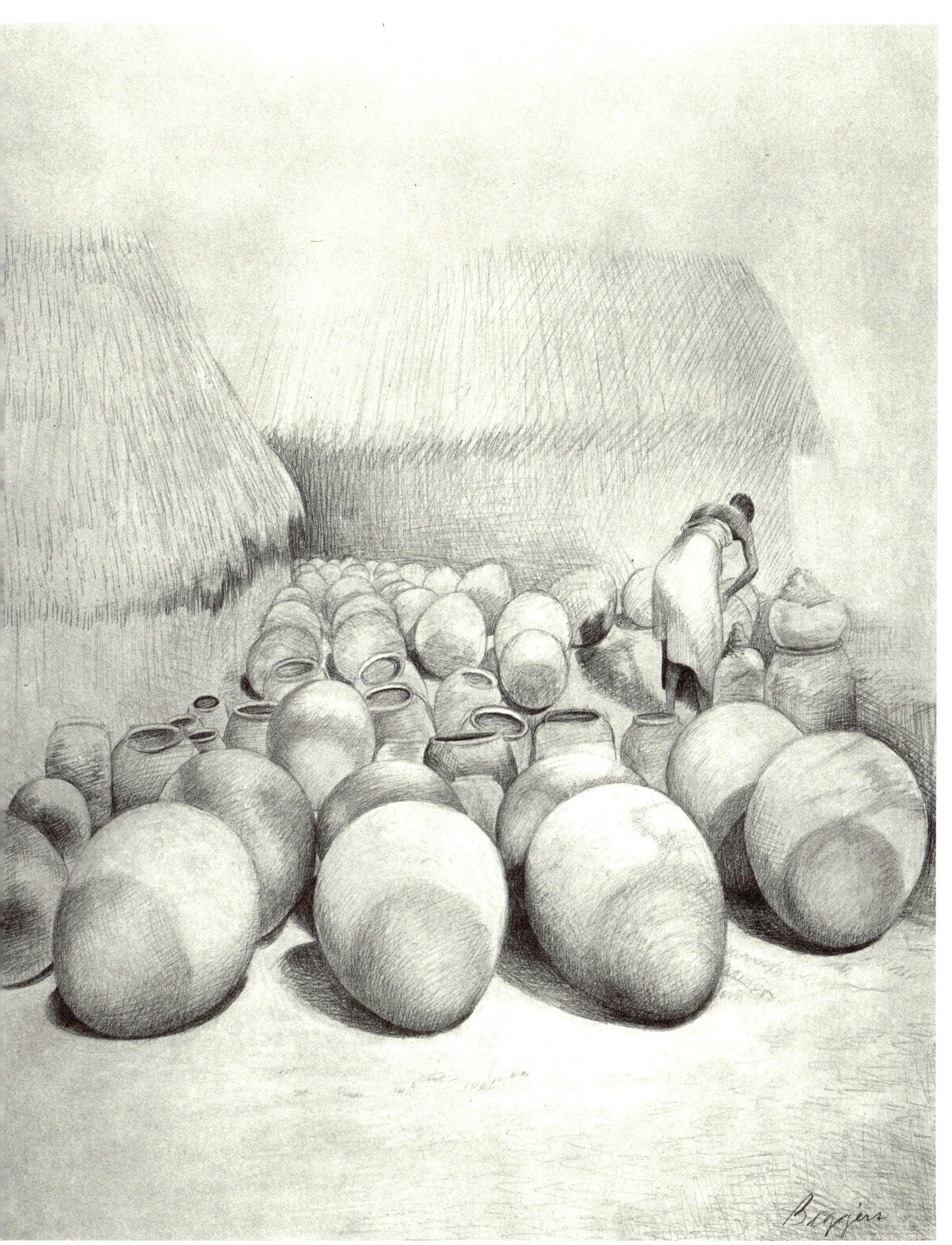

Throughout Ghana and Nigeria women produce traditional pottery by the coil and slab method—and without using a potter's wheel. Thatch and wood are then placed over the pots and burned. Modern ceramic factories, worked by men, are replacing this old way of making pottery.

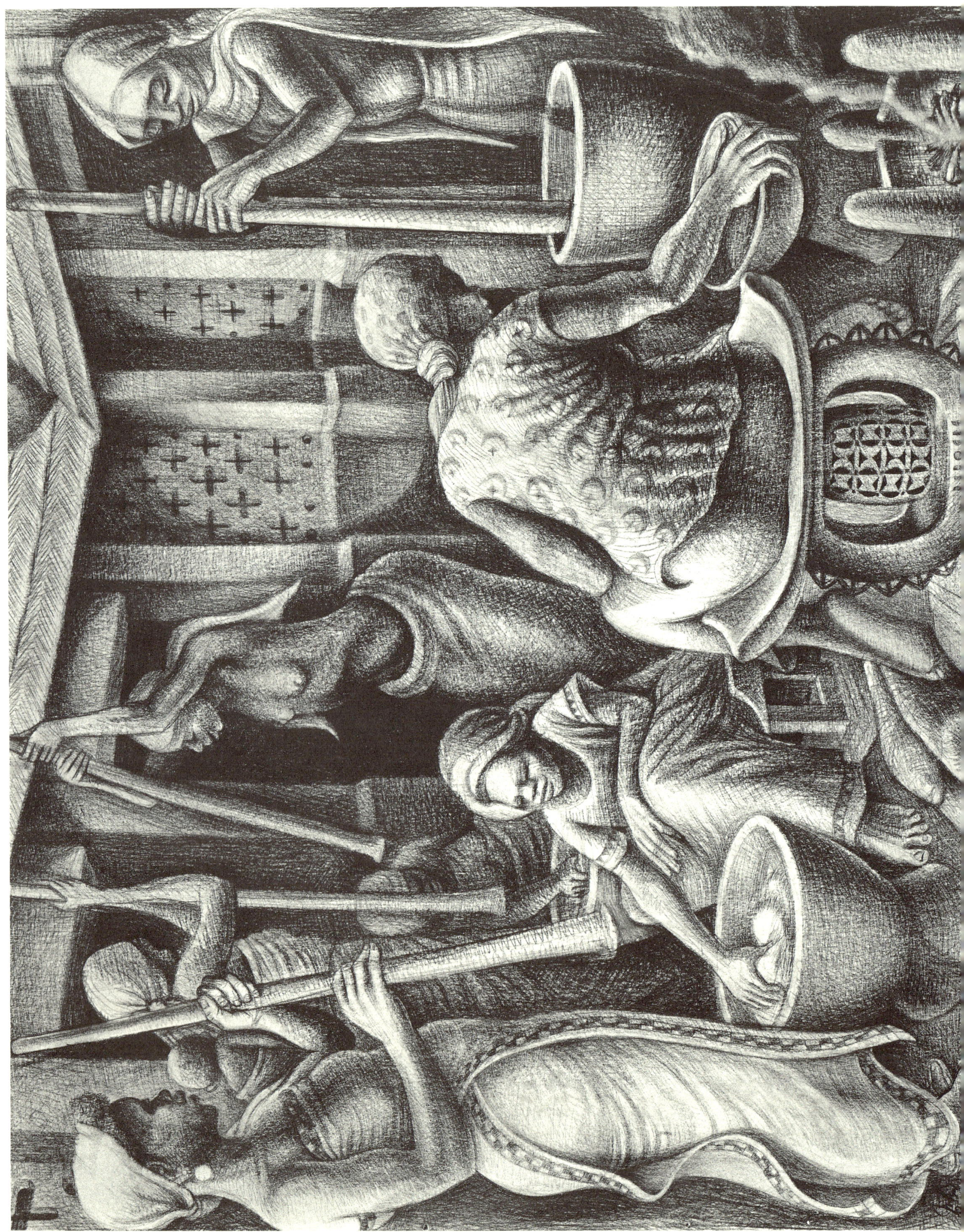

A warm, hospitable atmosphere prevails when womenfolk cook the evening meal. A muffled pounding of pestle in mortar signifies the preparation of *fu-fu*. Blue smoke rises gently from hearths in the courtyard. Conversation becomes lively among the women, while, nearby, working men and boys seated on stools stir impatiently.

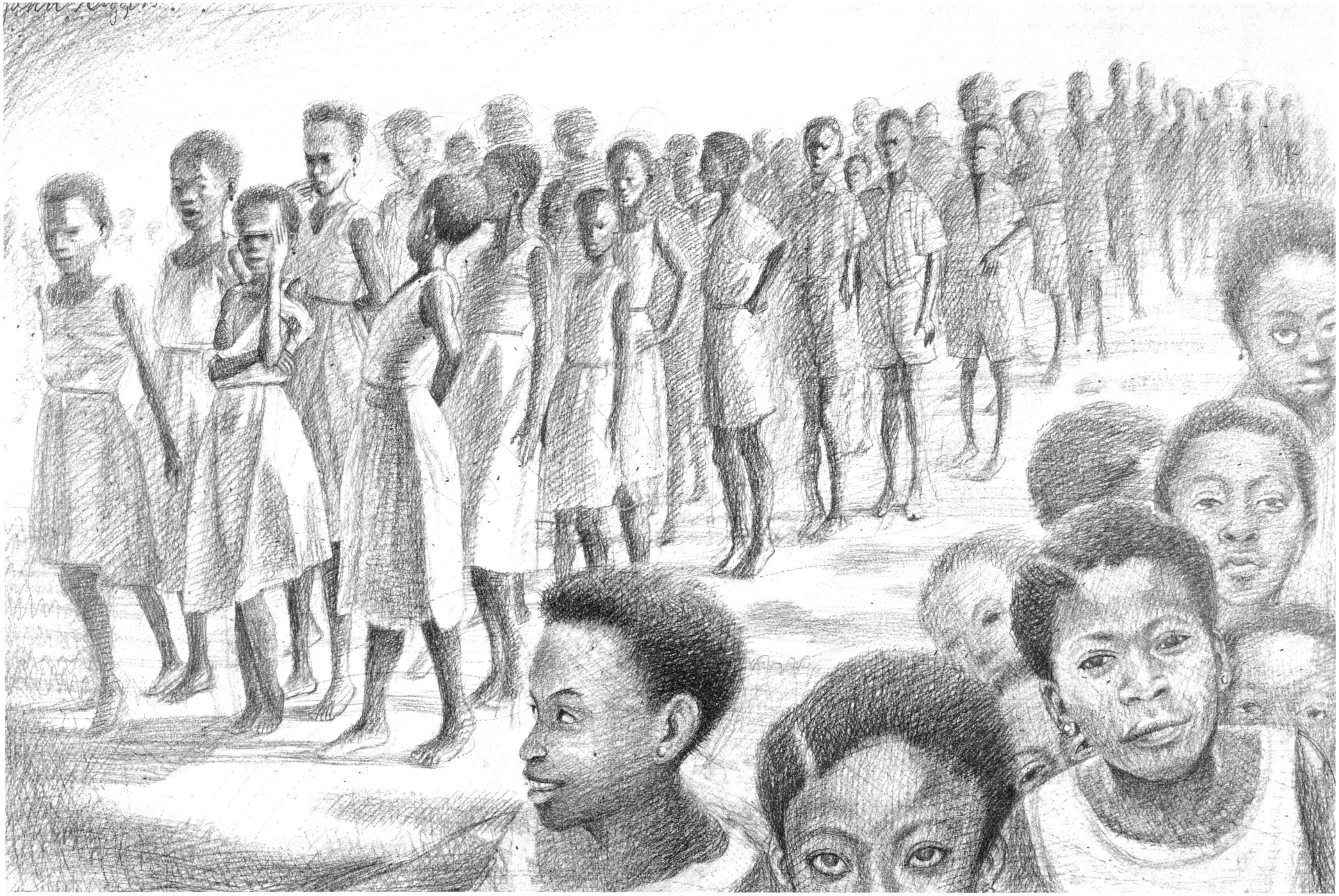

African children like these waiting to re-enter their school building after a recess are among the best-mannered to be found anywhere. Fear of hard discipline could never produce such sensitive poise. But a parent's hand is always near, for an African mother considers proper rearing her primary duty.

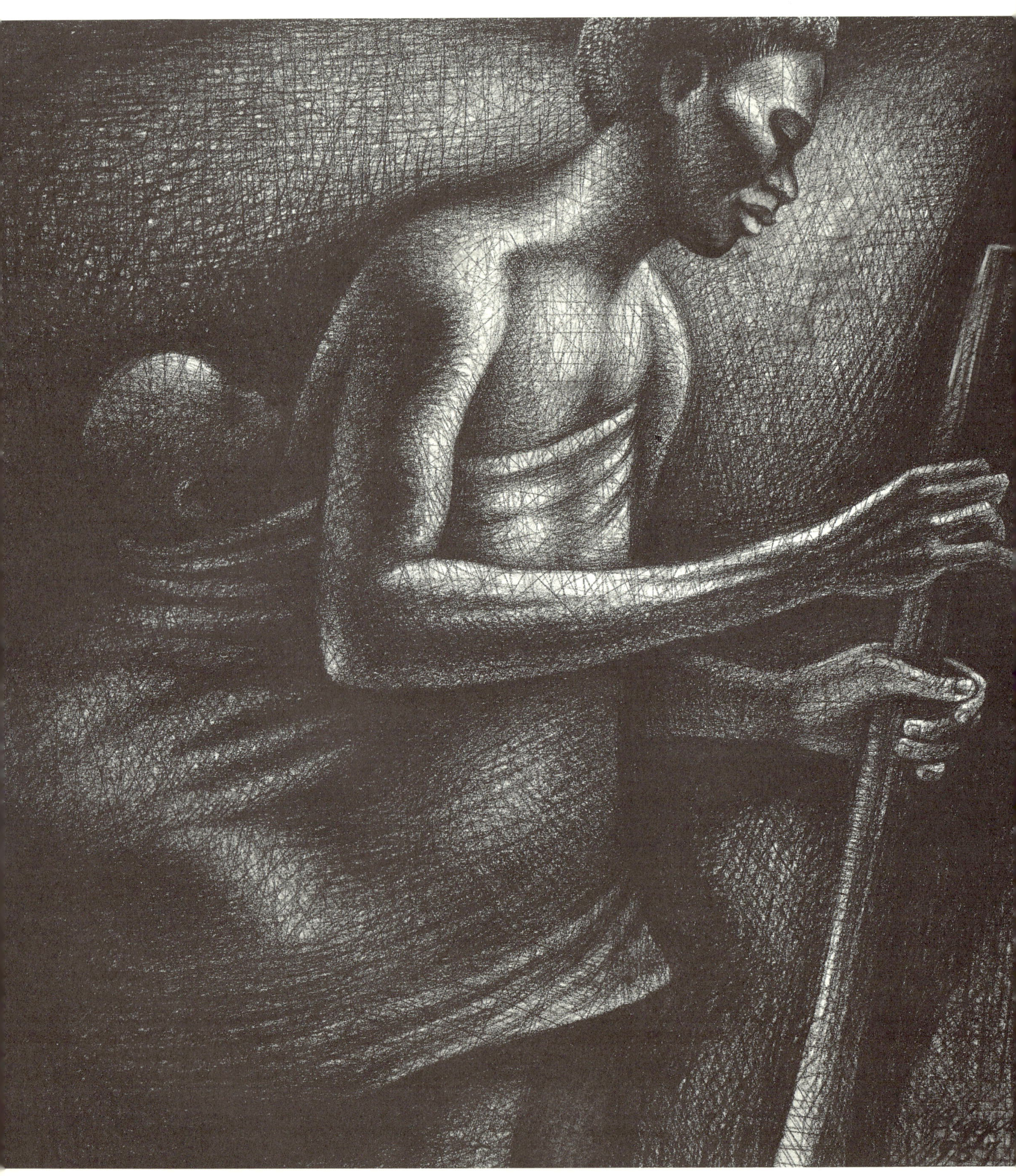

In Africa a child remains with its mother until old enough to walk confidently. An under cloth, tied around the mother's waist, provides a saddle for the infant; an outer cloth serves mainly as a covering for her breast. A mother's back thus becomes a warm, soft, syncopated cradle.

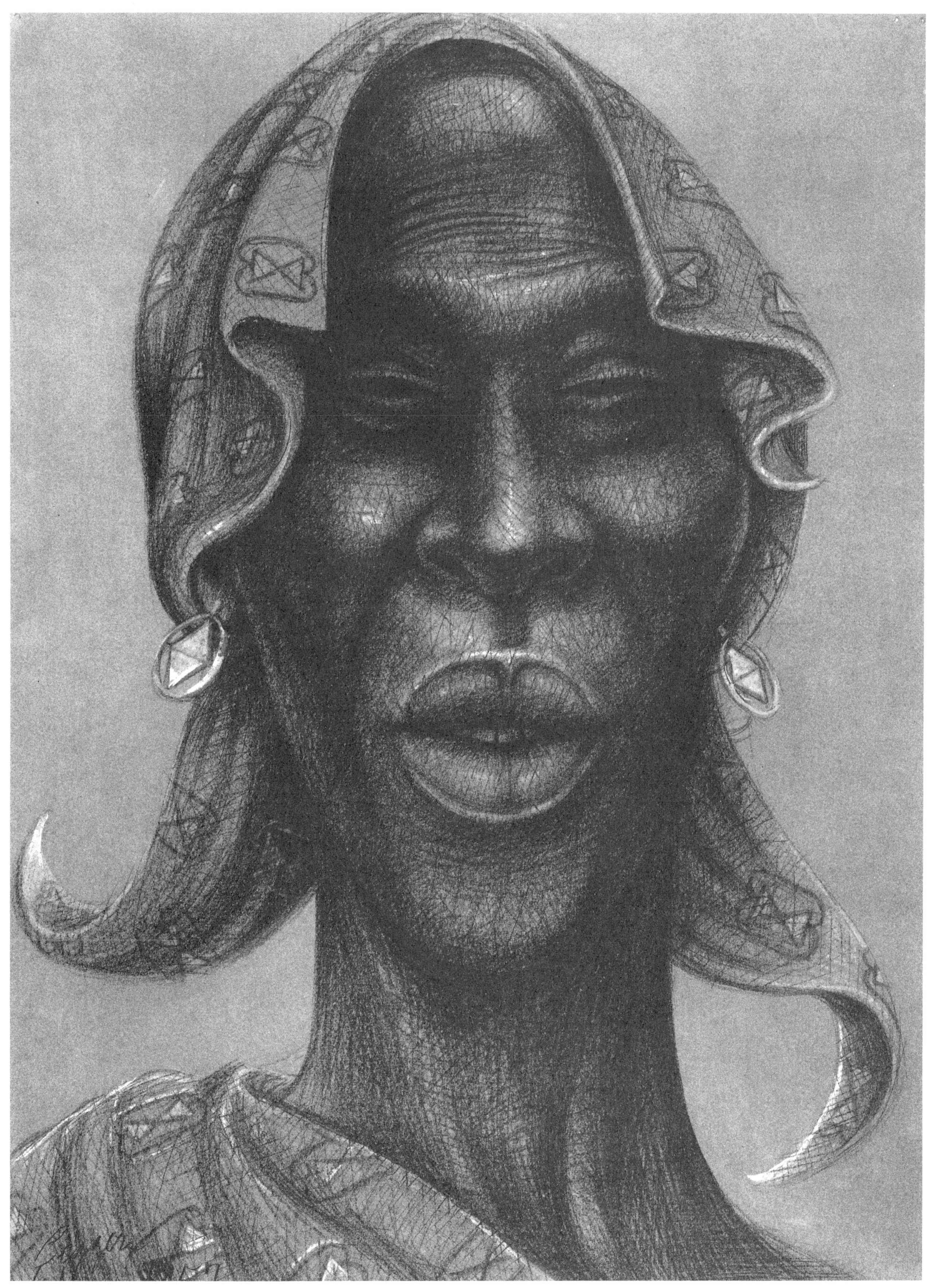

The market woman of West Africa maintains complete control of certain business activities and can keep in her head numerous accounts running into thousands of dollars, with errors never amounting to more than a few pennies. She and her colleagues, well organized, play a decisive role in politics.

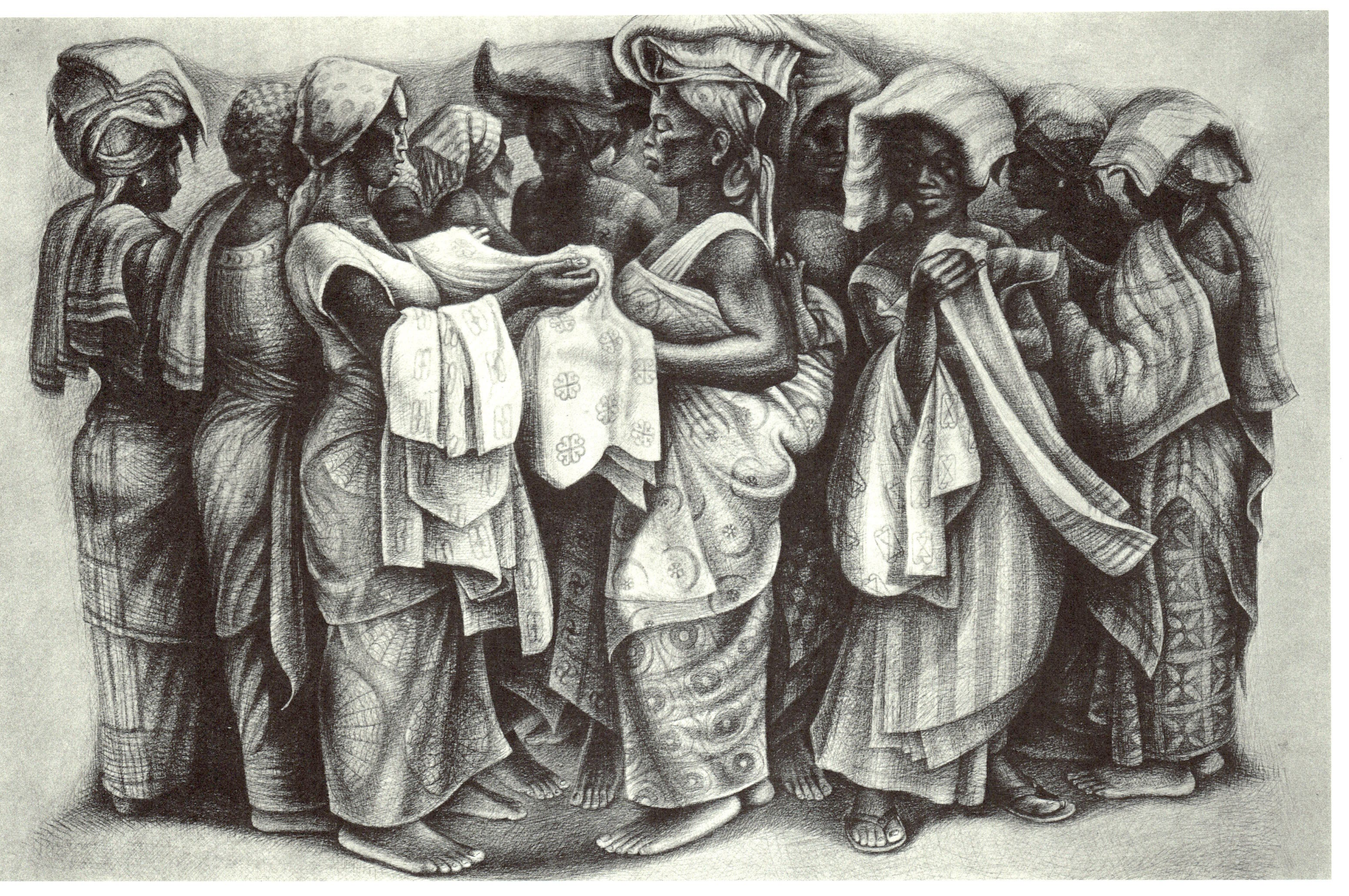

Women eagerly examine a cloth called *adinkera*, on which are stamped colorful religious symbols. Imported, printed cotton goods have almost eliminated the African craft of weaving.

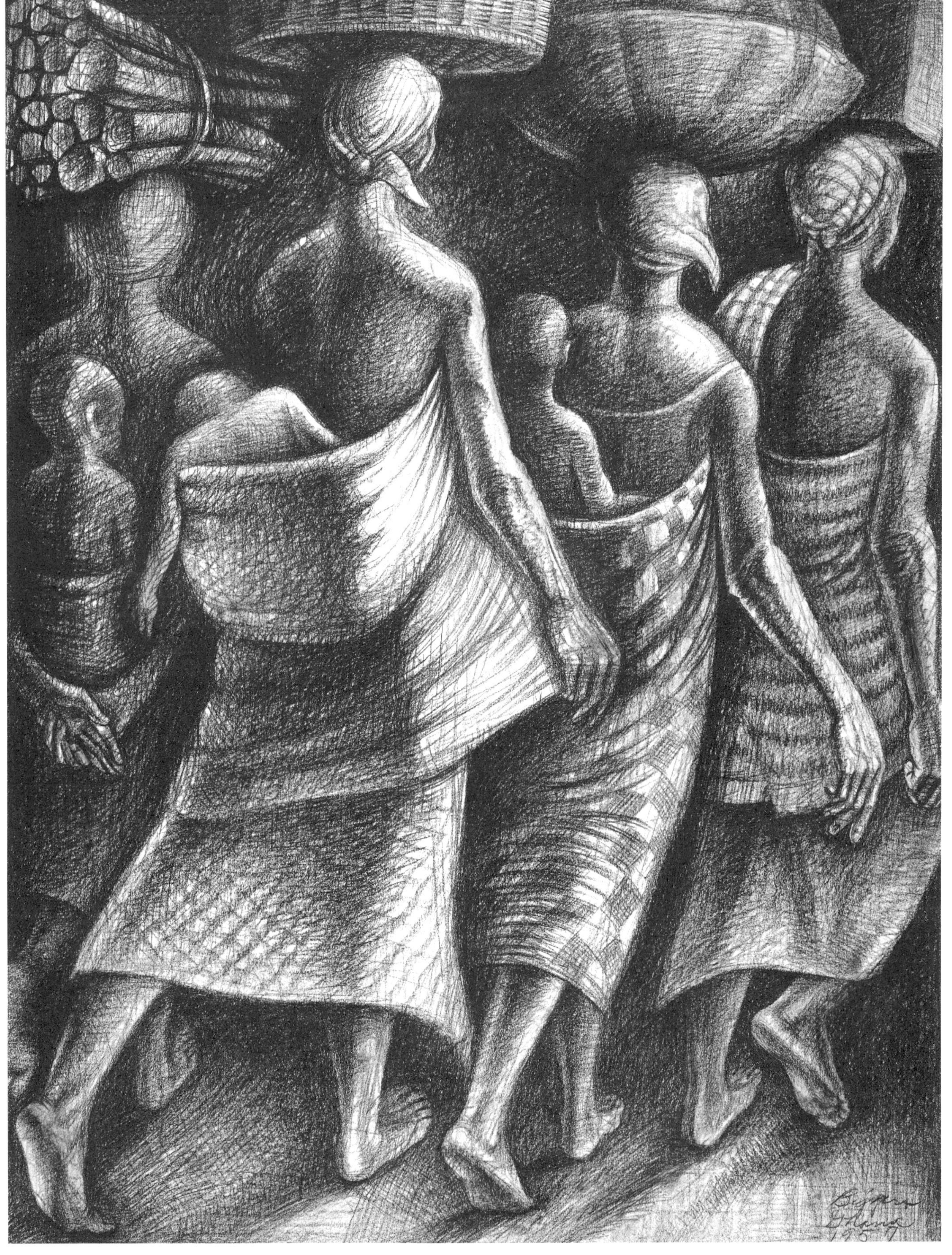

Moving with liquid ease, these market-bound women swing babies on graceful backs and balance goods of every description on proud heads.

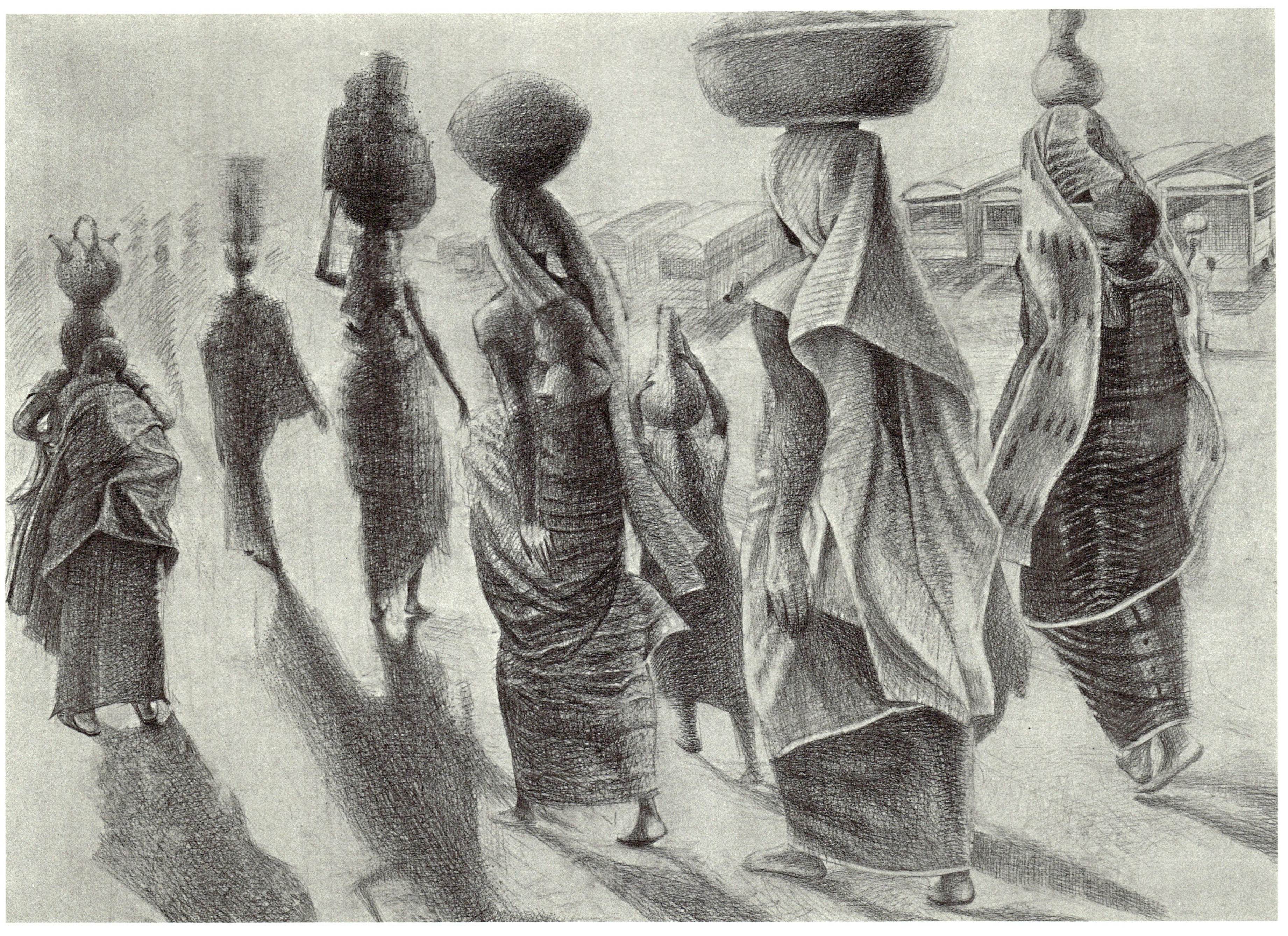

The stately feminine forms gliding along market lanes of West Africa are remindful of how actresses and models in some other countries are taught to walk with grace and poise.

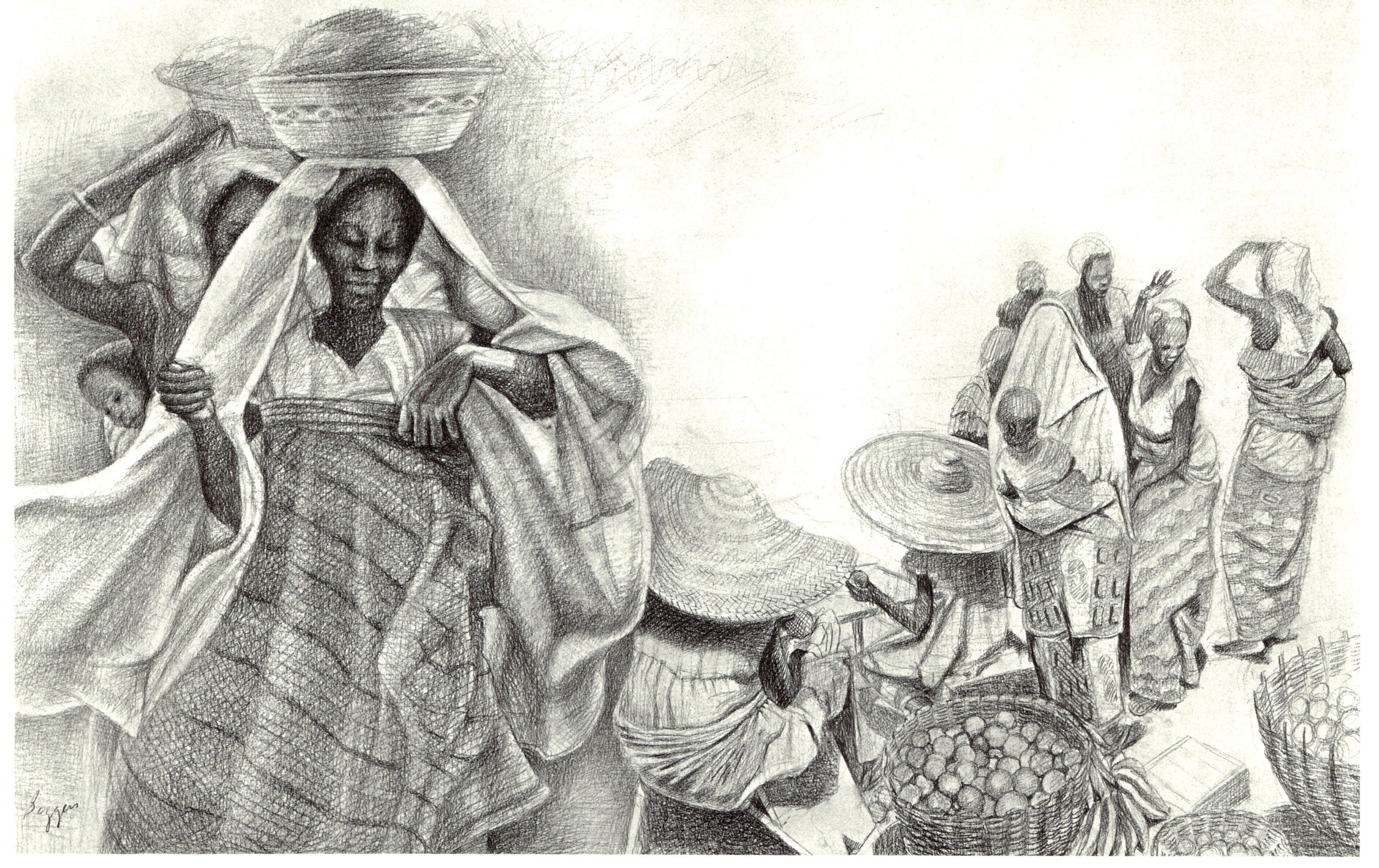

Adjusting her billowing clothing with an easy hand movement, meanwhile not missing a graceful step, this African woman appears to be some elegant, dancing, winged creature that has alighted upon an earthly stage.

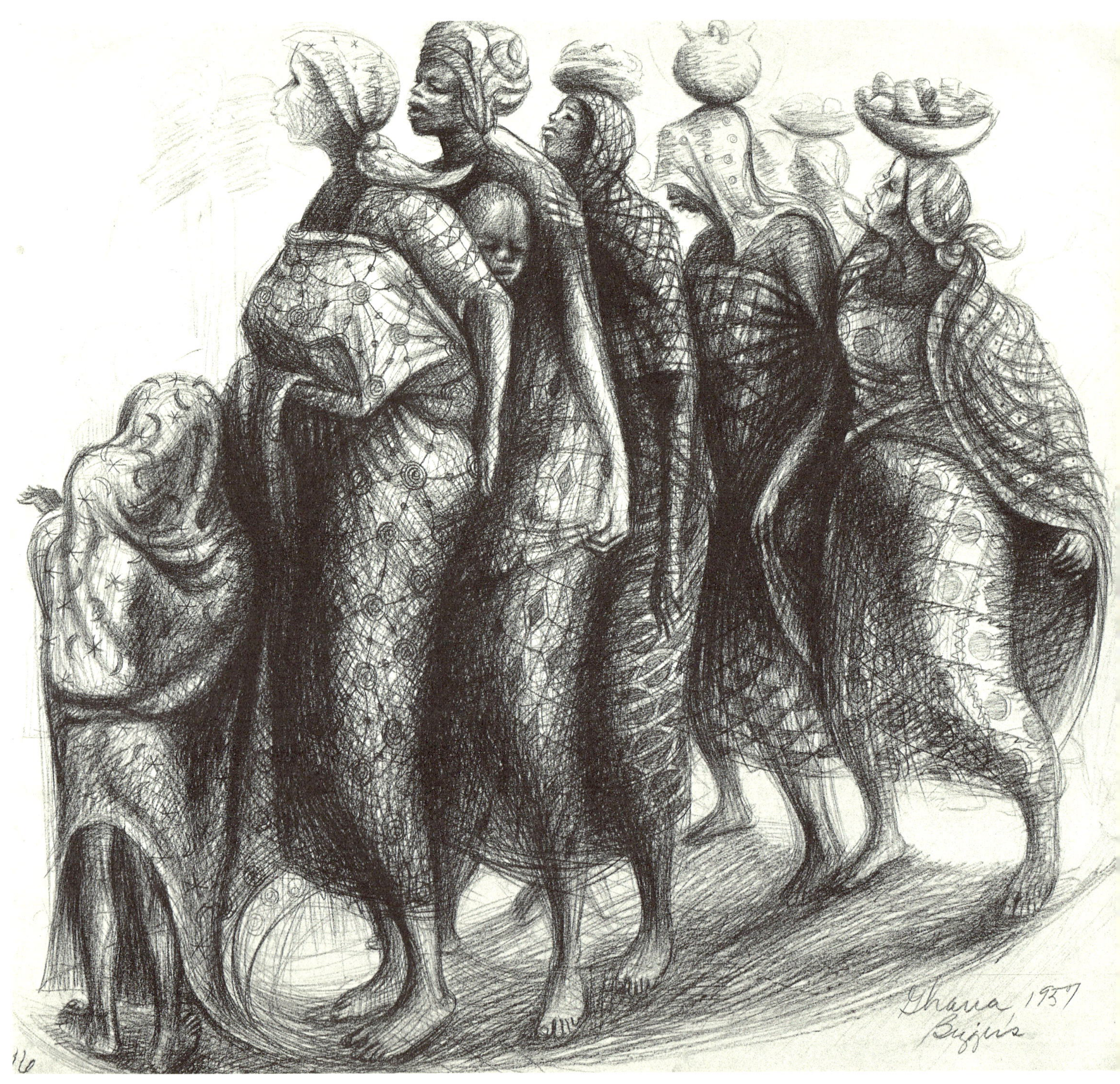

Standing patiently and respectfully, without pushing or shoving, African market women wait in a succession of lines—to load on their heads the produce from the land, to catch "mammy lorries" to distant markets, and to make their purchases.

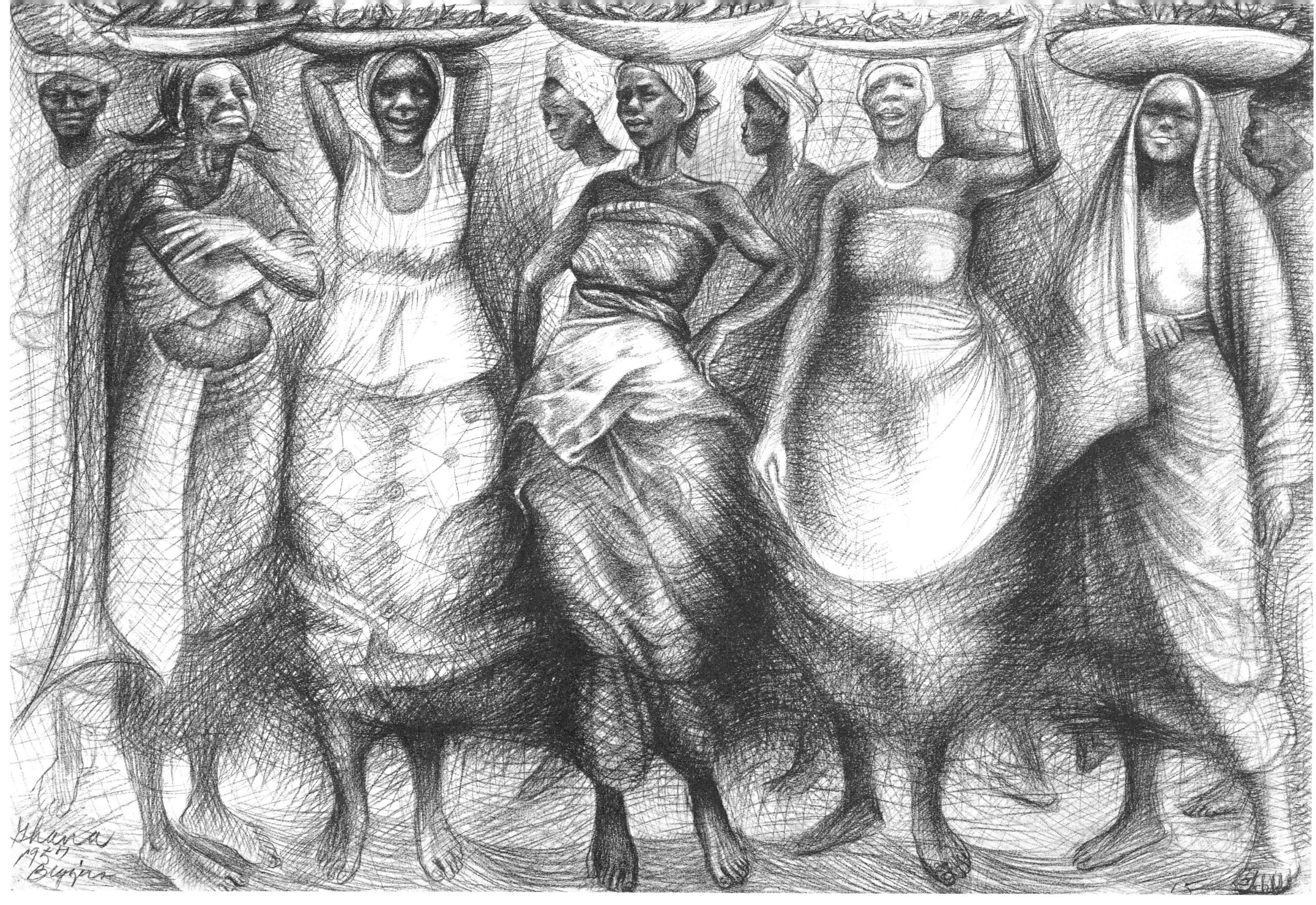

Fishmongers in the Accra market are a hearty, coquettish group, but one in which individuality is obvious. They do share at least one common characteristic: an odorous togetherness, the result of a small, spiny-finned perch they sell—fresh, dried, and smoked.

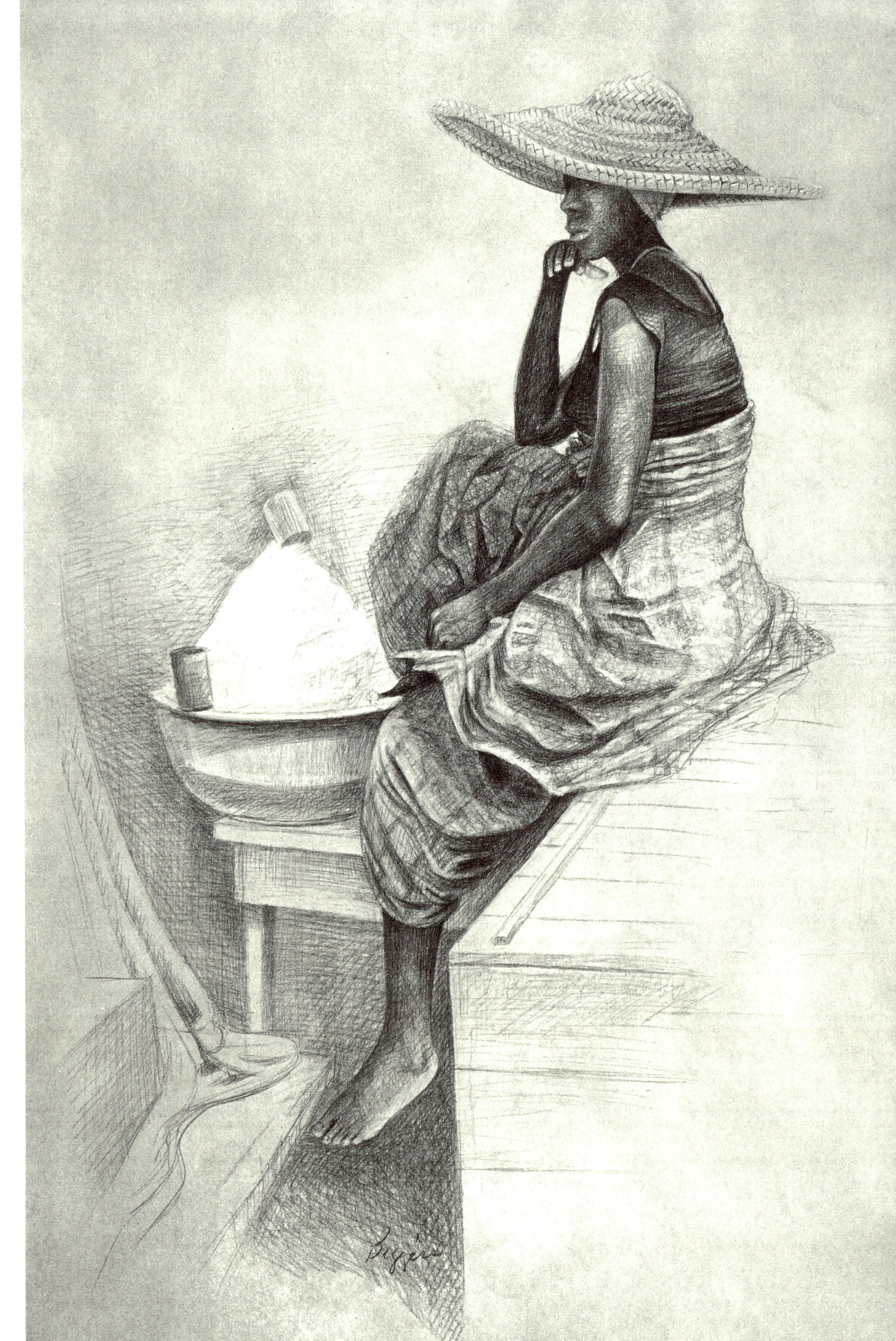

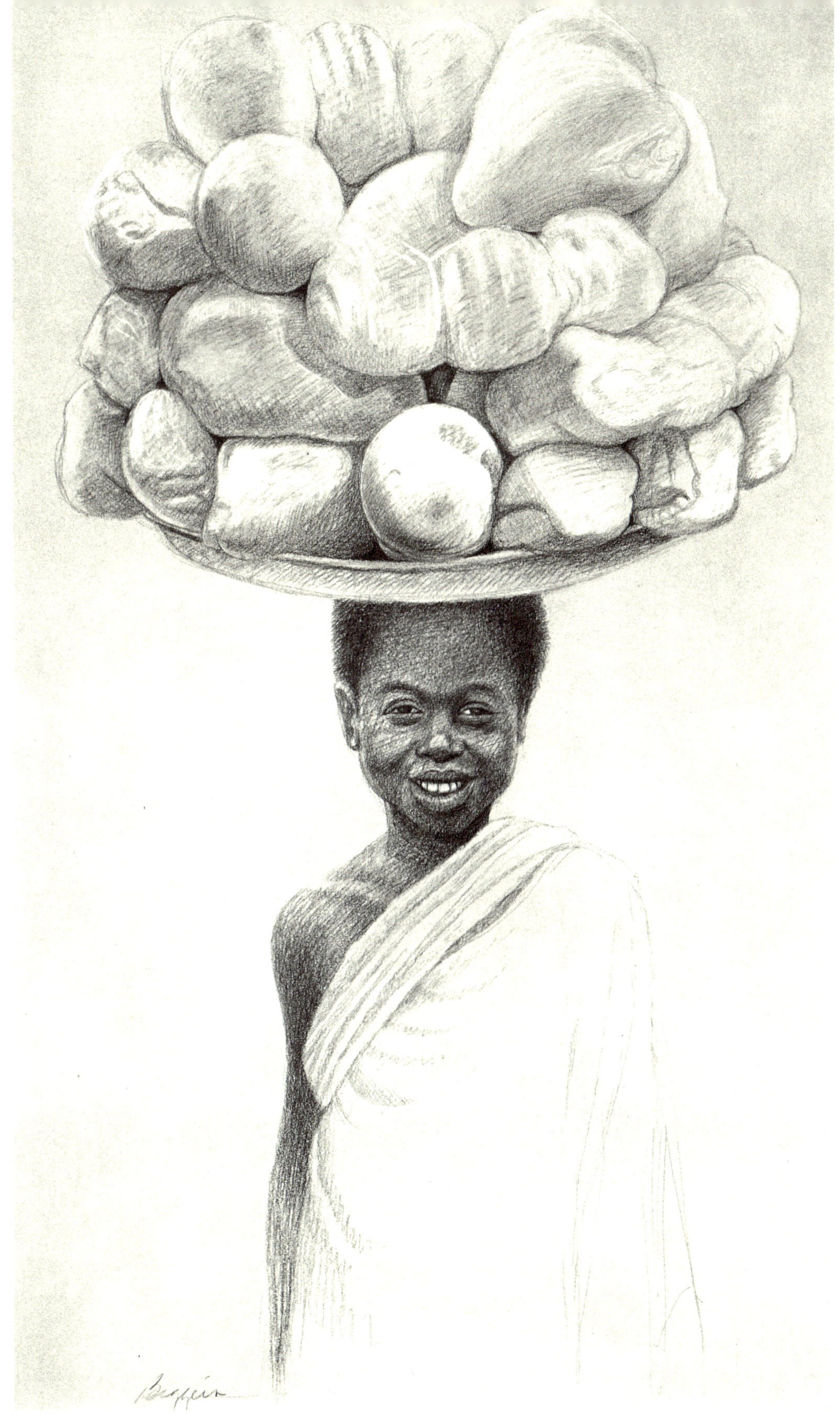

The golden brown, cinnamon-flavored product sold by this bread boy is heavy, savory, and filling.

The girl who sold *gari* did not object to having her likeness captured. She sat in quiet confidence, and her composure seemed to deaden the market bustle.

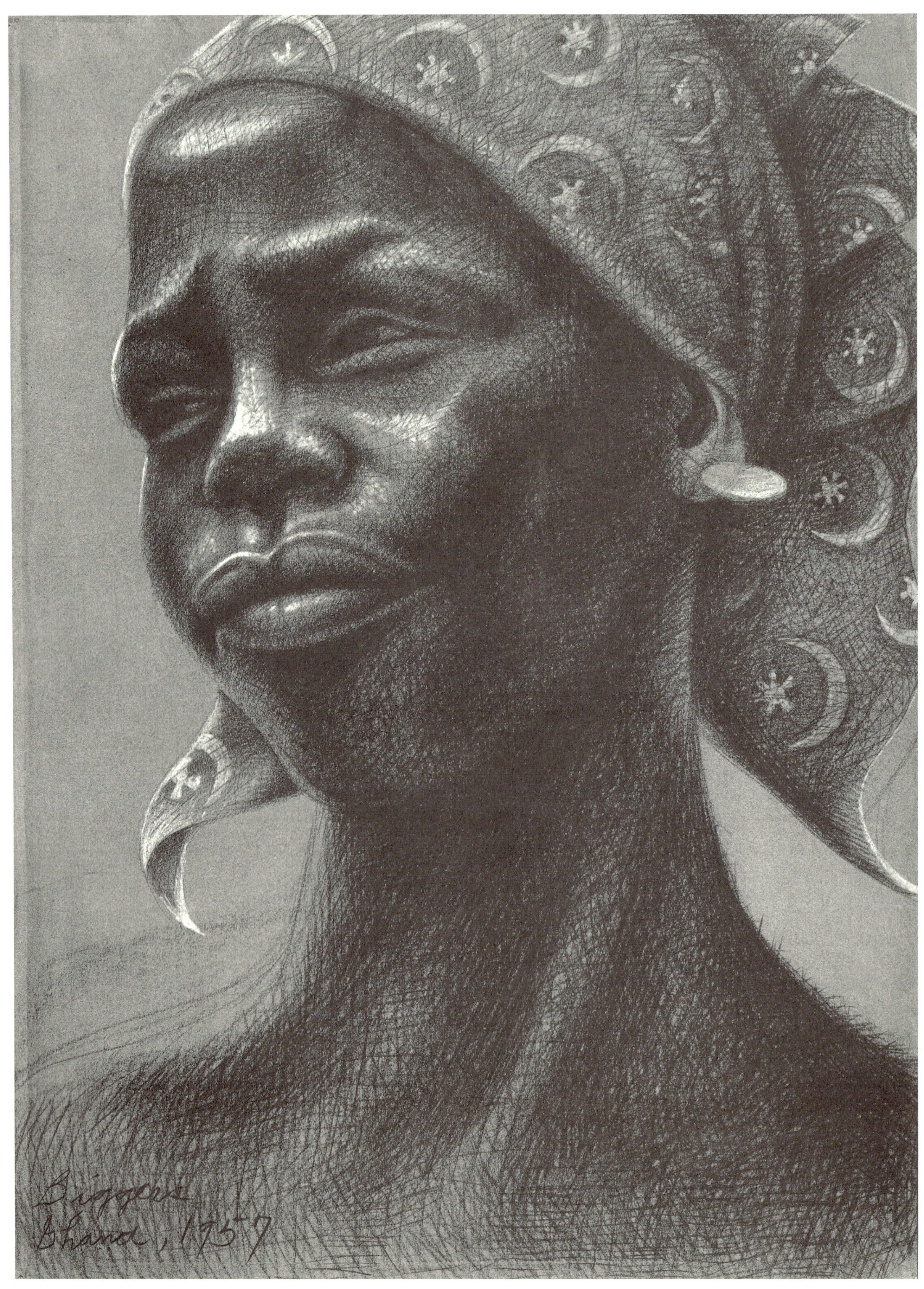

The queen mother of the Akan people of Ghana is regarded as the daughter of the moon; she dresses in garments of moonlight silver. Many other women also dress themselves in white or gray cloth embroidered with silver, and they adorn themselves with silver jewelry.

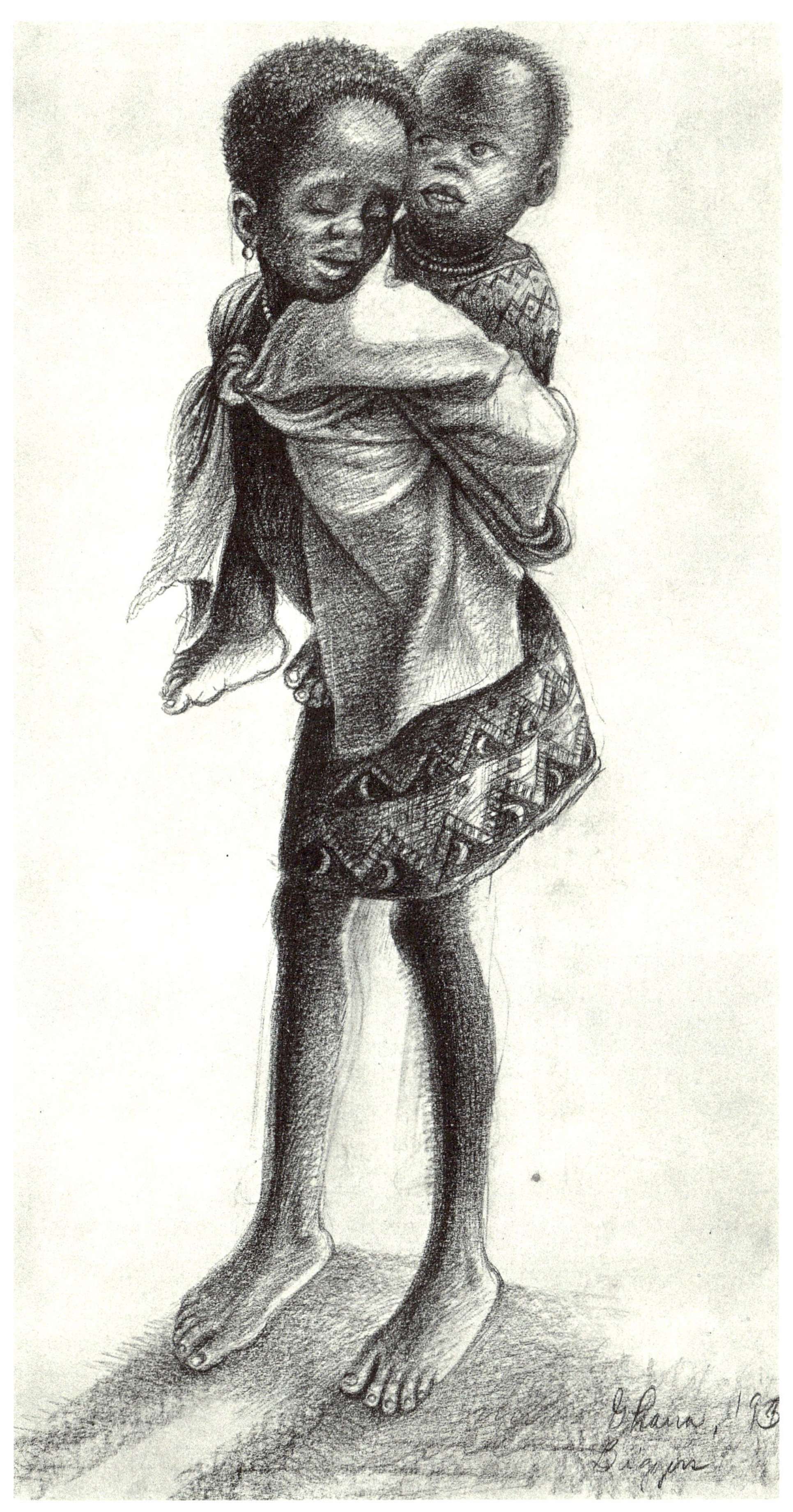

At an early age girls begin carrying their younger brothers, sisters, or cousins on their backs. Sometimes this is merely play, but often it is a preparatory course for motherhood. Occasionally it is even a necessity: The girl's mother might have another baby to tend.

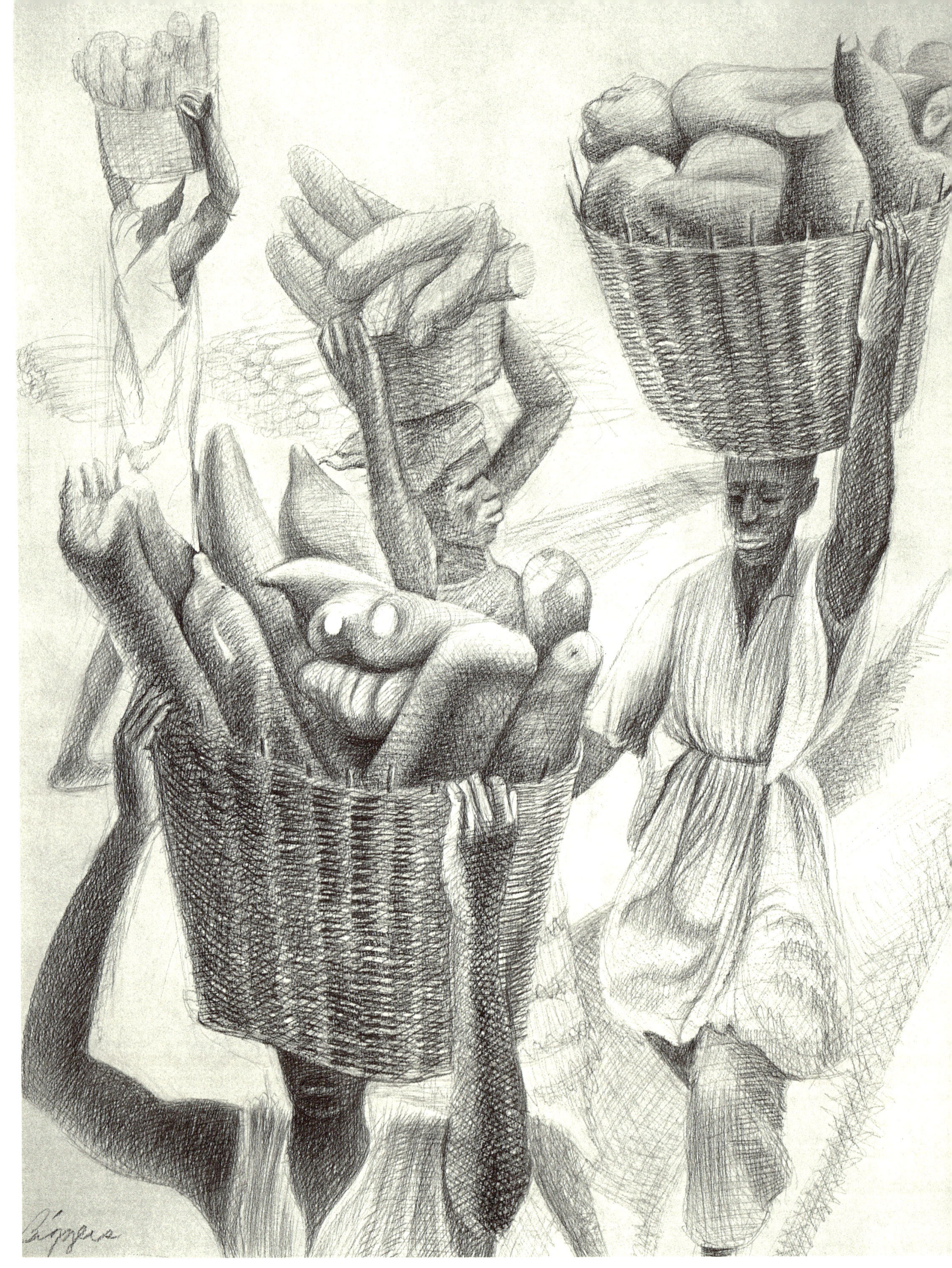

Strong farming men usually replace women in carrying the heavy yams that abound on the northern plains of Ghana.

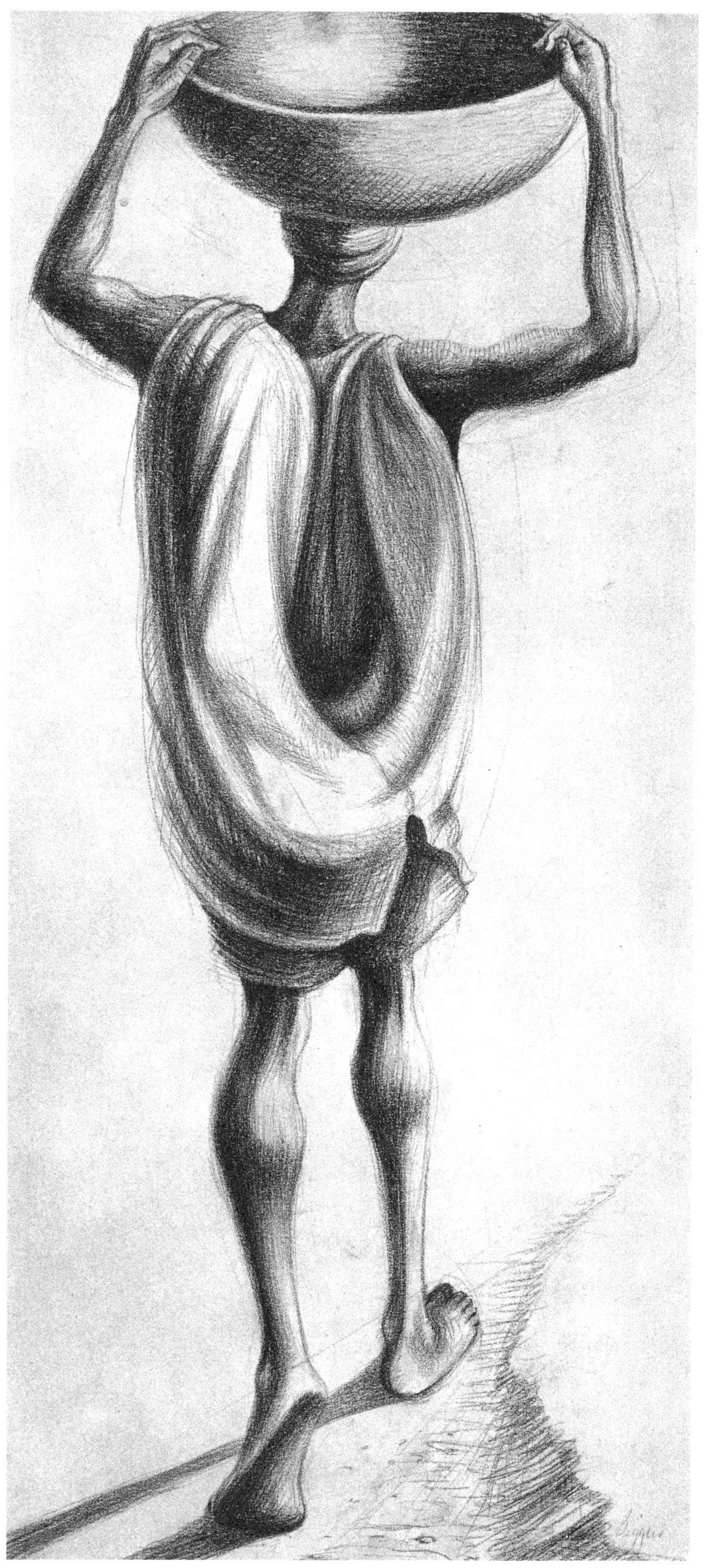

Men in the Ghana working brigades carry pans of cement and other building materials on their heads. This African hod carrier is returning for another load.

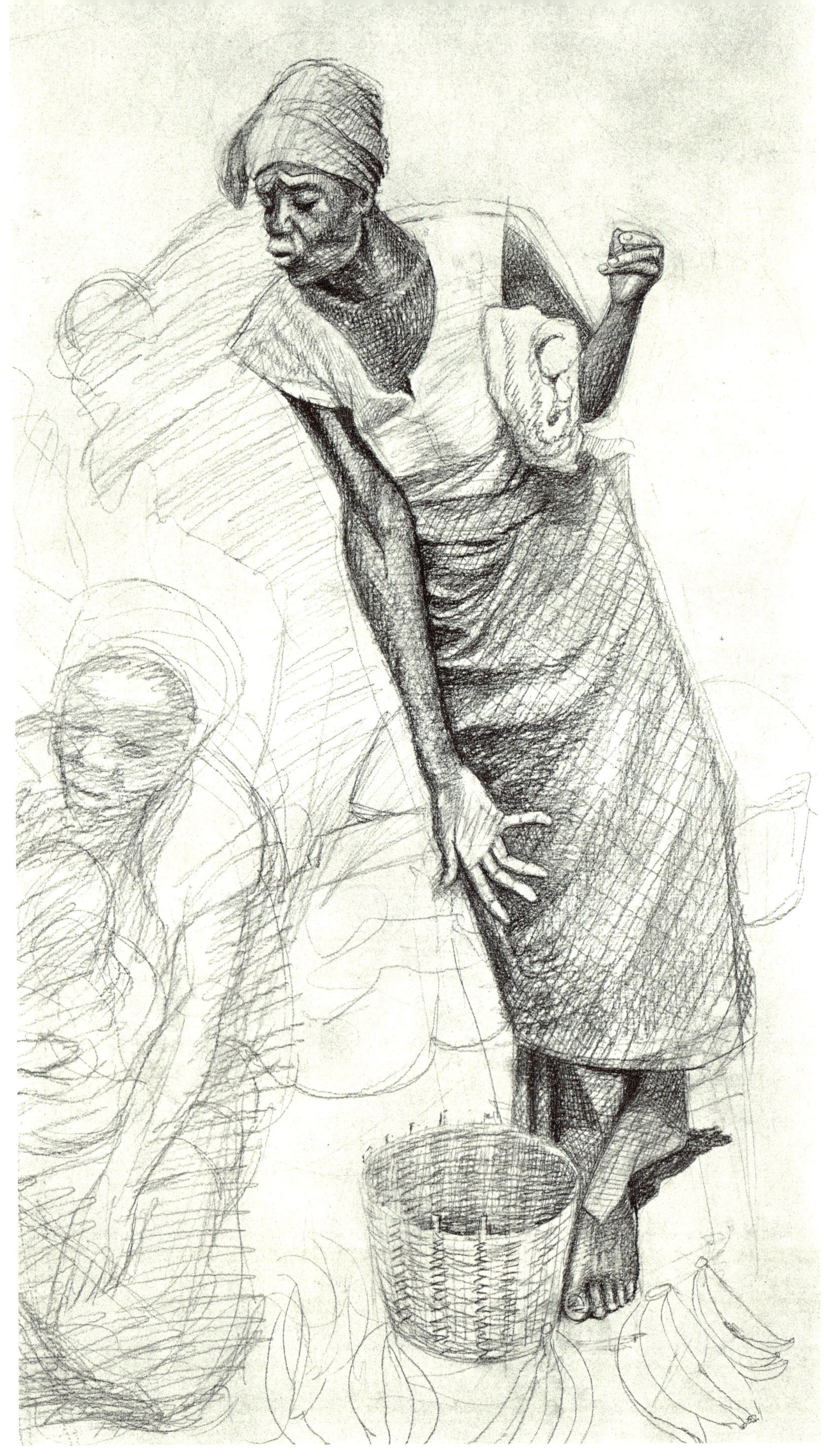

Africans are enthusiastic conversationalists. Their language has a marked tonal quality, and a great degree of sensitivity is required for both speaking and listening. Highly animated body movements and gesticulation add emphasis to the words.

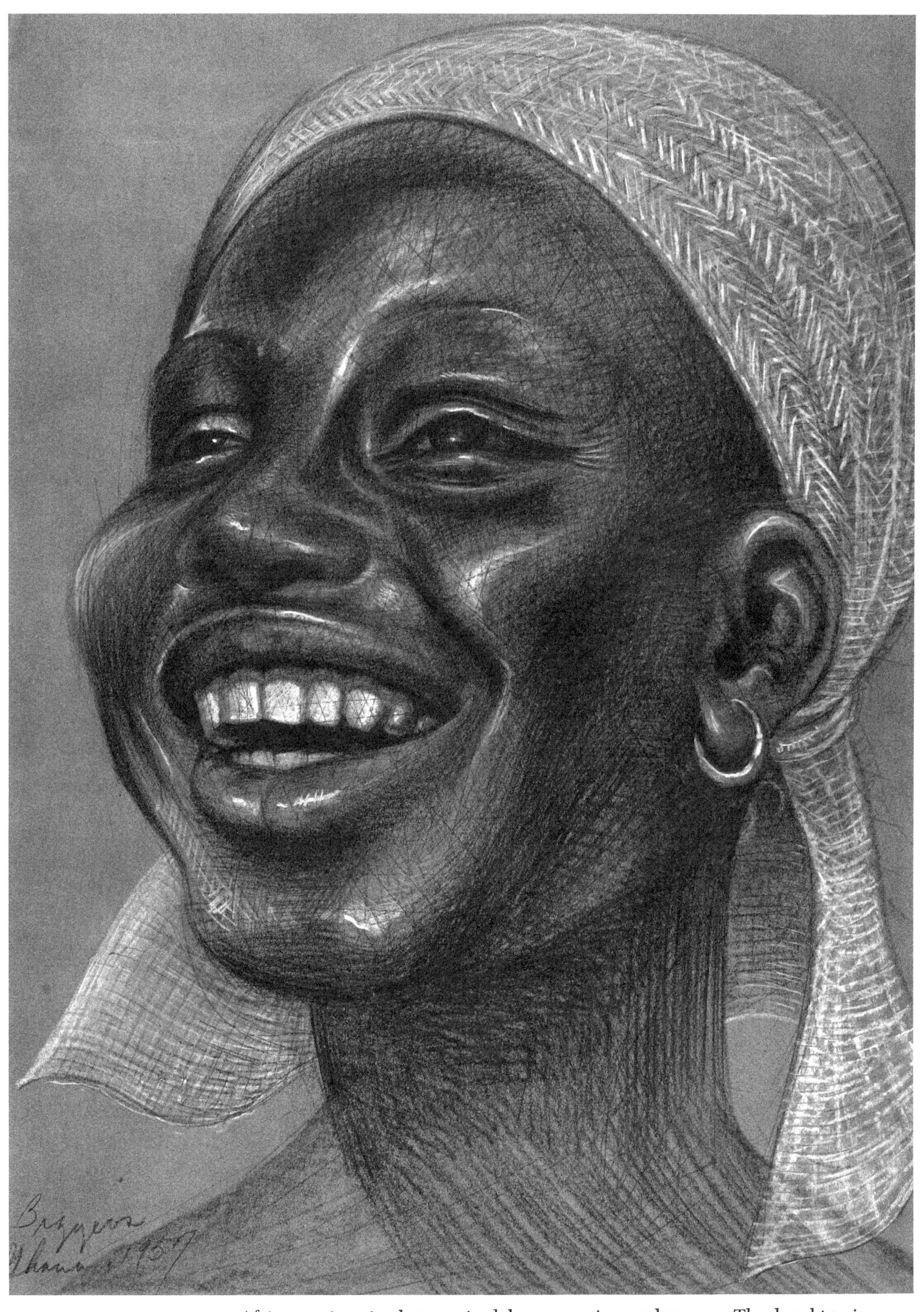

African gaiety is characterized by a genuine exuberance. The laughter is warm, infectious, invigorating.

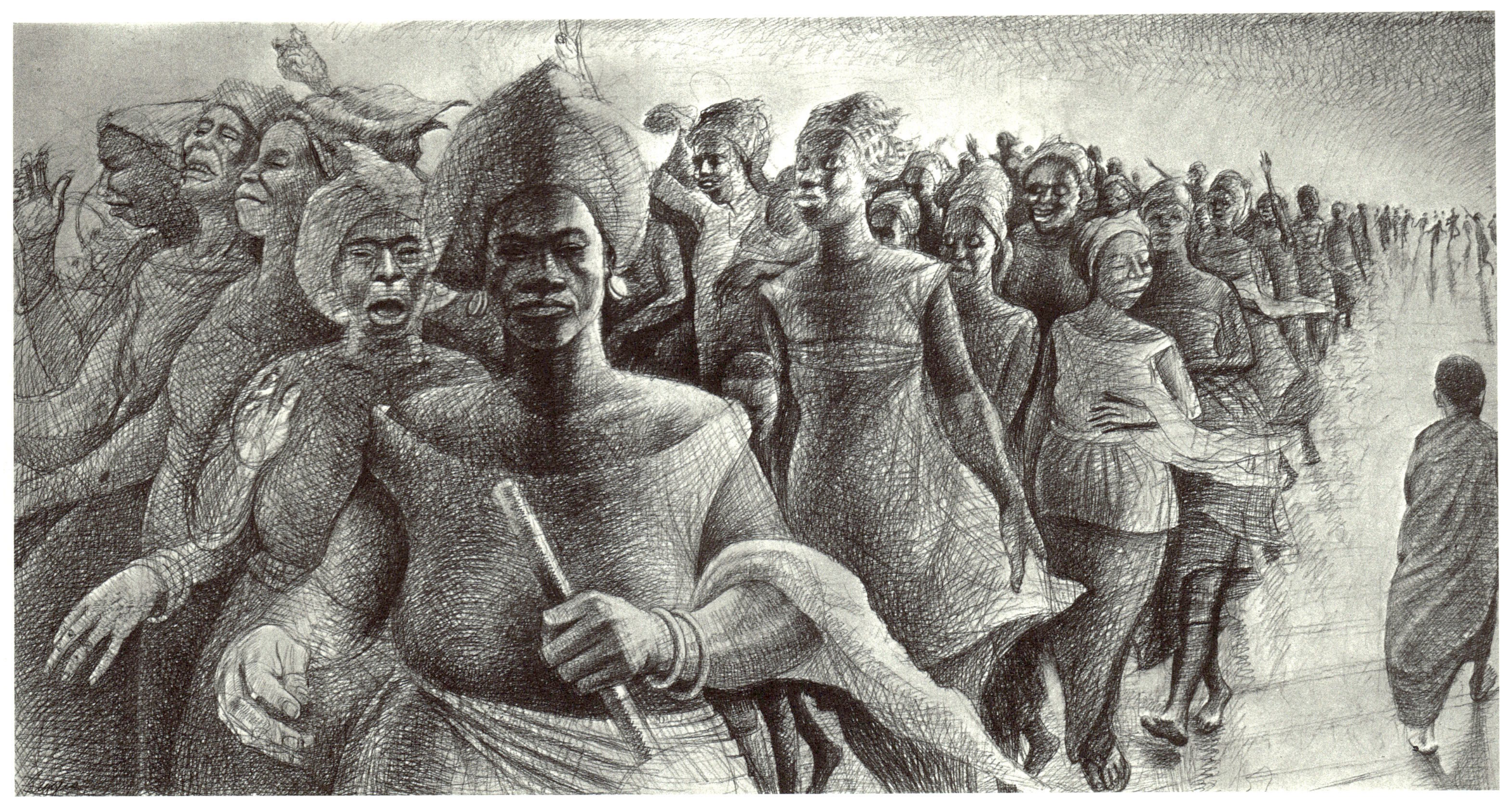

Women's organizations in Africa are numerous, and some are powerful politically. The Ghana market women, for instance, were instrumental in bringing into power the Convention People's Party. These market women have joined other groups in a holiday parade.

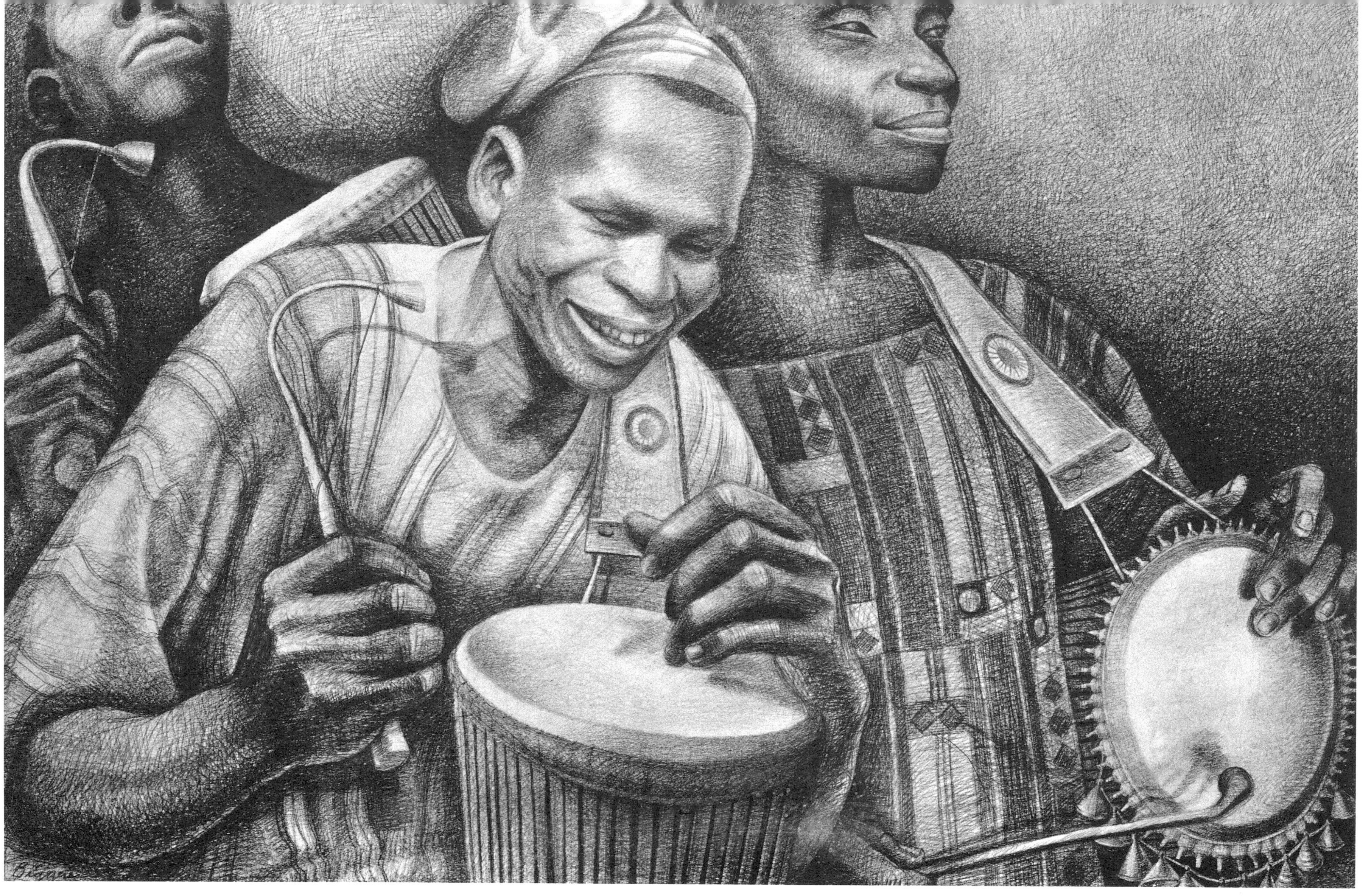

Many words and phrases of the tonal West African languages can be reproduced on a drum, which sometimes actually serves as a master of ceremonies at certain celebrations. It gives directions to each participant, telling him when and where to take his place in the ceremonial formation.

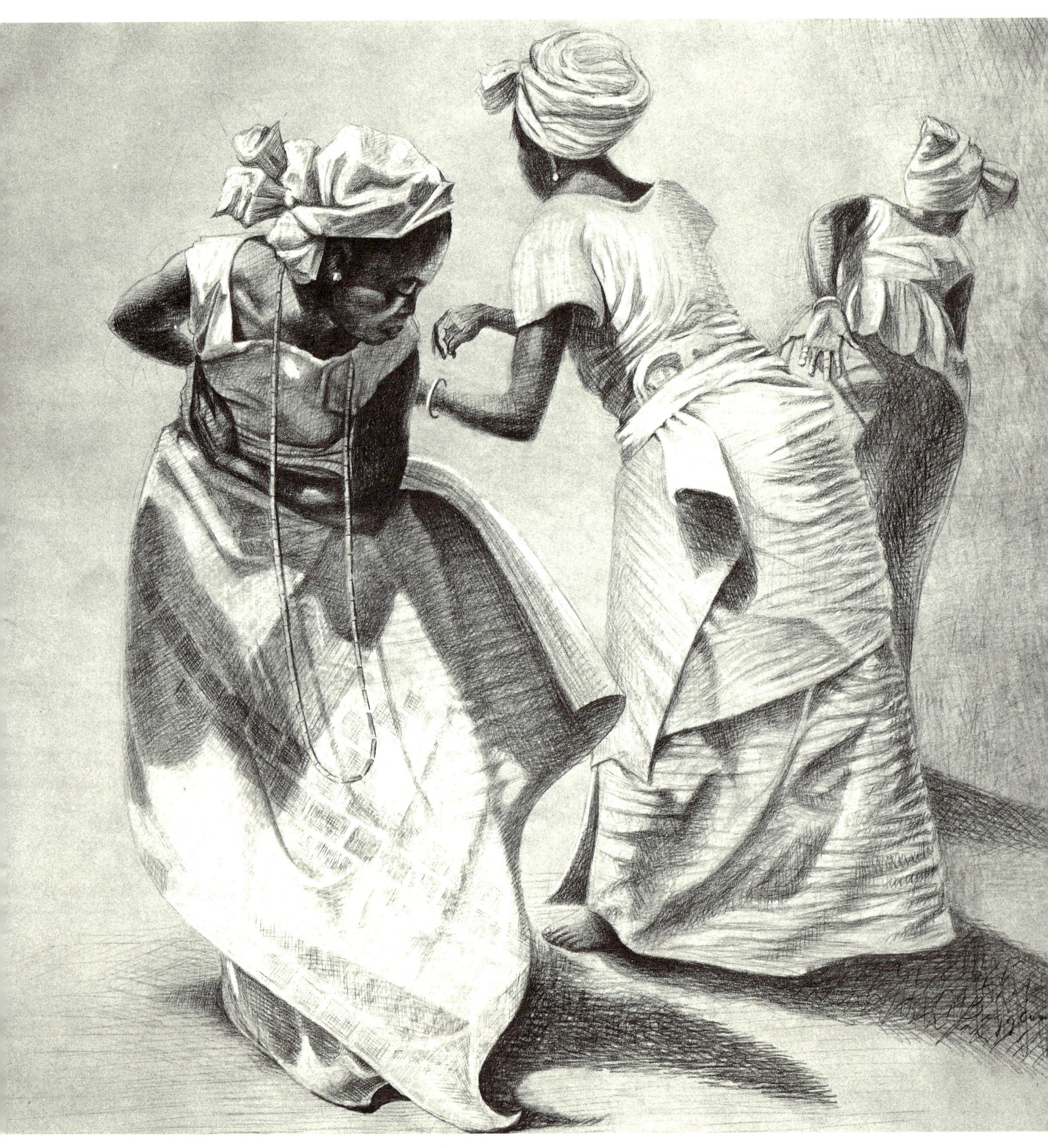

The *durbar*, a harvest festival, lasts for several colorful days. At Odumasi, Ghana, many women's societies participate in the group dancing. Members of each society are uniformly dressed, one group in yellow costumes and others in white, green, lavender, and brown.

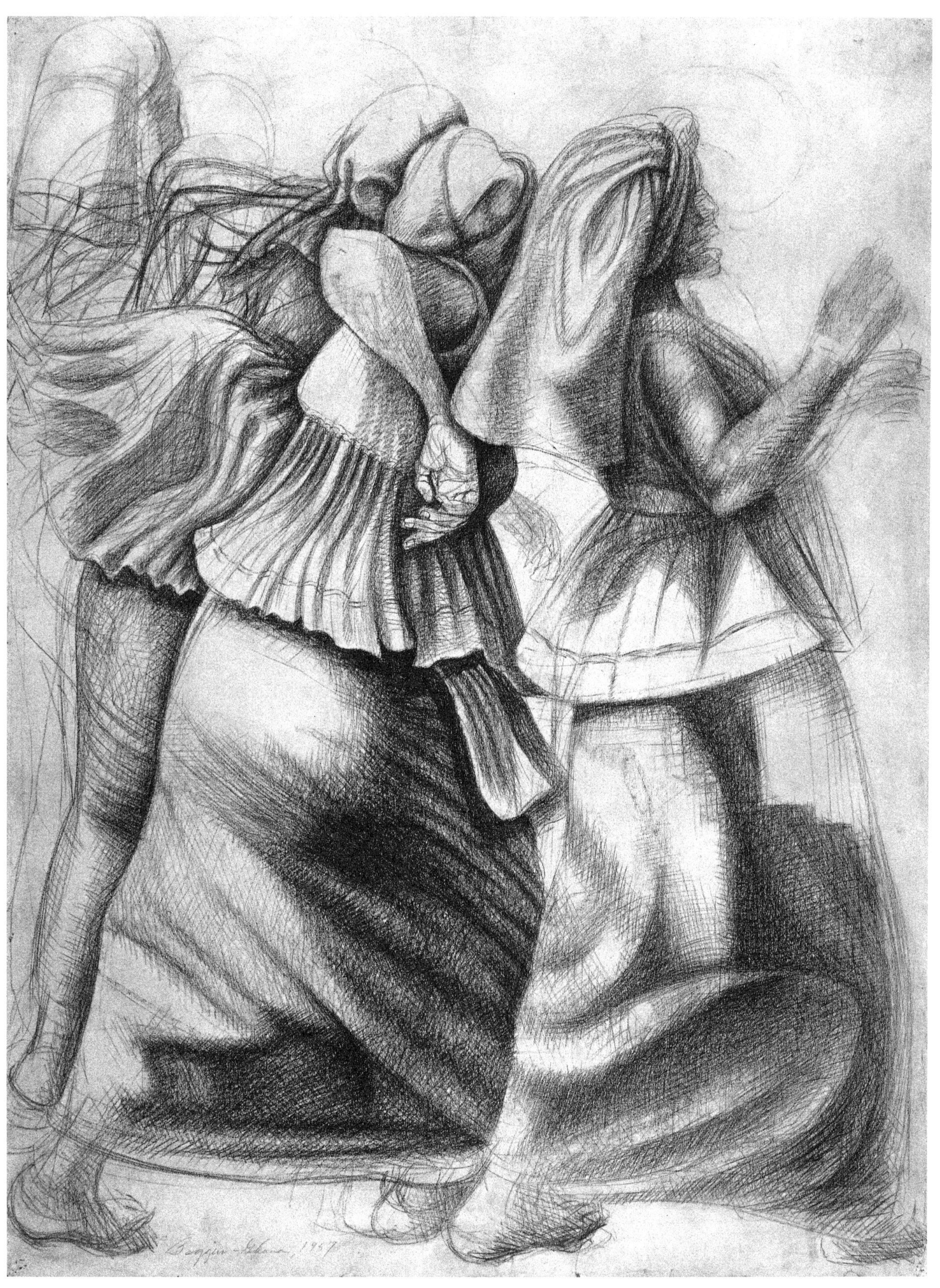

Drummers enchant the crowd with a pulsating rhythm that excites performers and spectators alike. Women dancers glide harmoniously across the ground, their feet weaving intricate patterns, their bodies swaying gracefully.

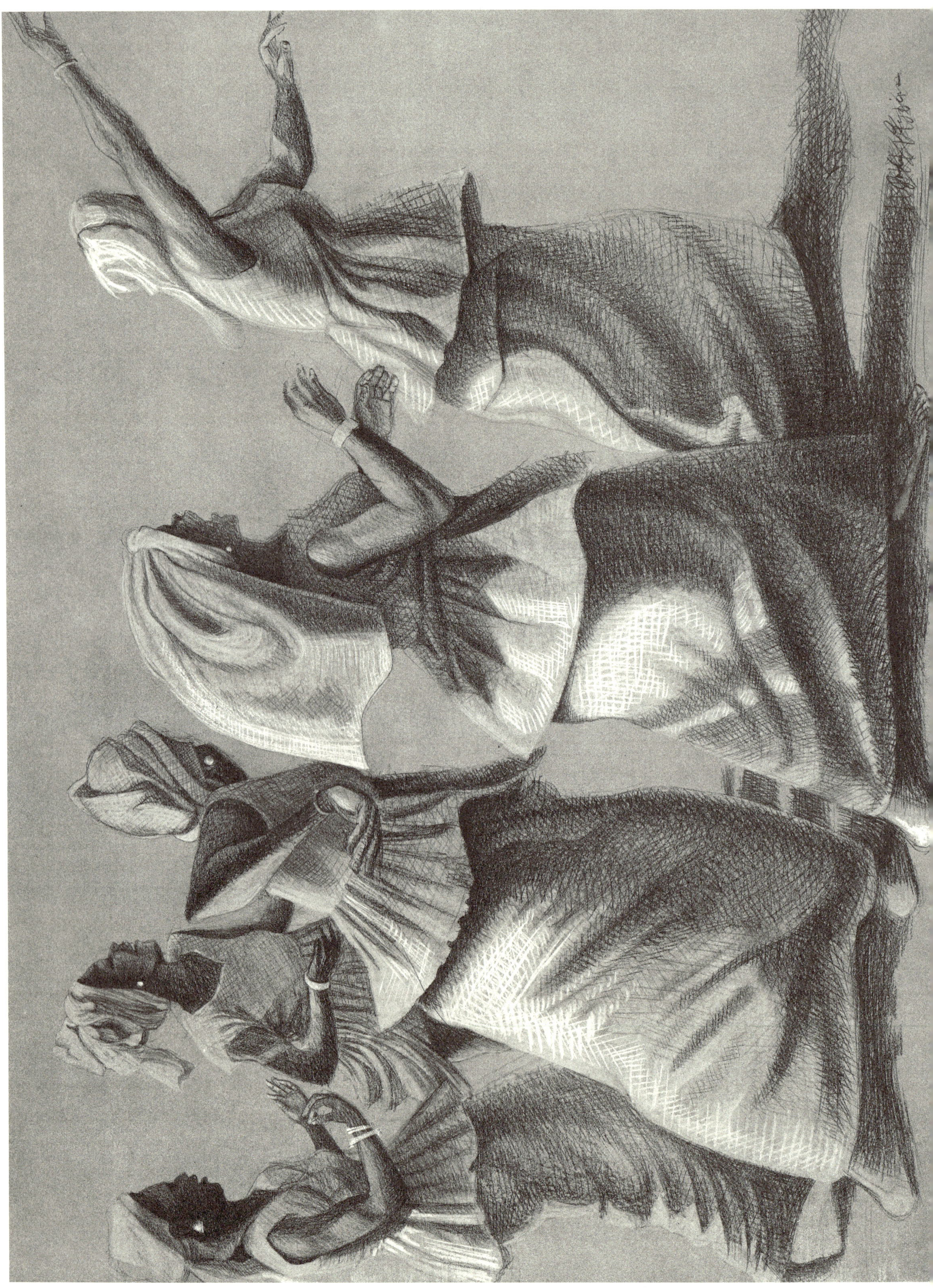

Drums throb in a stepped-up tempo. With rapid movements of exploding vigor the dancers still keep time, finishing with a series of quick little steps that leaves their arms outstretched as they vent utterances of ecstasy.

With her headdress fluttering and her beaded necklaces swinging freely, this dancing woman reflects other-world ecstasy. Her vigor brings to mind that of Pieter Brueghel's peasant dancers.

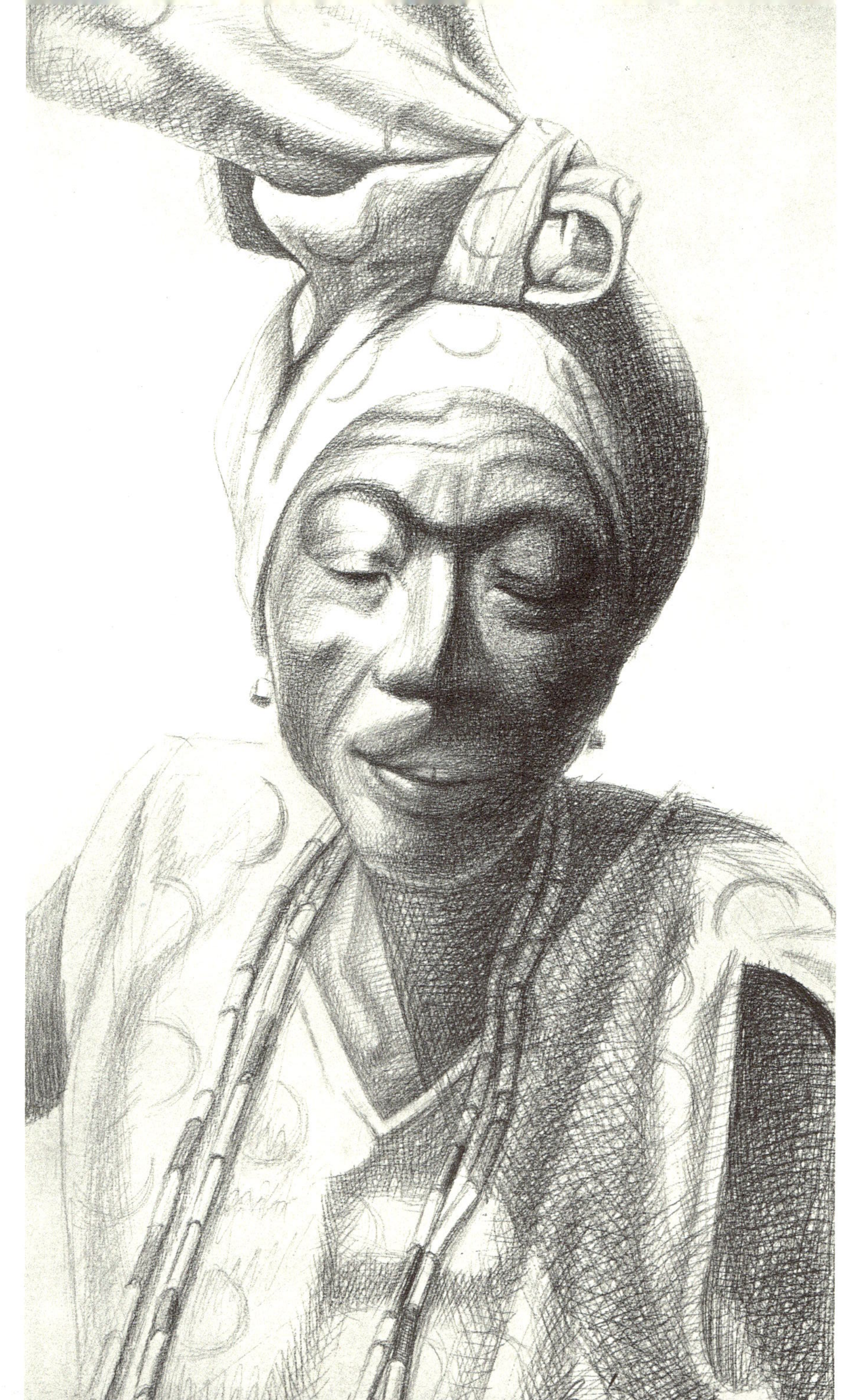

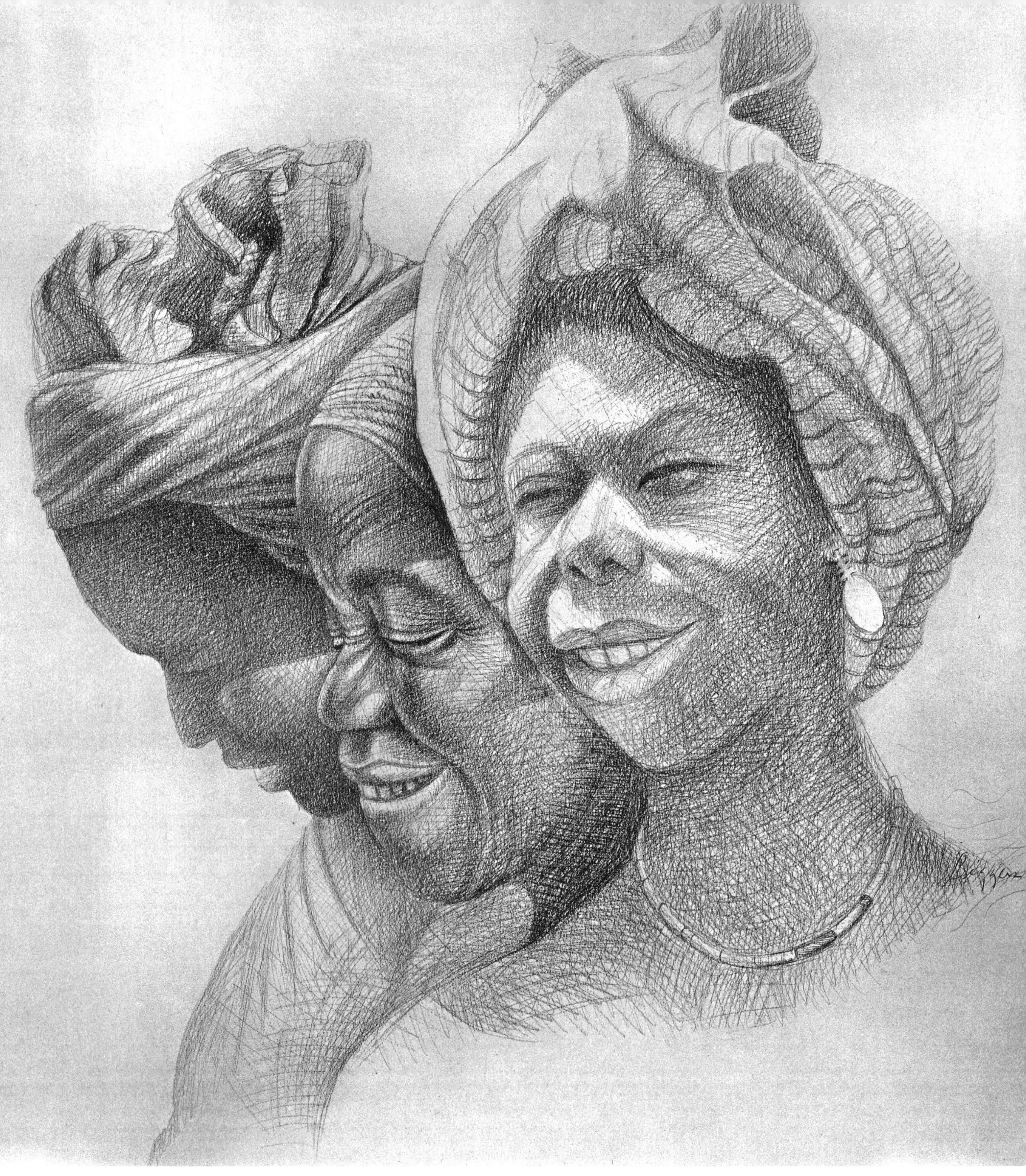

The inner happiness that can be shared only with one's dearest friend as well as the outgoing gaiety that one can share with all the world seem mirrored in the faces of these harvesttime merrymakers.

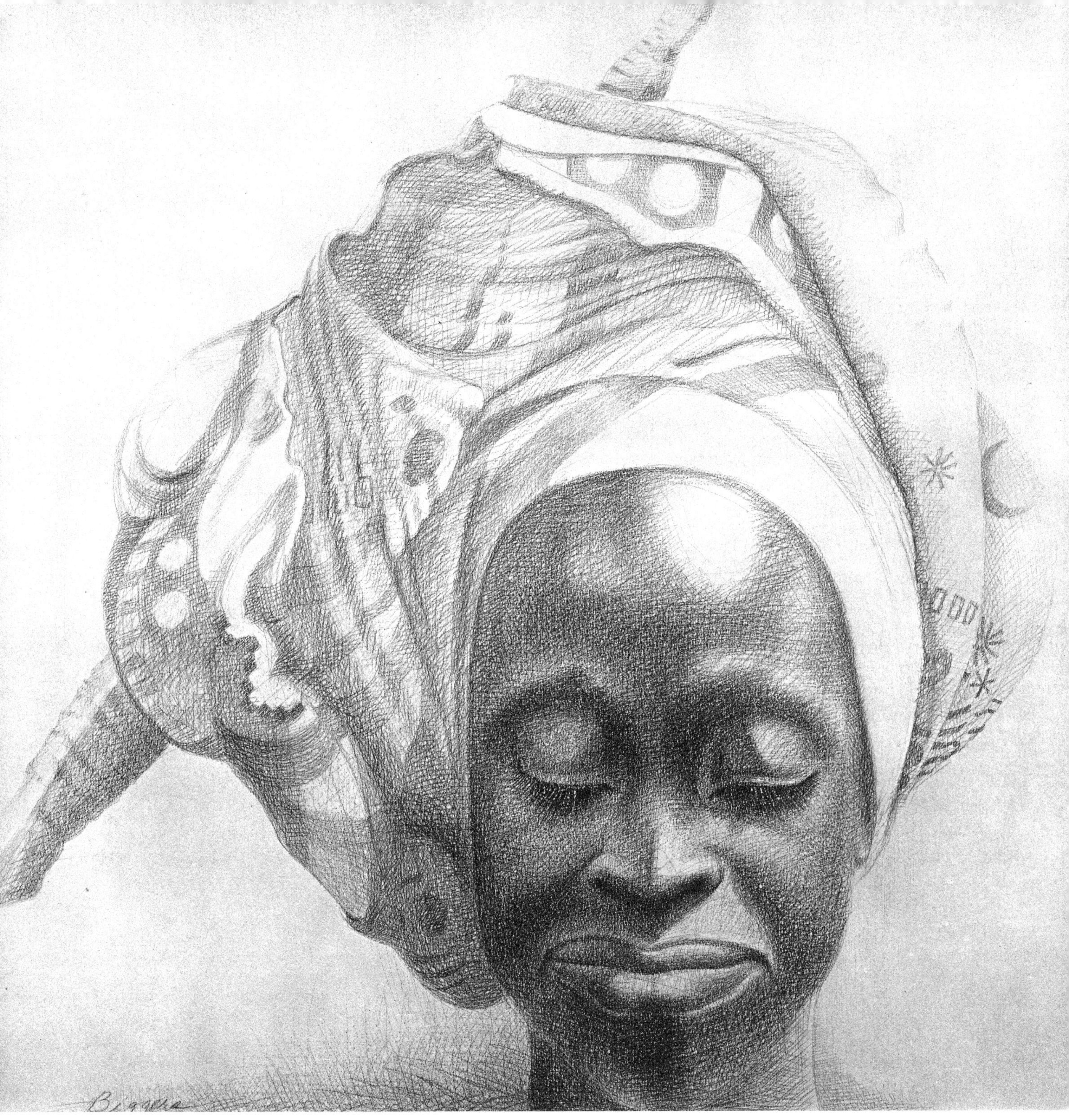

An exalting headdress enhances the classic beauty of this Yoruba girl and serves as an elegant crown.

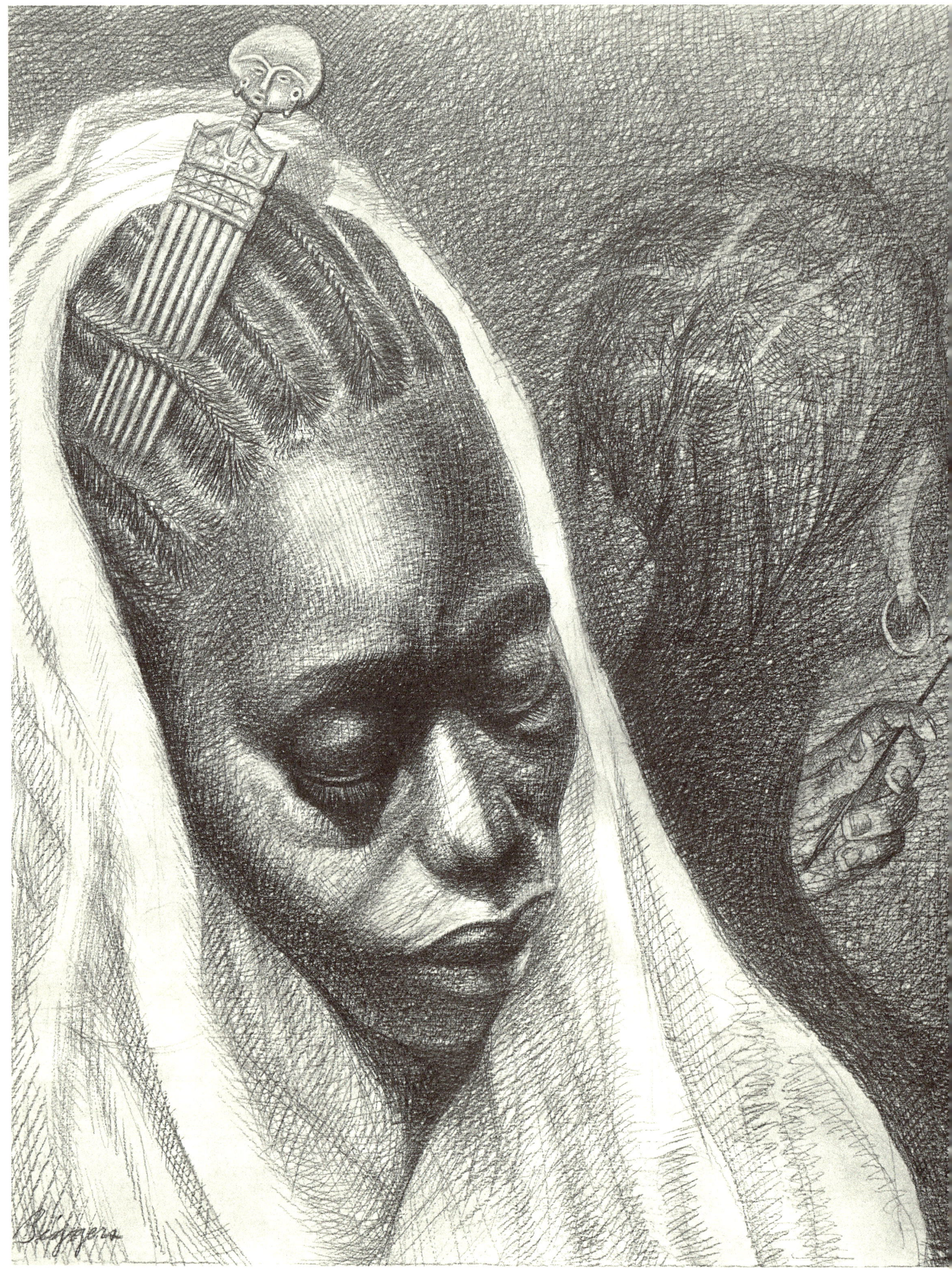

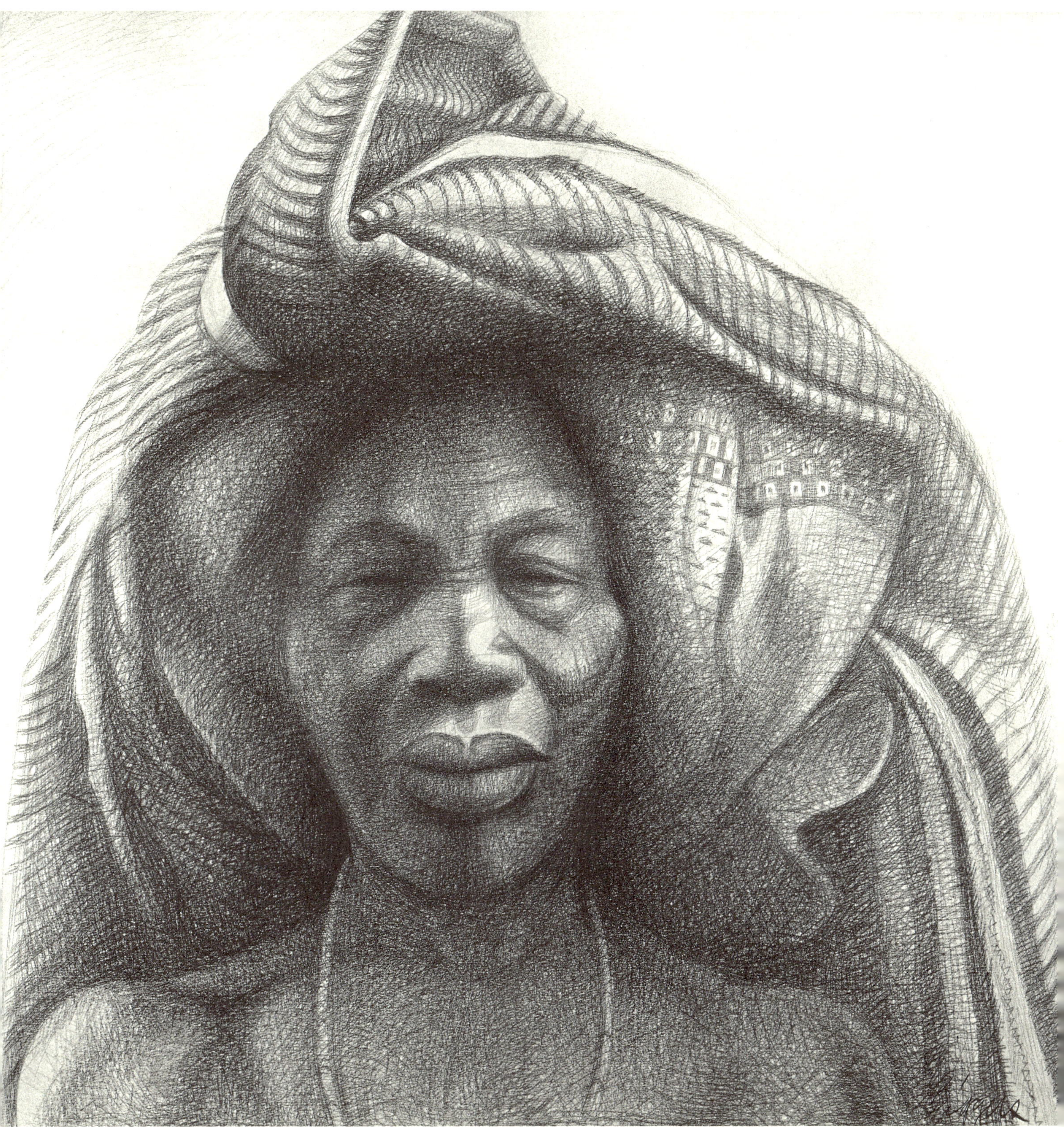

The headdress of the Nigerian woman is flamboyant, as shown here; her blouse is long-sleeved, open, airy; her wrap-around skirt is relatively short, the hem coming down to her knee.

lany West African hair styles are worn by Negro women in the Jnited States, including this one—"corn rows." The hair is greased, ombed, and tightly plaited. The ends of hair that fall upon the eck are tied by a string. The comb has been carved from hard vood.

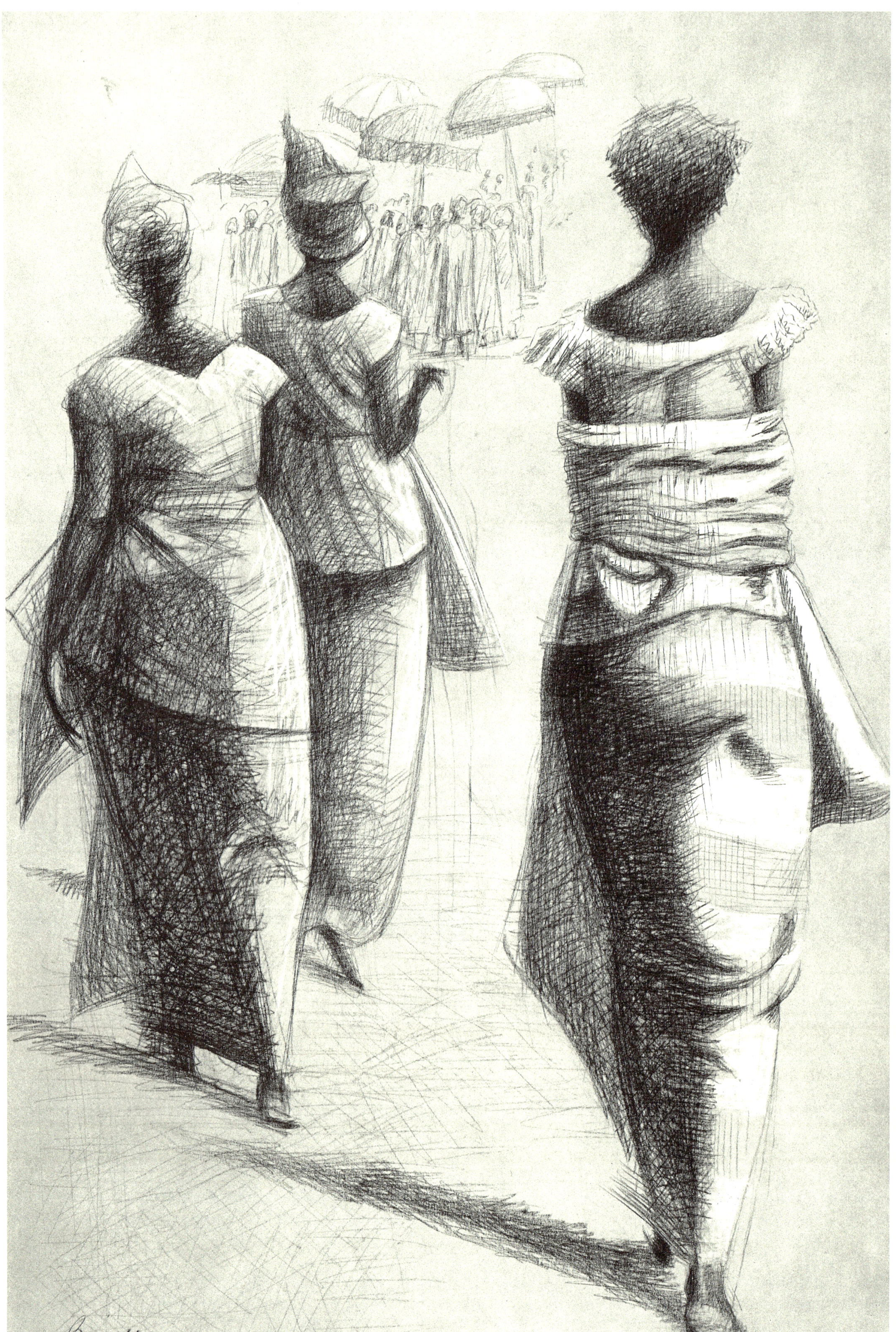

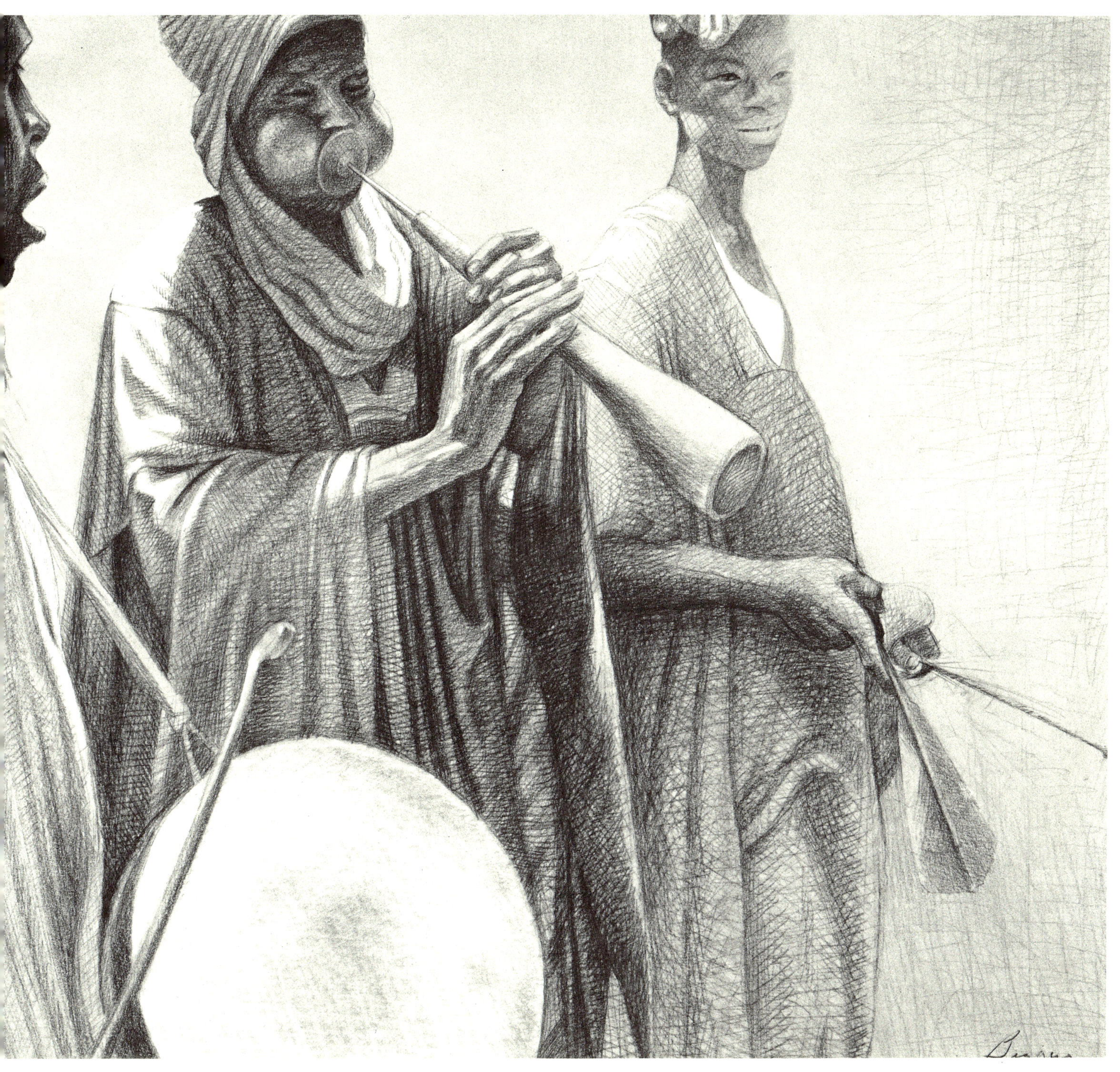

Drum, flute, and gong (from left to right) are popular musical instruments in Ghana.

The headdress of the Ghanaian woman is worn tightly, emphasizing the shape of the skull; her blouse is sleeveless, also fitting tightly; her wrap-around skirt is long, the hem covering her ankle. The colorful umbrellas, in satins and silks, are a mark of distinction.

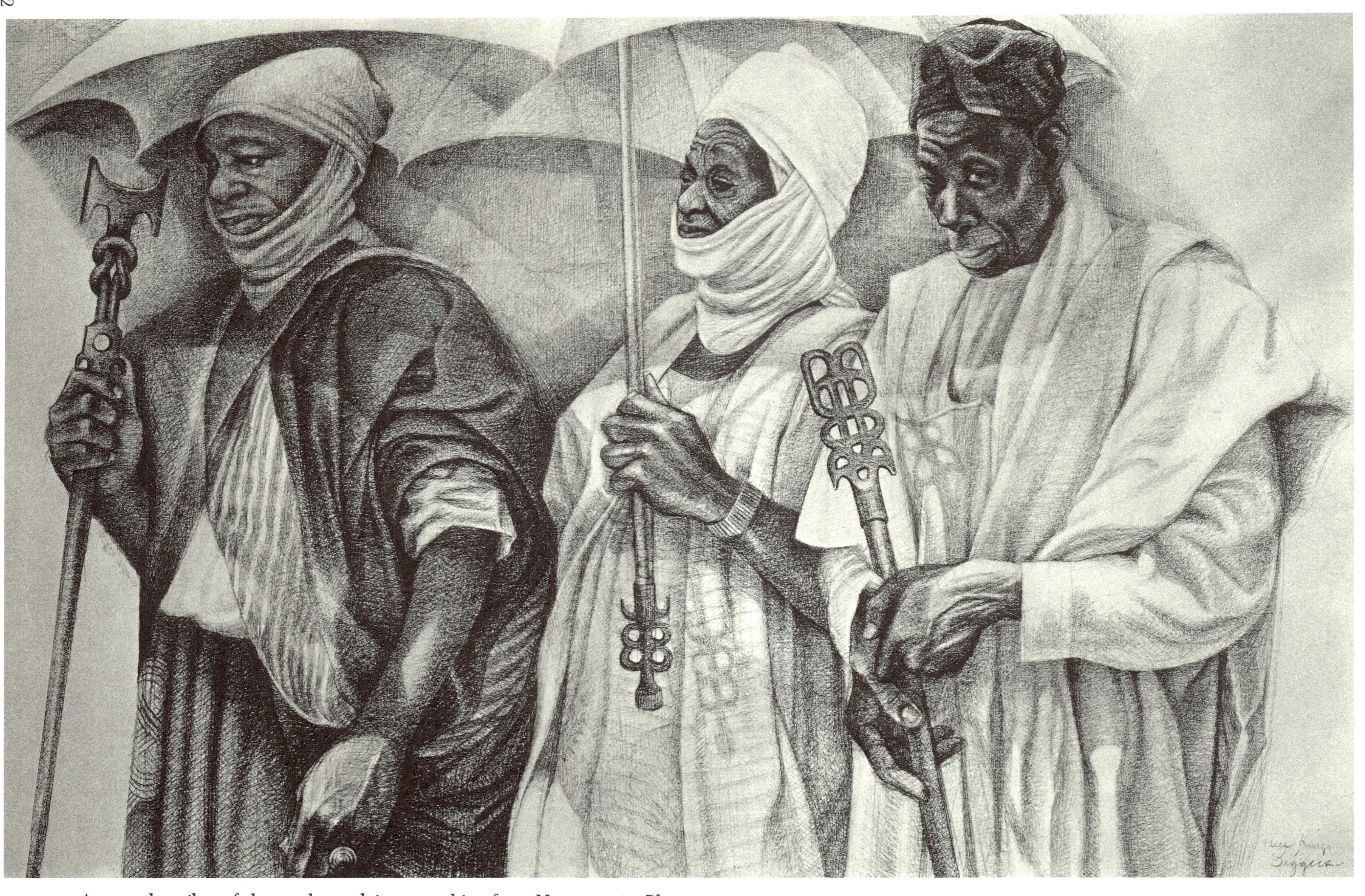

Among the tribes of the northern plains, stretching from Navrongo in Ghana to Kano in Nigeria, there is similarity of clothing style and design of ceremonial objects, as indicated in this drawing, "Three Kings."

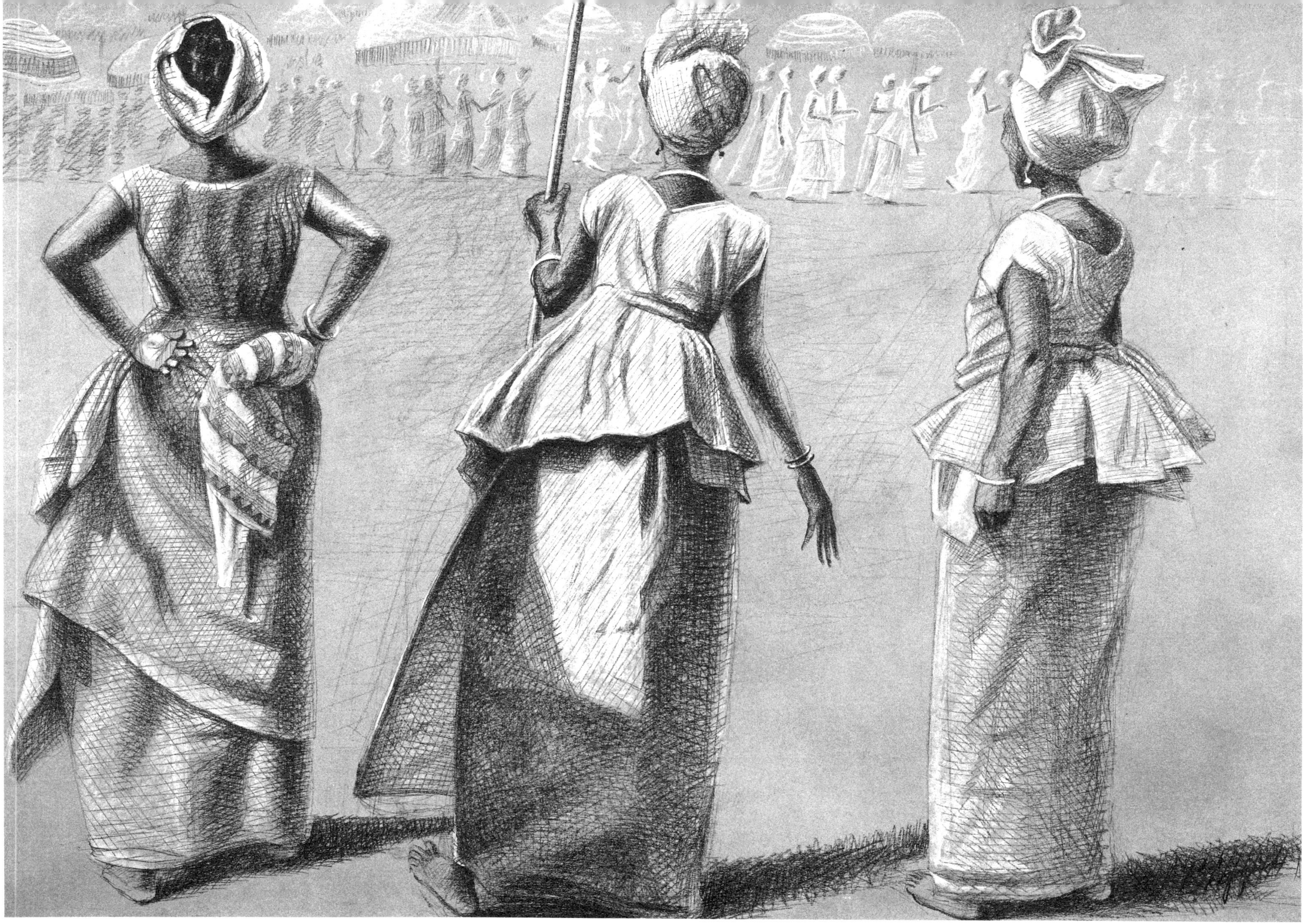

Ghanaian women, proudly attired in new garments, watch a parade at Odumasi.

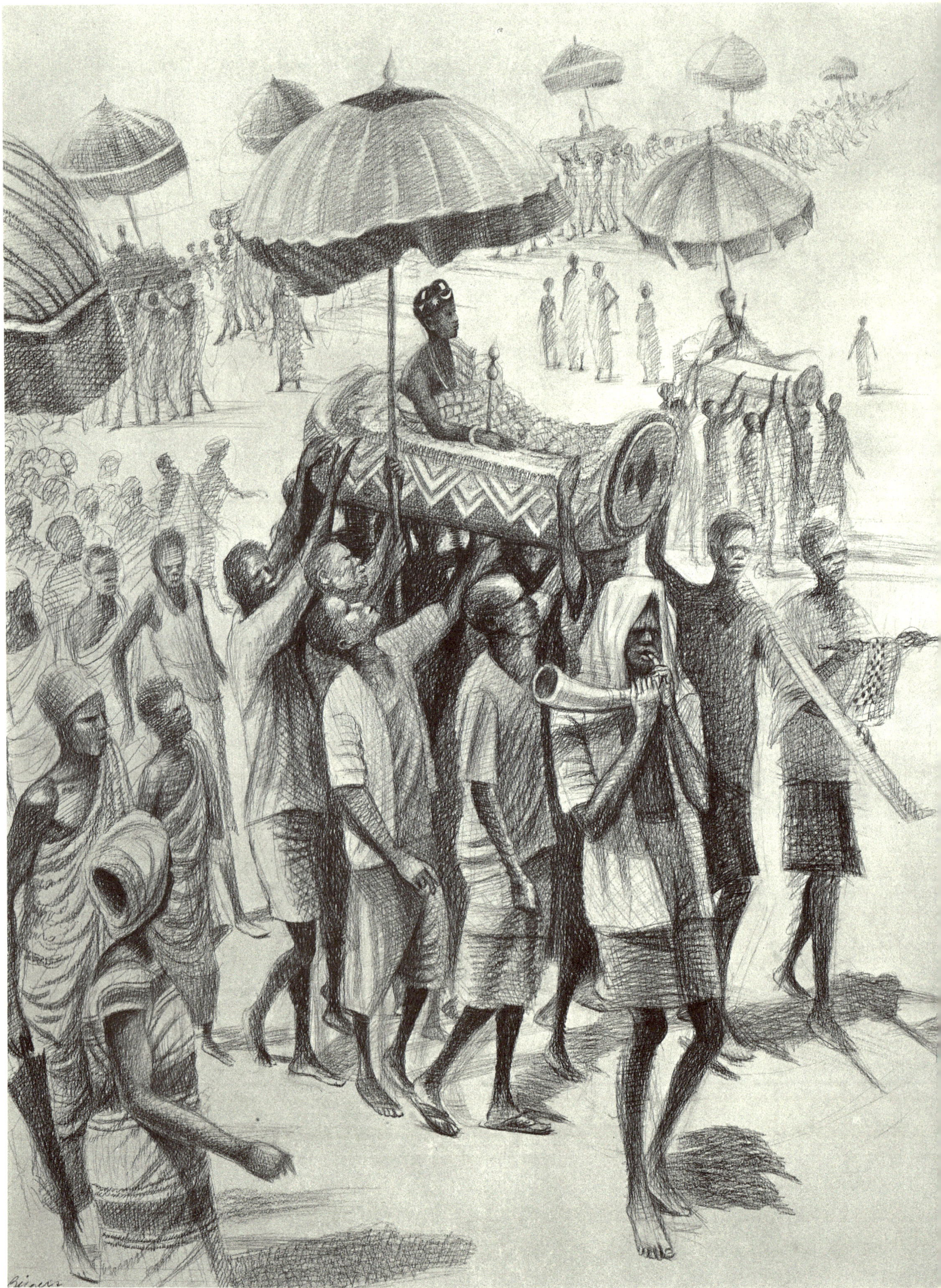

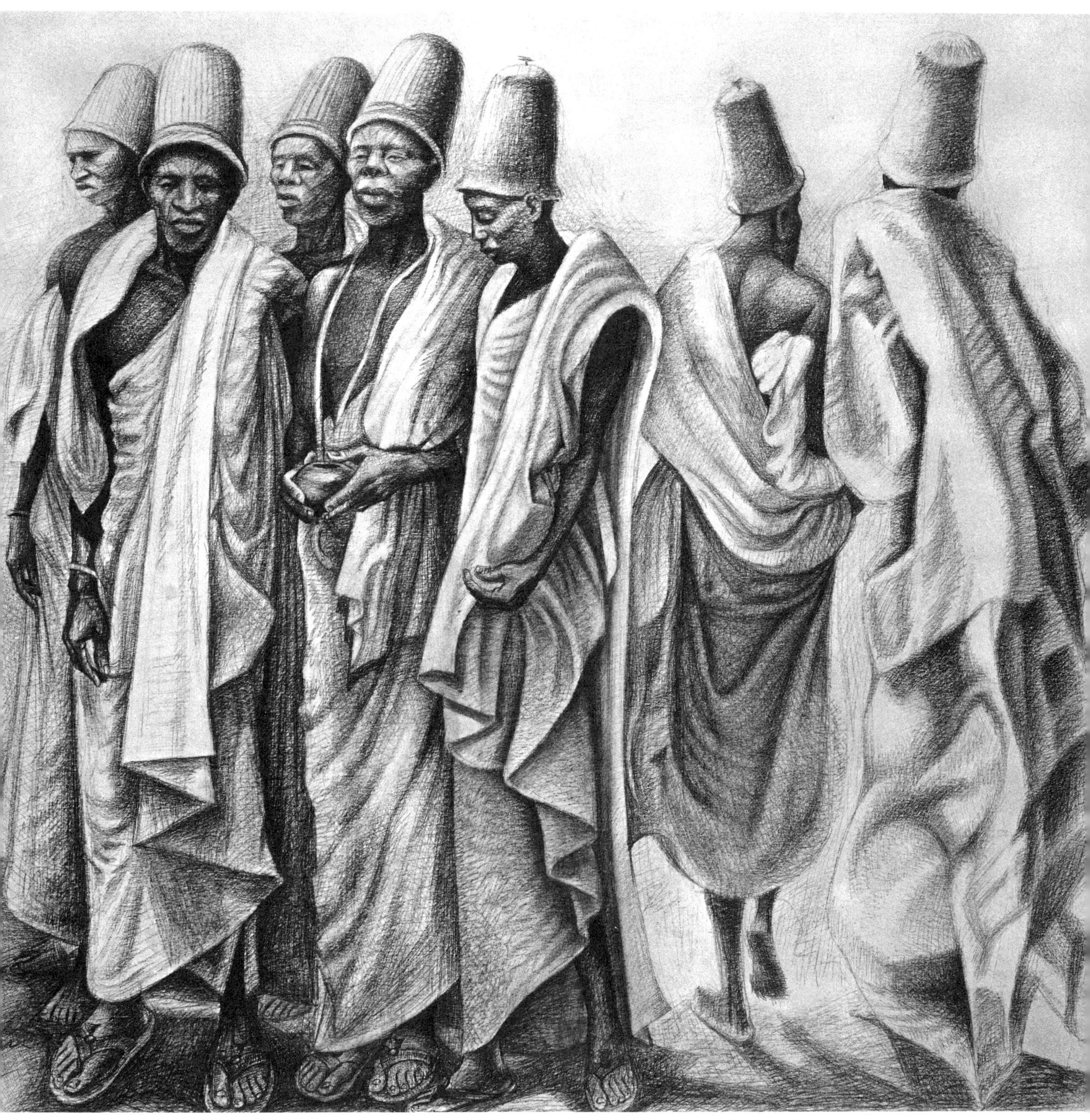

High priests dress in flowing white robes and tall hats woven from thatch.

Following the *durbar* at Odumasi the many chiefs in attendance are paraded in dazzling palanquins. Ahead of each chief marches his retinue—including trumpeters who blow instruments carved from ram horns and elephant tusks. Later, at the palace of the Chief of Odumasi, there will be feasting and drinking.

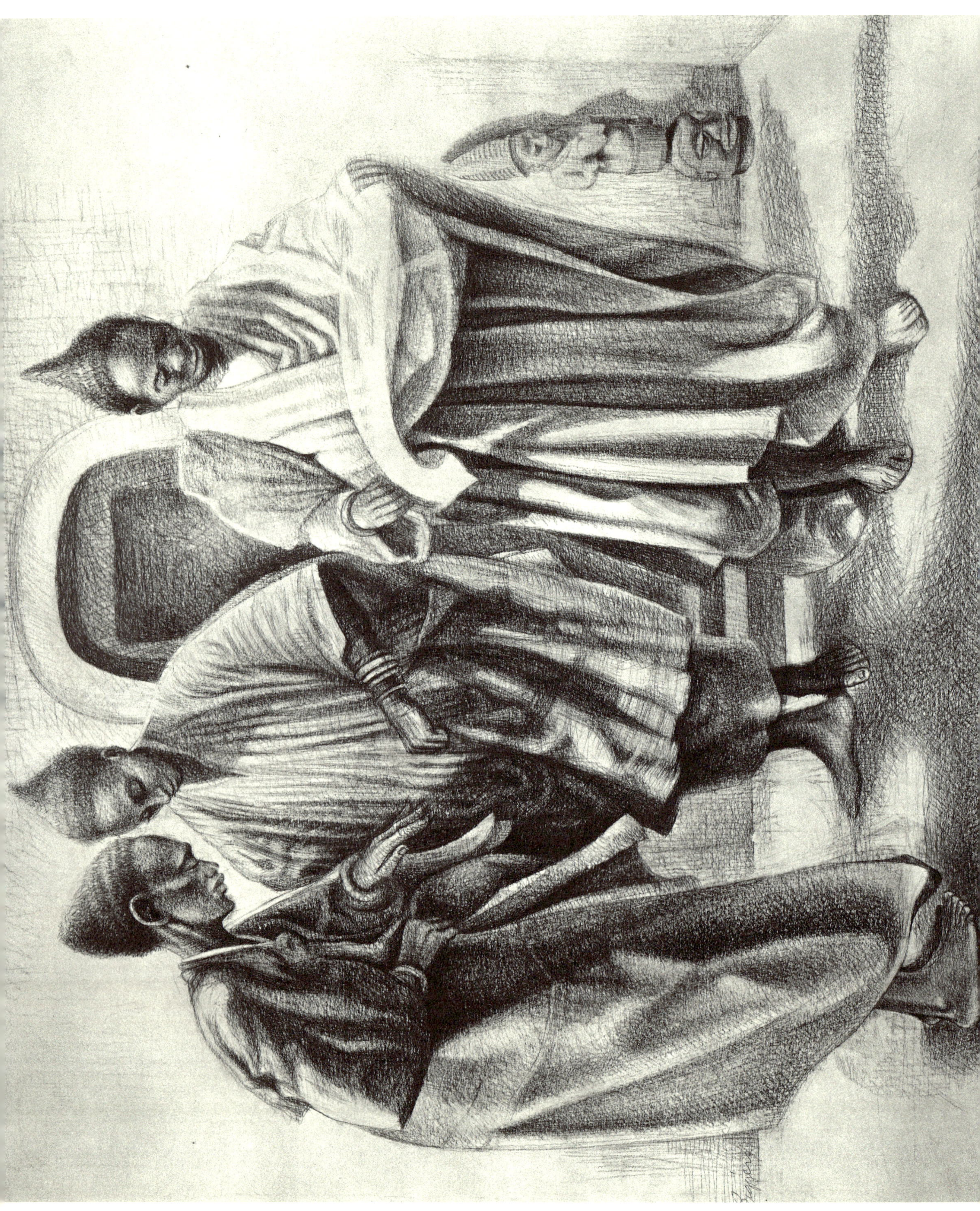

These priests in Ilobu, Nigeria, greet us with drumming and dancing. Their pyramidal hair style copies the shape of crowns fashioned in Yoruba sculpture.

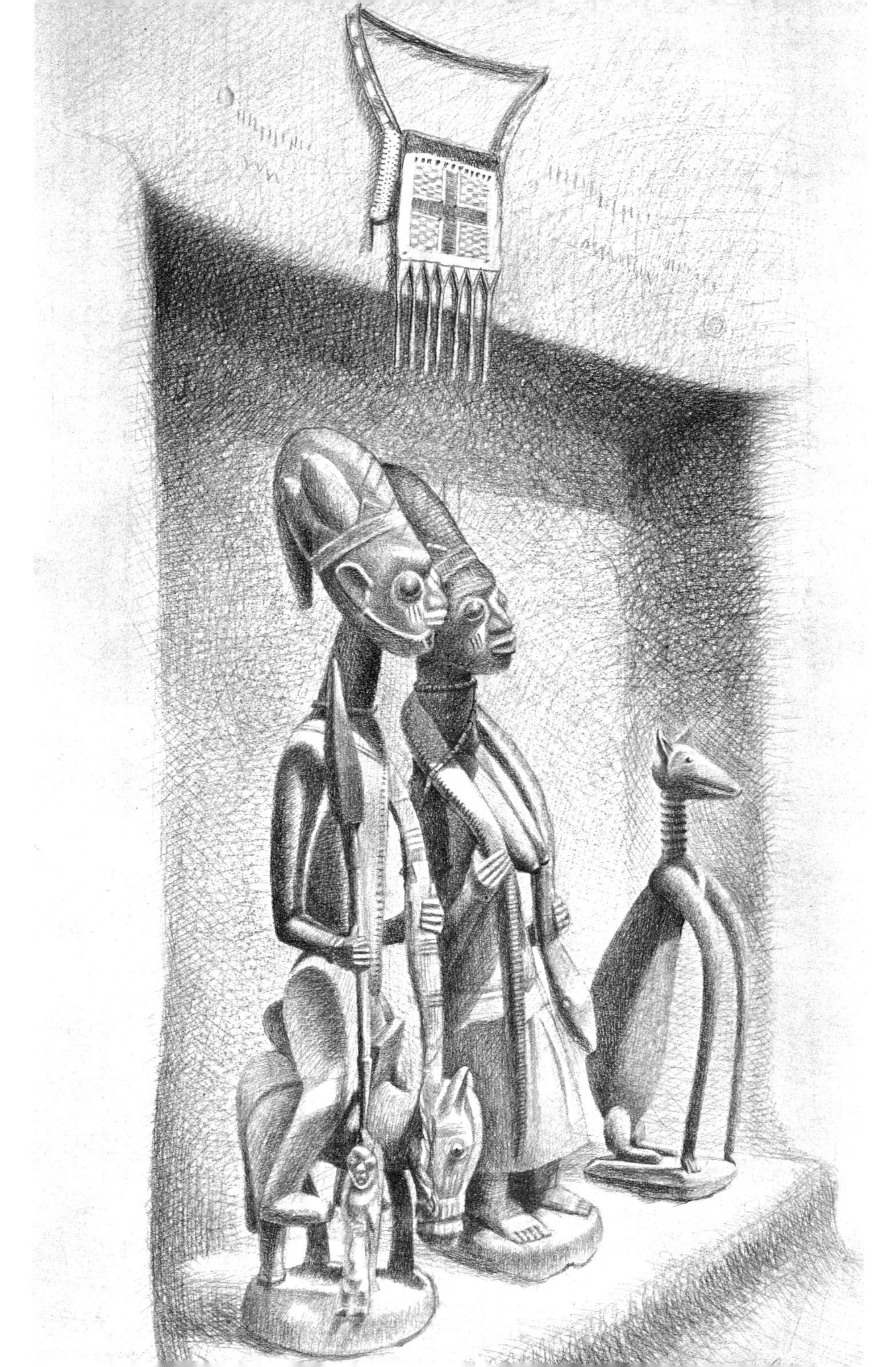

Erinle, a mighty warrior-god, and his wife, horse, and dog are depicted in sculpture near Ede, Nigeria.

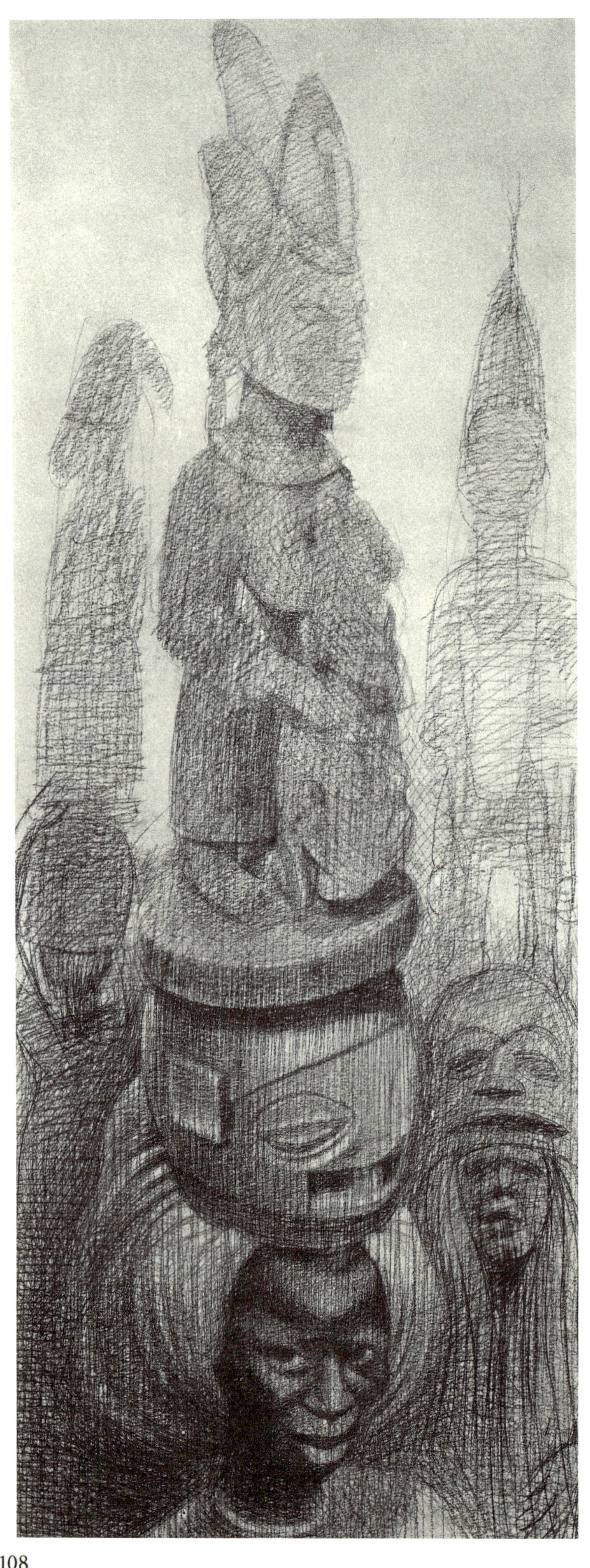

Maintaining what appears to be a precarious balance, Nigerians carry sculpture the same way they carry everything else. Occasionally they defy gravity completely by bending or stooping so that children (as well as adults) may touch the images.

The talking drums of Kumasi are sometimes mated, as seen in the left foreground. The male drum has a deep, resonant tone, the female a high-pitched sound. Drummers must serve an apprenticeship, the same as wood carvers, metalsmiths, and other craftsmen.

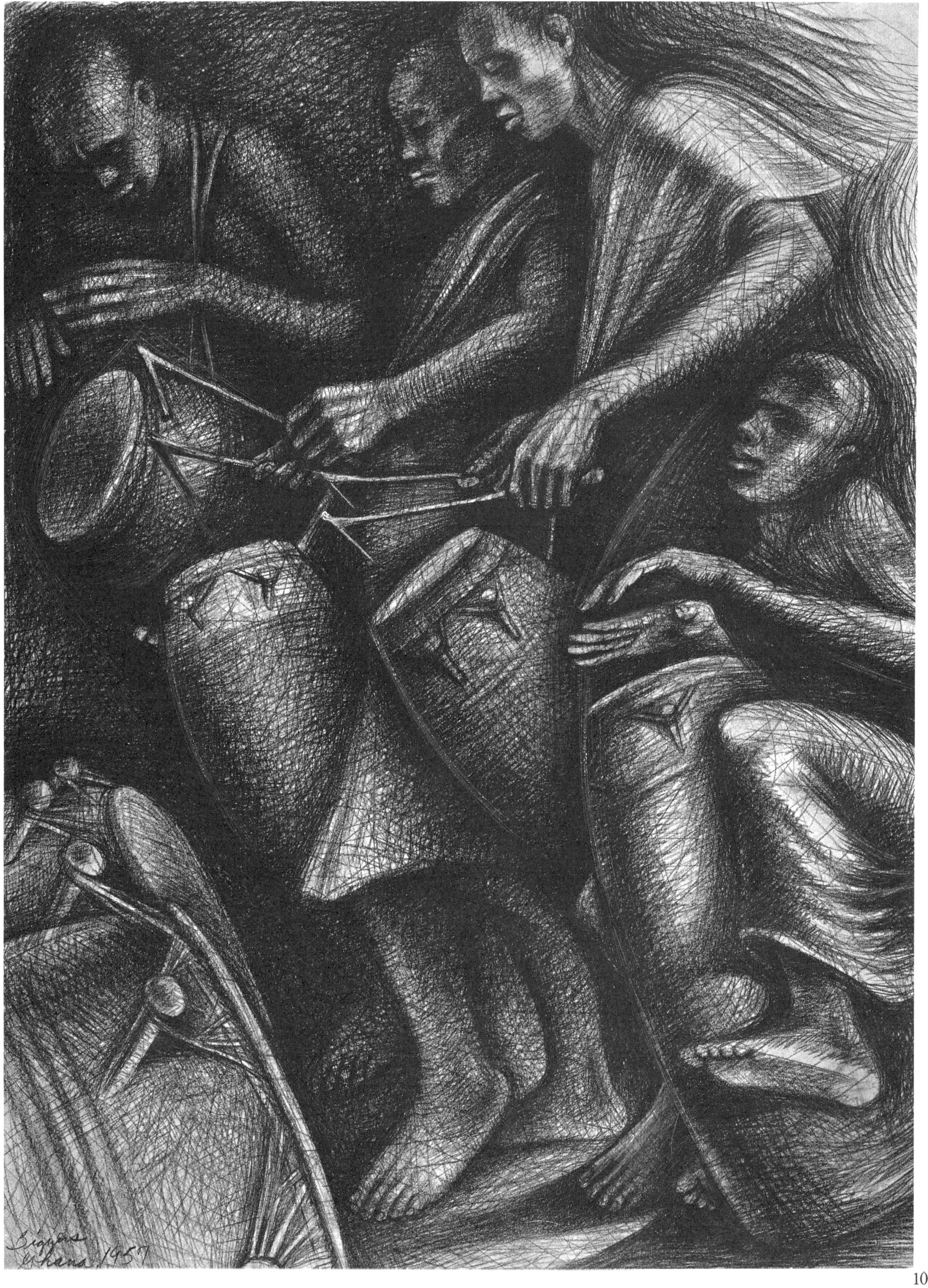
Biggers
Ghana 1957

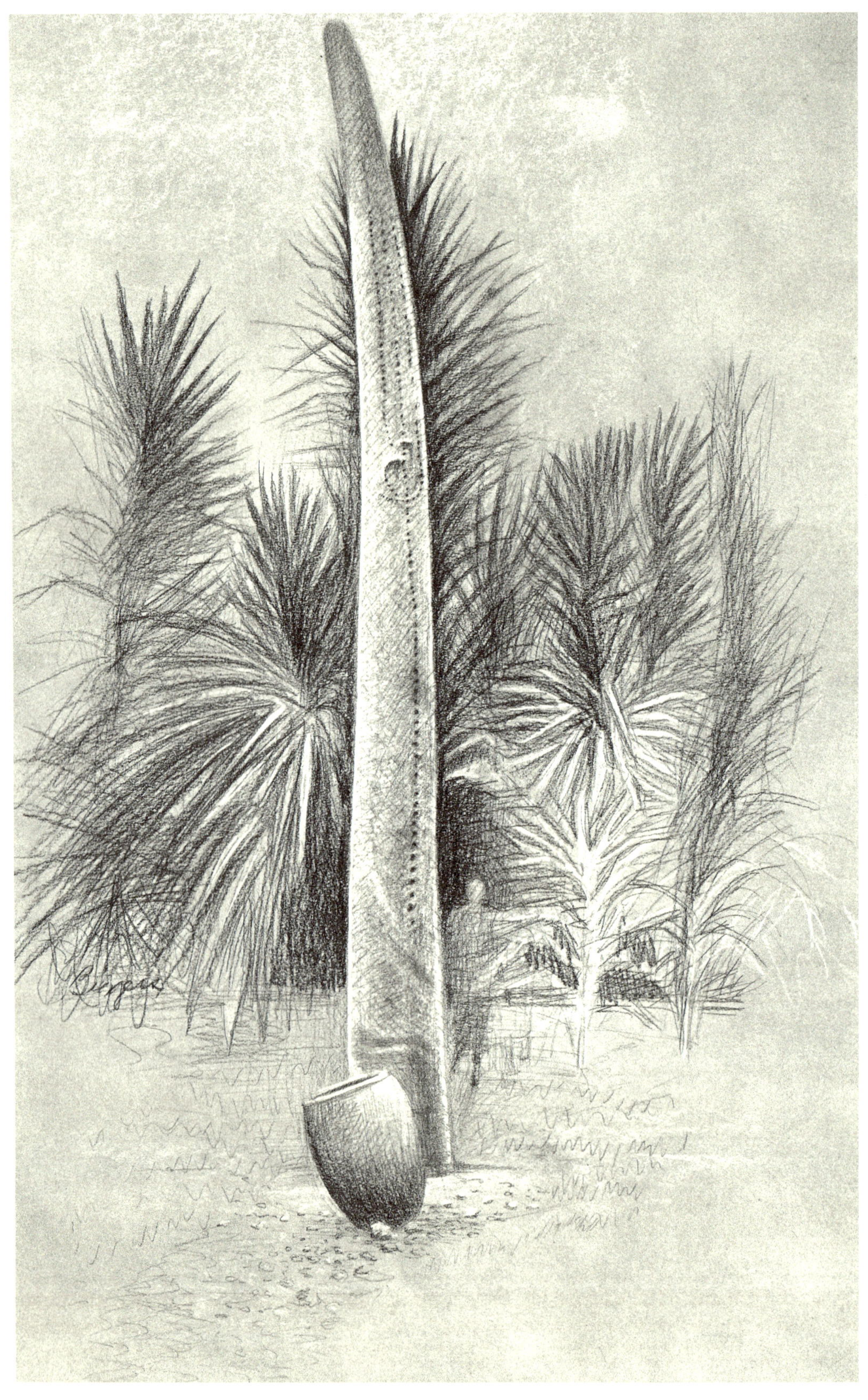

The same inscriptions found on this and other Nigerian shrines have been found on the obelisks of ancient Egypt.

This old Yoruba priestess is a living storehouse of African lore. Her commanding manner reflects wisdom and understanding; she acts as soothsayer, physician, and foster parent. She reminded me of Negro matriarchs I knew as a North Carolina youth; in their heads they carried hundreds of remedies for many illnesses.

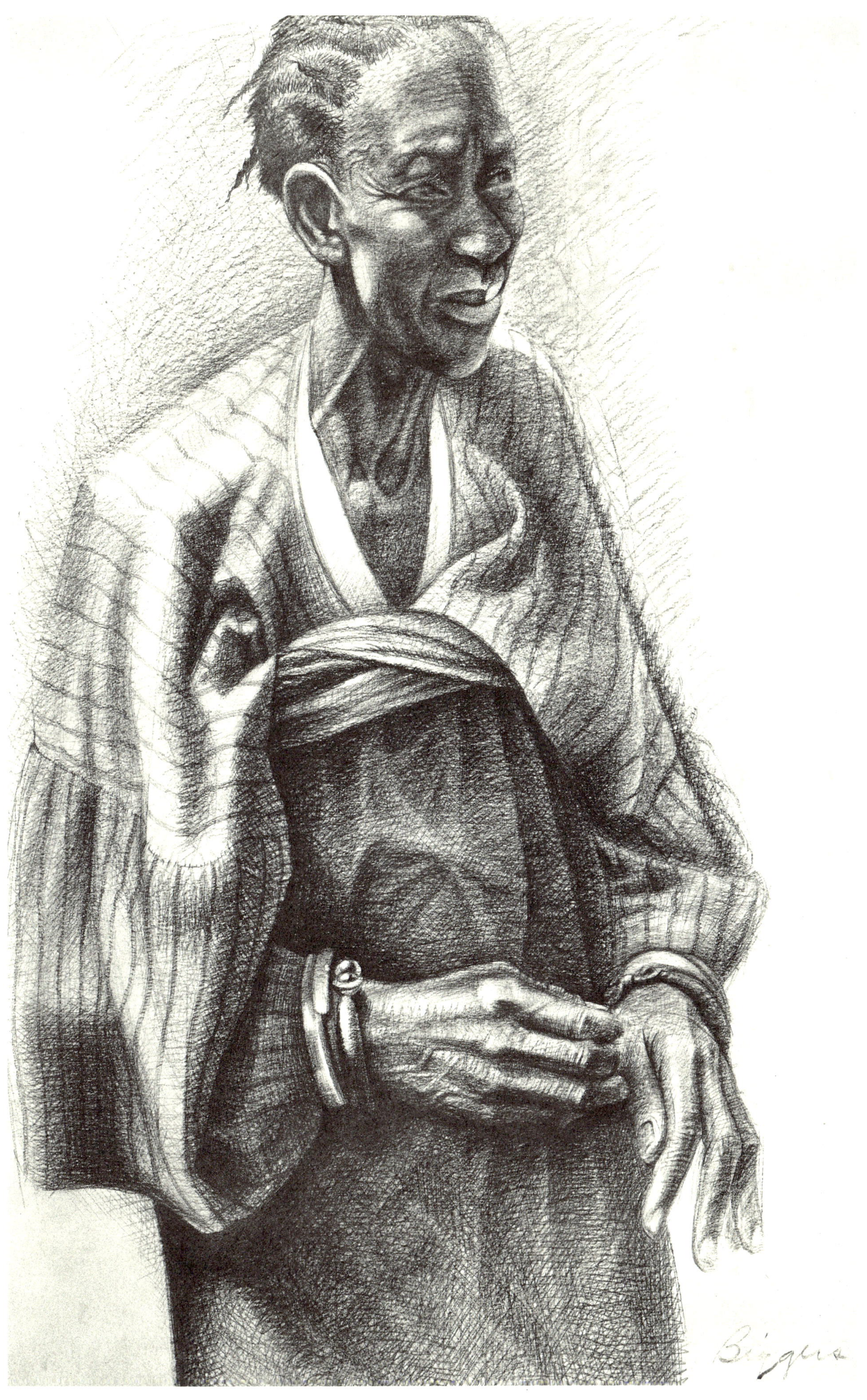

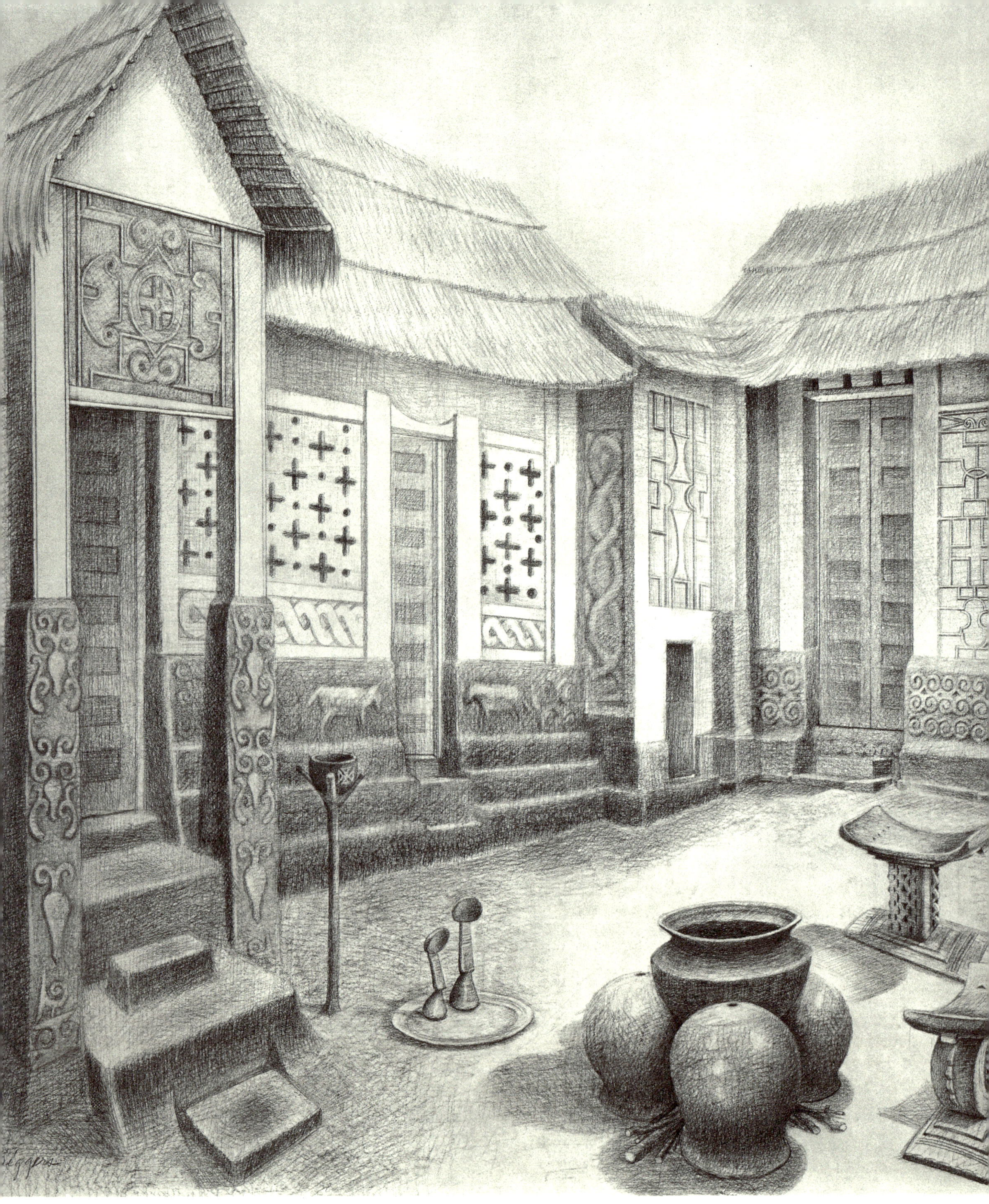

Many years ago houses in the forest region of Ghana were built from a tough, reddish clay, into which had been molded, in low relief, exquisite abstract patterns. Not many houses with such decorations survived the British conquest of 1895, and few new ones have been built. This view is from the courtyard.

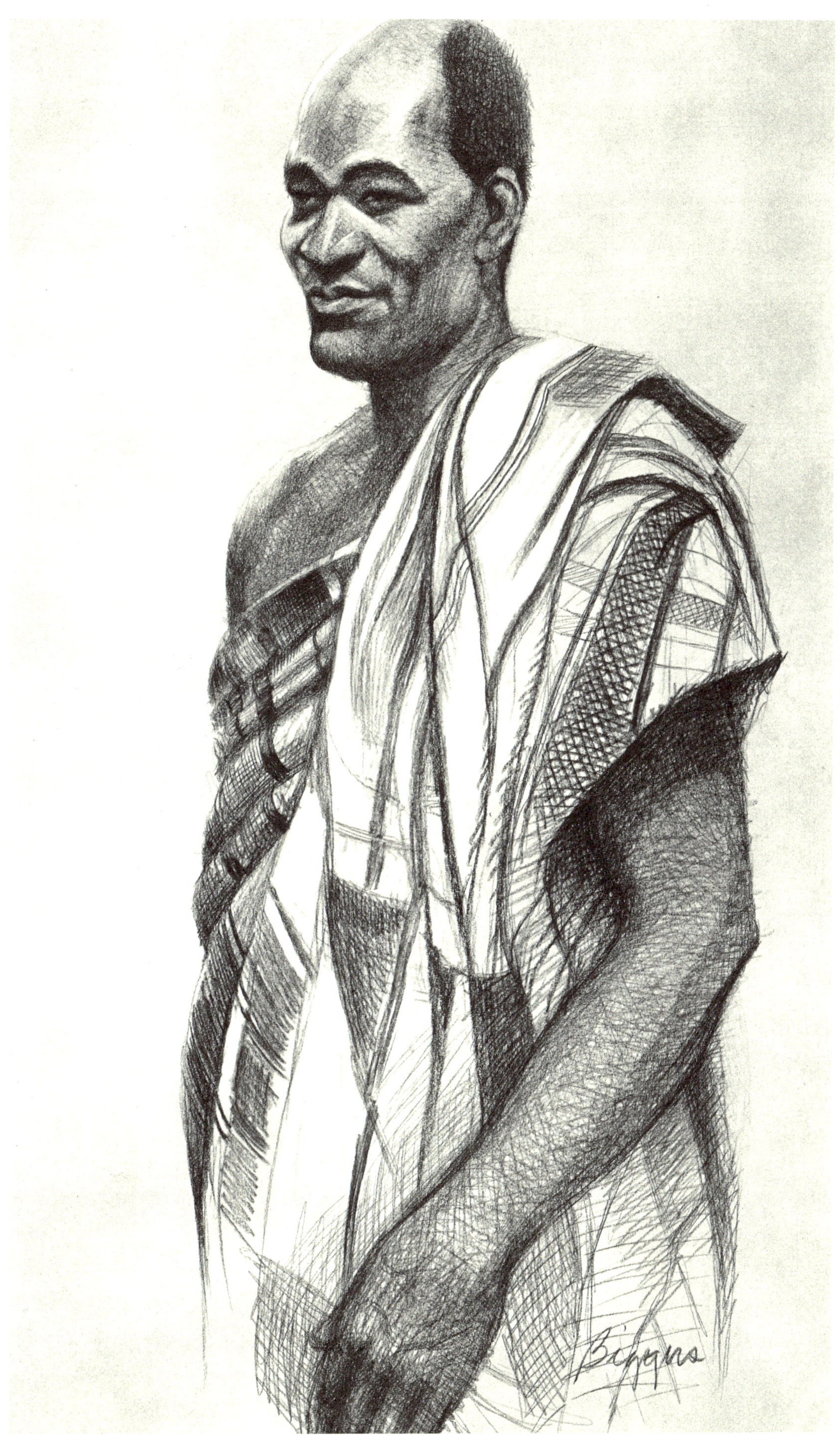

Patrick Hulede, a professor in the College of Technology at Kumasi, welcomes us cordially. Later he will share his home as if we were his Ewe brothers and introduce us to hundreds of Ghanaians, enabling us to observe many ceremonies.

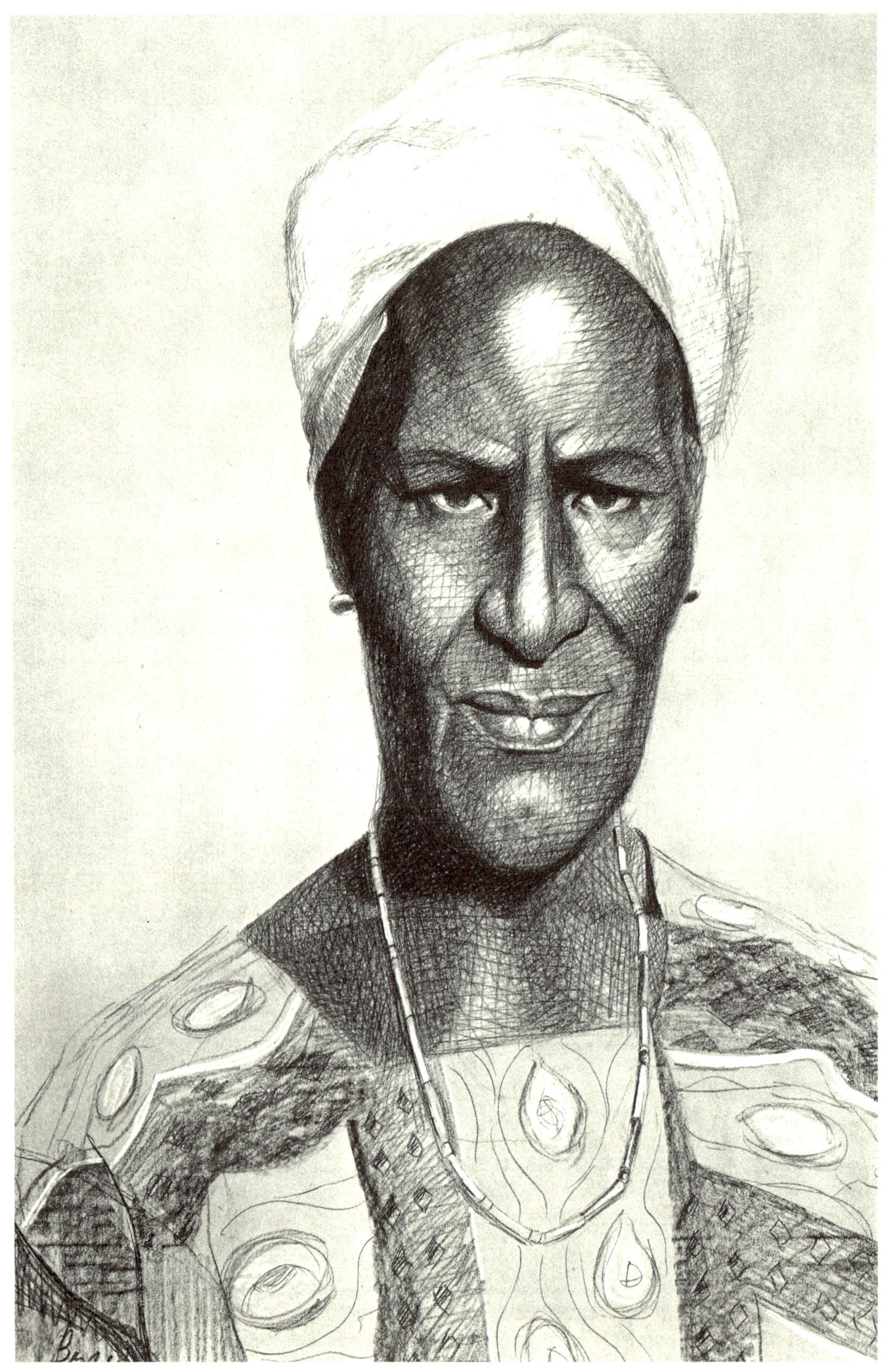

Patrick Hulede's mother speaks the Ewe language, which is lost on us. But her kind, penetrating eyes communicate easily.

A Nigerian queen mother acts as arbiter in problems concerning birth, marriage, and family life, and serves as legal adviser in disputes arising from marriage payments, divorce, rape, seduction, and other matters involving women. Despite the many troubles with which she deals, she is as tranquil as the full moon.

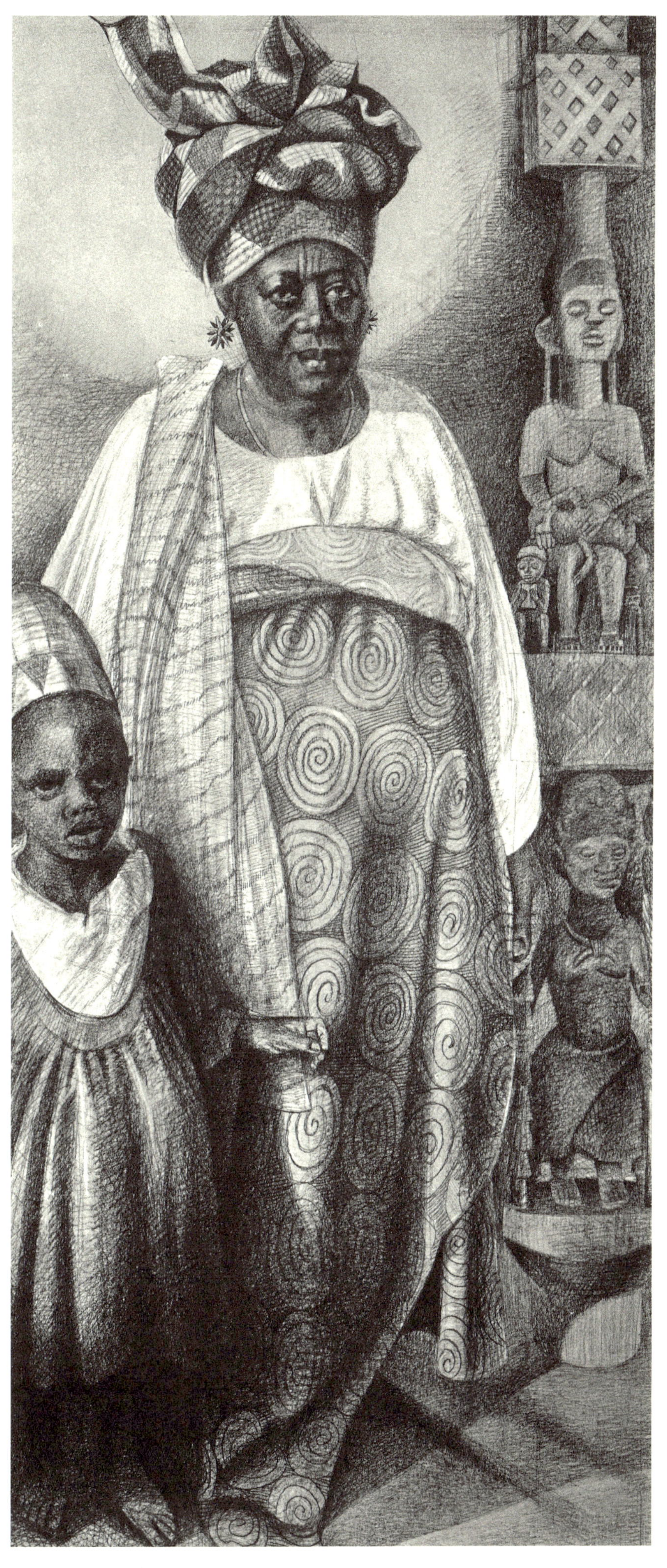

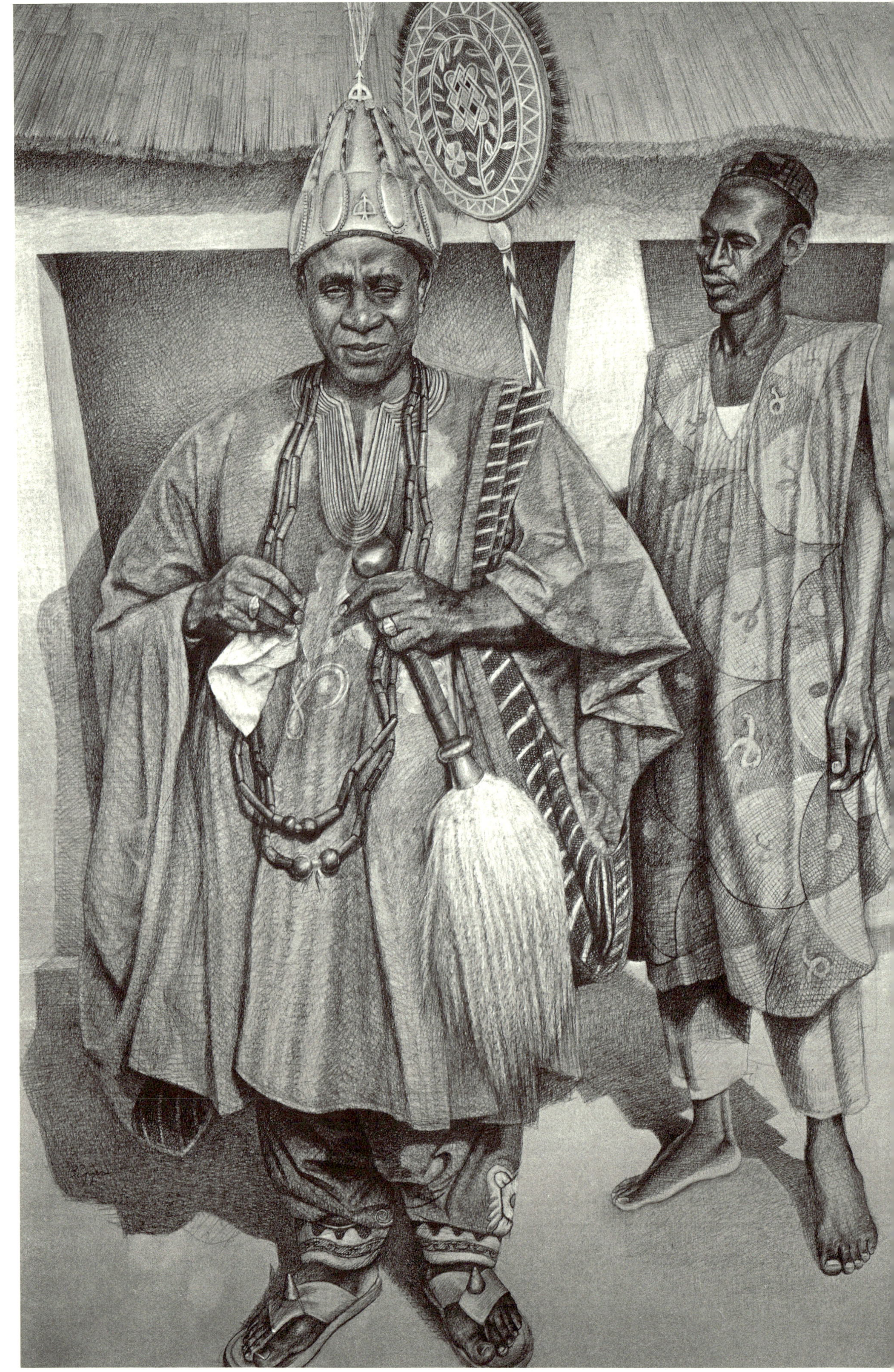

His Highness the Timi of Ede, one of the most respected leaders in Nigeria today, is descended from kings and queen mothers who possessed great power, material wealth, many slaves. He greeted us as if we were brothers who had been separated for three hundred years.

ACKNOWLEDGMENTS

THE NATURE OF THIS PROJECT made the cooperation and advice of many individuals and groups necessary. I wish to thank the United Nations Educational, Scientific, and Cultural Organization for providing a fellowship which made the visit to Africa possible. I wish to thank also those persons who performed the difficult task of arranging accommodations and contacts throughout Ghana, Togo, Dahomey, and Nigeria. This was the responsibility of Mr. Edward Read, director of the Vernacular Literature Bureau in Ghana, and his assistant, Miss Ella Griffin. Assisting them were Mr. Patrick Hulede, professor at the Kumasi College of Technology, and Mr. Donald W. MacRow, editor of *Nigeria Magazine*.

I am especially indebted to my gracious hosts, who provided invaluable information regarding certain aspects of African culture: The Honorable K. A. Gbedemah, finance minister of Ghana; Dr. J. B. Danquah, author, philosopher, and statesman; His Highness the Timi of Ede; Mr. Ephraim Amu, professor at the Kumasi College of Technology; Mr. J. H. Gambra, businessman of Kumasi; Dr. Seth Cudjoe, Accra Mental Hospital; Dr. Oku Ampofo, Akwapim; Bishop Amissah of Ghana; Miss Mary Mensah, Kumasi schoolteacher; Miss Doris Dodzie, Miss Alberta Addo, Kumasi College of Technology; Mr. and Mrs. J. S. Boston, Lagos Museum of Art; and Mr. R. B. Nu Noo, director of the Accra Museum of Art.

I acknowledge gratefully the encouragement given me by the following African artists, writers, and teachers: Messrs. Kofi Antubaum, Osei Bonsu, Vincent Kofi, Berti Opoku, George Obeng, and Joseph Colman DeGraft of Ghana; Ben Enwonwu, Felix Idubar, and H. U. Beier of Nigeria; Selby Mvusi of South Africa; and James Nyoike Hinga of Kenya. And I offer wholehearted thanks to friends and colleagues who gave so much valuable time, advice, and inspiration: Dr. J. Mason Brewer, professor at Livingstone College, who through his own work has made me aware of the need for the preservation of Negro culture and lore; Carroll H. Simms, professor at Texas Southern University; and Miss Vivian Ayers, Houston poet.

I am deeply grateful to Dr. S. M. Nabrit, president of Texas Southern University, without whose encouragement and cooperation the project might not have been completed, and to the Faculty Research Committee of Texas Southern University.

My heartfelt gratitude goes also to a great teacher and leader who imbued me with a philosophy of creative expression through self-identification with my own roots and background, the late Dr. Viktor Lowenfeld, head of the Department of Art Education at Pennsylvania State University.

And my sincere thanks go to Mr. and Mrs. John Blaffer of Houston for their interest and encouragement in connection with the publication of this book.

Finally, I would like to express my deep appreciation to my wife, Hazel, for her sacrifices and her full cooperation, which made this project possible.